WONDERS OF THE ANCIENT WORLD

WONDERS OF THE ANCIENT WORLD

ANTIQUITY'S GREATEST FEATS OF DESIGN AND ENGINEERING

JUSTIN POLLARD

Quercus

Contents

Stonehenge, England

The Pharos of Alexandria

The Library, Petra, Jordan

Preface

Around 140 BC the Greek poet Antipater of Sidon began to write a poem which included a list of *themata* – a word which can be translated as 'must-sees'. Such lists were popular in the ancient world and we know that the historian Herodotus, who was an inveterate traveller, wrote one, as did the greatest Alexandrian librarian Callimachus of Cyrene. Diodorus of Sicily and the Roman geographer Strabo, amongst others, also followed suit. They were perhaps the first to codify that love of lists that we still have – from the top ten music singles to our hundred favourite films; from the 'rich lists' to the football league tables.

What all these ancient writers wanted to do was give us an itinerary, a table of the very best, most wonderful, most awe-inspiring sights that might be found in their world. Most of these lists have long since disappeared along with the monuments they once recorded, but what makes Antipater's list different is that it has survived:

> *'I have set eyes on the wall of lofty Babylon on which is a road for chariots, and the statue of Zeus by the Alpheus, and the hanging gardens, and the Colossus of the Sun, and the huge labour of the high pyramids, and the vast tomb of Mausolus; but when I saw the house of Artemis that mounted to the clouds, those other marvels lost their brilliancy, and I said, 'Lo, apart from Olympus, the Sun never looked on aught so grand.'*
>
> Antipater, *Greek Anthology* IX.58

We don't know if Antipater actually visited all these sights – certainly the Colossus of Rhodes had crashed to the ground long before his time, although he could still have seen its wrecked frame. If he did, it would have been a gruelling journey through Mesopotamia and Egypt, across the deserts of Asia Minor, the mountains of the Peloponnese and over the turbulent seas of the eastern Aegean. Many, no doubt, were content simply to visit these 'Seven Wonders of the Ancient World' in their minds and be the armchair travellers of the ancient world, trading superlatives and comparing sites as we still do today. And there was still some trading to be done, for the list of Seven Wonders was not set. Antipater's roll-call does not include the Pharos lighthouse but has instead the Walls of Babylon, making that the only city to ever hold two wonders. Indeed, our 'modern' list of ancient wonders was compiled after the sixth century, in the mediaeval period, when the still impressive remains of the Alexandrian lighthouse managed to supplant the crumbling walls of Babylon on what has since become the definitive list.

But there was so much more that Antipater had not seen, that he could never have seen and that no writer of *themata* ever would. He lived long before the sheer walls of the Colosseum reared up in Rome, before Justinian built the great church of Hagia Sophia in Constantinople and long after such wonders as Solomon's Temple in Jerusalem and the original Temple of Artemis at Ephesus had been destroyed. His was also a small world, inscribed around the Mediterranean Sea. He could never know of the caves of Ellora in India, or the Indonesian shrines at Borobudur. The Americas were unknown so the cities of the Maya and the Great Serpent Mound of the Adena meant nothing to him. And yet all these were also wonders of the ancient world.

This book tells the story of the greatest sights world travellers might have seen in antiquity had they been able to journey across the globe and through the centuries. It describes 40 sites, 40 examples of the most extraordinary feats of human engineering and design from around the globe created between the dawn of human civilization and the onset of the medieval period. It is, in many ways, a companion piece to *The Story of Archaeology*, my history of my own subject. That book could only deal with those discoveries that came about through archaeological investigation and which marked significant landmarks in the development of the subject. As such, there was no room for those sites that have never disappeared from human view, those that are now gone without trace or those whose excavation did not mark a turning point in the history of archaeology itself.

This book, I hope, fills in that gap and gives me the chance to tell the stories behind the rise and fall of the greatest monumental achievements of earlier societies across the world. It is my own list of *themata* for a now sadly impossible journey to see what humanity once achieved and survey the remains of the greatest accomplishments of civilizations that today lie in ruins.

Justin Pollard

DORSET 2008

Newgrange

Neolithic passage tomb and ritual site

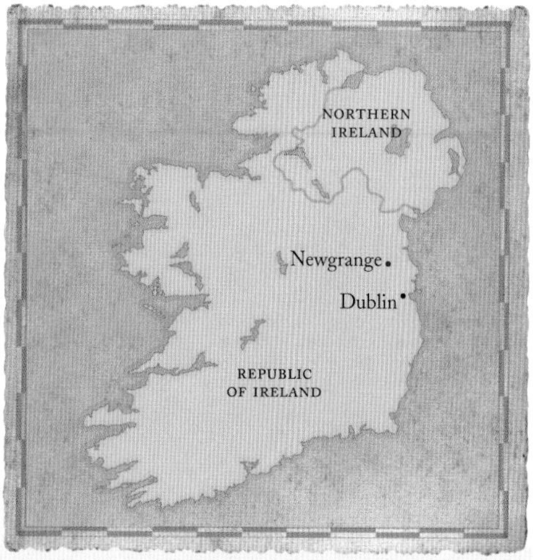

In a wide curve of the River Boyne between Slane and Drogheda, some 25 miles (40 km) northwest of Dublin, stands one of the oldest surviving buildings in the world. It predates the trilithons at Stonehenge by 700 years, is older than any pyramid in Egypt and represents perhaps the supreme achievement of the first farmers to till the rich soils of Ireland.

Newgrange is a type of monument known as a 'passage tomb' and consists of a circular stone retaining wall about 80 metres (262 ft) across enclosing a grassy mound that rises 12 metres (39 ft) above the base. From the southeast side a 19-metre- (62-ft-) long passage leads into the mound at a slight incline, terminating in a chamber in the shape of a cross with a 6-metre- (19-ft-) high corbelled roof that remains as sound and watertight today as it was when it was built over 5000 years ago.

During the Neolithic period, when the monument was first constructed, it was common for the cremated remains of some, or perhaps all, the inhabitants of a community to be buried in communal graves, and this appears to be the purpose of Newgrange. In the 'arms' of the central cross-shaped chamber stood large stone basins, two carved from sandstone and the third from granite, which originally held the ashes of these early farmers. To date, the remains of only five individuals have been found at the site, but there were originally probably many more. As is often the case in Irish passage tombs, the right 'arm' is the most elaborate and ornate, containing the double granite basin. However, it is unclear whether this represents the final resting place of people with a higher social status or simply formed a part of a series of communal burial rites long since lost to posterity.

'I was there entirely alone. Not a soul stood even on the road below. When I came into the tomb I knew there was a possibility of seeing the sunrise because the sky had been clear during the morning.'

PROFESSOR MICHAEL J. O' KELLY – *NEWGRANGE: ARCHAEOLOGY, ART AND LEGEND* (1982)

Contentious Reconstruction

Around the outside of the monument can be seen some of the finest megalithic carving in the whole of Ireland. The base of the retaining wall of the mound consists of 97 massive kerbstones, some of which are decorated with the distinctive spiral and lozenge-shaped patterns that reappear at several other megalithic sites such as the passage tomb at Gavrinis in the Gulf of Morbihan in Brittany, France. In particular, the entrance slab that stands directly in front of the passage is carved with a design known as the 'triple spiral', a motif

The reconstructed mound at Newgrange. It has been estimated that it would have taken a workforce of 300 some 20–30 years to build the original passage tomb.

that is then repeated in the passage and the chamber itself. Deducing the meaning of these abstract patterns from deep prehistory is fraught with difficulty, but it has been suggested that these interlocking spirals represent supernatural maps, aspects of their makers' belief in life, death and eternity, the changing seasons or even the three main buildings of the Brú na Bóinne complex (see Disrepair and Rediscovery opposite) of which Newgrange forms a part. In truth, understanding the inspiration behind carvings made five millennia ago by artists who left no other record may always be too much to ask.

Above the kerbstones of the retaining wall is the most contentious part of the site. When excavations began here between 1962 and 1975 the mound, which contains around 200,000 tons of stone, had slumped down, leaving a jumble of rocks around it. In reconstructing the original appearance of the mound, Professor Michael J. O'Kelly of University College, Cork, chose to reconstruct this mass of granite and white quartzite boulders into a near-vertical retaining wall, bonded with concrete and reinforced with steel. It has since been pointed out that concrete and steel technologies were patently not available in the early Neolithic and, considering the enormous lateral thrust that would be exerted by the mound on such a wall, the original makers of Newgrange could never have successfully built such a structure. Instead, critics have suggested that the quartzite, which was brought to the site probably from the Wicklow Mountains some 50 miles (80 km) to the south, may have been laid as a cobbled apron around the mound. This interpretation has been followed in reconstruction work elsewhere in the Boyne Valley, such as the site at Knowth.

Midwinter Light

What is not in doubt, though, is Professor O'Kelly's discovery of the most extraordinary feature of Newgrange. During excavations of the doorway, which had been almost completely blocked, O'Kelly noticed a strange slot directly above the entrance, then partially obscured by grass and weeds. A section of this slot – which he later termed the 'roofbox' – was covered by a square block of quartz, which appeared to have been designed to slide back and forth over the opening like a shutter. A local tradition claimed that the sun shone into the tomb during the midsummer solstice, but O'Kelly knew that the orientation of the entrance made this completely impossible. Instead, he surmised that the alignment of the shaft leading to the roofbox might actually be with the midwinter solstice. Once the site was cleared, he decided to visit the site at dawn on the shortest day of the year in 1967 to see if his prediction was correct. Entering the tomb he made his way to the inner chamber and turned to look back down the passage and wait as the sun broke the horizon. As he later reported:

> *'I was literally astounded. The light began as a thin pencil and widened to a band of about 6 in. There was so much light reflected from the floor that I could walk around inside without a lamp and avoid bumping off the stones. It was so bright I could see the roof 20 feet above me. I expected to hear a voice, or perhaps feel a cold hand resting on my shoulder, but there was silence. And then, after a few minutes, the shaft of light narrowed as the sun appeared to pass westward across the slit, and total darkness came once more.'*

The roofbox was an astounding discovery. The enormous mound at Newgrange had been constructed with such precision in terms of its orientation, angle of passage and construction of the roofbox that between 19 and 23 December, and only between those dates, the dawn sunlight floods into the central chamber between 8.58 a.m. and 9.15 a.m. So impressive is the effect that the local visitors' centre runs a lottery each year to allocate tickets to witness the event. In 2006, no fewer than 27,485 people applied for the 100 places, and even the winners had to depend on the midwinter skies being clear enough to see the sun.

TIMELINE

c.3250 BC Probable date of construction of Newgrange

AD 1142 The land on which Newgrange stands is granted to Mellifont Abbey

1699 Newgrange first comes to light in modern times, as local landowner Charles Campbell accidentally discovers the entrance while excavating material from the hillside for road-building; Oxford scholar Edward Lhuyd makes extensive notes and sketches of the site

1725 Antiquarian Thomas Molyneux of Trinity College, Dublin, visits the site; in his report, he claims that Newgrange was built by the Danes between the eighth and ninth centuries

1882 The Ancient Monuments Protection Act places Newgrange and other sites in the British Isles under state control

1890 Irish archaeologist George Coffey begins work on the site

1962–75 Michael O'Kelly of University College, Cork, undertakes major excavation and rebuilding works at Newgrange, including the controversial step of restoring the quartzite facing stones

1967 O'Kelly successfully tests his hypothesis that the roofbox at Newgrange faces the midwinter sun

1993 UNESCO designates Newgrange a World Heritage Site

DISREPAIR AND REDISCOVERY

Newgrange continued in use throughout the Neolithic Age and was augmented later by other monuments, including a double circle of wooden posts 91 metres (300 ft) in diameter. Some time after 2000 BC a standing-stone circle was also built enclosing the whole site, although only 12 of the original 38 stones, each around 2.5 metres (8 ft) tall, survive. During the Bronze and Iron Ages the site seems to have fallen into disuse; even so, the presence of Roman coins and jewellery at the site, and its appearance in Celtic mythology, suggest that it was still considered a significant place. The mound was no longer maintained, however, and over the ensuing millennia it slumped down and was lost to view.

In 1142 the site became part of the lands granted to the new foundation of Mellifont Abbey and the area became one of the monastery's outlying farms or 'granges' (hence its modern name). The tomb itself was only rediscovered by workmen employed by a local landowner to excavate building stone in 1699. Fortunately, antiquarian interest in the tomb prevented it from being quarried away and from 1962 extensive excavation and restoration work was carried out at the site.

Work has also expanded beyond the monument itself. Newgrange is now known to be a part of the Brú na Bóinne – a collection of passage tombs, henges (continuous circular ditches, with a bank outside the ditch, sometimes with stone or wooded circles inside), standing stones and enclosures which form one of the major Neolithic ritual landscapes in Europe. Contained within a 780-hectare (1926-acre) site in a bend on the River Boyne, the area is home to over 40 passage tombs, of which the three largest and most highly decorated are Newgrange, Knowth and Dowth. Each of these stands in a prominent position in the landscape and two, Newgrange and Dowth are aligned on the winter solstice. Meanwhile Knowth, the largest tomb in the complex, is home to over one-third of the total number of pieces of megalithic art known in Western Europe.

View of the granite-lined passageway within the Newgrange mound, part of the Brú na Bóinne ('Palace of the Boyne') complex in County Meath.

Like the ritual landscape around Stonehenge in Wiltshire, England – whose earliest phases are contemporaneous with the construction of the Irish passage tombs, and which is also contained within a bend in a river (the Avon) – the Brú na Bóinne landscape contains several other monuments whose uses are still uncertain. Running from the Mattock Valley up to the ridge on which Newgrange stands are the remnants of a 20-metre (66-ft) wide Neolithic cursus (a set of parallel earthworks) similar in form to the Stonehenge cursus and which perhaps symbolically linked the tomb site to the valley below.

Further down the valley four henges are probably contemporary with this structure; indeed, all three of the main passage tombs appear to have associated henges. At Knowth a timber circle was built around 2700 BC to the east of the main mound, while at Dowth to the northeast an earth henge was added around 2500 BC.

Stonehenge

Britain's most iconic megaliths

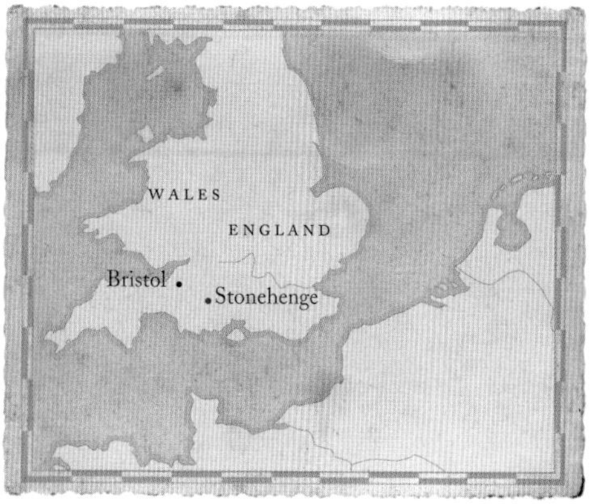

A few miles northwest of the city of Salisbury in southern England, on the exposed chalk down of Salisbury Plain, stands the most iconic ancient monument in the United Kingdom and a site unique in world prehistory. Yet exactly who built it and what it was used for remains largely unknown, and may perhaps remain forever unknowable, making it one of the greatest and most enduring mysteries in modern archaeology.

Stonehenge is not a single monument built at one time, nor can we be sure that those people who added to and altered it were using it for the same reasons as those who built it in the first place. Today the site is most famous for its surviving massive upright stones, with 'lintel' stones on the

'And when I spide those stones on Sarum Plaine,
Which Merlin by his Magicke brought, some saine,
By night from farr I-erne to this land,
Where yet as oldest Monuments they stand:
And though they be but few for to behold,
Yet can they not (it is well knowne) be told.
Those I compared unto my plaints and cryes
Whose totall summe no numers can comprise.'

Alexander Craig – 'To His Calidonian Mistris' (1604)

The standing-stone circle at Stonehenge. Visitors were once permitted to wander at will, touching and even climbing the stones. Now, to preserve this unique site, they are confined to a walkway around the stone circle.

A fanciful artist's impression of a druidic ceremony at Stonehenge in its prehistoric heyday, by the early 19th-century Italian illustrator Angelo Biasioli (1790–1830).

top of them – an arrangement found in no other stone circle on earth. But these were not a part of the first Stonehenge, whose origins lie centuries further back.

The First Phase

The first monument at Stonehenge was begun around 3100 BC, some 500 years before the building of the Great Pyramid of Khufu at Giza in Egypt (see pages 18–23). At this time a circular ditch about 98 metres (320 ft) in diameter was dug on the plain – which had not long before been hazel and pine forest – and the rubble from it piled up in a bank on the inner side. Since this was the Neolithic (New Stone Age) period, the work was carried out without the use of metal tools, the chalk ditch being cut with antler picks, some of which have survived and given us the carbon-14 dates for this phase of the construction. At the northeastern edge of this circle, two stones were put on end to make an entrance. One of these stones, nowadays called the 'Slaughter Stone' (due to the misguided belief that it had one been a place of druidic sacrifice) still survives, although it has toppled over. Just inside the ditch were cut 56 shallow holes, known as 'Aubrey holes' after the 17th-century antiquary and writer John Aubrey (1626–97) who first discovered them. These were probably post holes, holding a circle of timber uprights, similar to the Woodhenge site nearby, although no evidence of wood has been found in them and they seem to have been filled in shortly after being dug.

This arrangement of ditch, bank, post holes and stones remained in use for around 500 years, although exactly what that use was is now impossible to ascertain. It certainly seems likely that this was a meeting place and probably had some ritual significance but there is no evidence left from which we can honestly attempt to reconstruct what happened here.

Arrival of the Stones

Sometime after 2500 BC – in other words, nearly a millennium after its first use – the Stonehenge site again underwent development. At this stage 'bluestones' (whose name derives from the fact that they look blue when wet) were brought to the site to form 80 upright stone pillars in two concentric circles inside the ditch, although this plan was never completed. What is most extraordinary about the presence of these stones here is that they came from the Prescelli Mountains of South Wales almost 250 miles (380 km) away. Even if, as some archaeologists now believe, glacial action brought these boulders nearer than their original source, to reach Salisbury Plain these rocks, weighing up to 4 tons each, would still have to have been hauled by land, sea and river, a massive undertaking in a prehistoric culture. Indeed, all the stones, of whatever period, had to be imported to the site, since there is no workable local stone supply.

A Changing Landscape

If we have any intimation of the use of Stonehenge, it comes from this time, as the entranceway into this circle, which was approached by a ditch and bank avenue, was aligned with the rising sun on the summer solstice. This alignment was made even clearer as 'heel stones' were placed in the avenue over which the sun rose on that one morning when viewed through the two entrance stones. This very precise alignment definitely suggests some astronomical significance to the site.

ERECTING THE SARSEN STONES

Sometime between 2300 and 2000 BC, the builders of Stonehenge dragged 30 massive blocks of silicified sandstone ('sarsen stones'), 20 miles (32 km) from the Marlborough Downs in Wiltshire to the site. These stones, each of which weighed up to 45 tons, were then hauled upright to form a circle the same diameter as the original ditch at Stonehenge (98 metres/320 ft). Once erected, the sarsen stones stood 5 metres (16 ft) high. They were then capped with a continuous circle of stone lintels, each shaped into an arc so that they formed a perfect circle. The lintels were linked to one another by tongue and groove joints, and were held in place on the sarsens by mortice and tenon joints (both woodworking techniques). Inside this circle stood another horseshoe-shaped arrangement of trilithons – two upright stones with a lintel stone over them. These stones were from a more local source. Each stone was smoothed and shaped simply by repeatedly hitting the rough blocks with hammer stones known as 'mauls'. The construction of Stonehenge represents an extraordinary feat of engineering and organization but the precise method by which its prehistoric builders managed to heave the huge stones upright and surmount them with lintels remains a mystery.

After this stage of development, the site appears to have been abandoned for a while, but was back in use by sometime between 2300 and 2000 BC, when the monument was extensively remodelled. In this phase, the bluestones were removed and the huge 'sarsen' stones that are so emblematic of the site nowadays, were erected.

Possibly as little as a century later, in what was now the Bronze Age, the bluestones were reinstated in an oval inside the horseshoe. Later still holes (now known as the 'Z' and 'Y' holes) were dug outside the main stone circle, presumably to hold the other 60 bluestones but this never happened, and indeed the bluestones in the middle were later removed. Minor alterations continued to be made throughout the second millennium BC, with groups

TIMELINE

c.3100 BC Initial stage of construction of Stonehenge. The ditch and bank and 56 post holes ('Aubrey holes') that held timber uprights date from this period

c.2500–2100 BC Bluestones from the Prescelli Mountains in Pembroke, South Wales are erected at Stonehenge

c.2300 BC Bluestones are removed and the largest stones (sarsens) dragged from the Marlborough Downs and erected with lintels to form trilithons

c.1100 BC Final phases of building at Stonehenge

AD 1918 Stonehenge is given to the nation

1986 Stonehenge is declared a UNESCO World Heritage Site

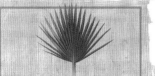

of bluestones being reinstated and removed, indicating that the site was still important to local people. Finally, around 1100 BC the avenue from the henge, which consisted of two parallel ditches and banks, was extended as far as the River Avon, further connecting the monument into a ritual landscape replete with burial mounds and other henge monuments.

After this date, however, Stonehenge seems to have fallen out of use. Having survived from the Stone Age of the fourth millennium BC into the Bronze Age of the late second millennium, the importance of such places rapidly declined. It may be that this development reflected changes in belief or social structures in society during that period. In any event, it is still so deep in prehistory that we have few clues to help us understand what those changes might have been. What the last users of Stonehenge were doing at the site in 1100 BC is still as shrouded in mystery as the motivation and activities of its first builders some 2000 years earlier.

From Private to Public Custodianship

Throughout the late Middle Ages and beyond, Stonehenge remained in private ownership, initially belonging to the nuns of nearby Amesbury Abbey before the dissolution of the monasteries by Henry VIII in the 1530s, and passing thereafter into the hands of various aristocrats, including the Duke of Somerset and the Marquis of Queensbury.

Finally, Stonehenge came into the possession of the Antrobus family, who held onto this archaeological treasure right up to the First World War (1914–18). Then, tragically, in the opening months of the war, Edmund Antrobus, the heir to the family fortune, was killed and his father decided to sell up. One of the lots for sale at auction on 21 September, 1915 in Salisbury was Stonehenge, which was bought on the spur of the moment by Sir Cecil Chubb (1876–1934) as a present for his wife. Three years later, she gave the site to the nation and the process of restoring England's best loved monument could begin.

Over the millennia, Stonehenge has given up few of its secrets, but perhaps it is precisely this enigmatic silence that remains its strongest attraction. Although we do not and probably cannot know what it was for, it was clearly originally constructed for a very important purpose. Thereafter, over thousands of years ancient societies continued to invest huge quantities of time and effort into making this a special place. And it remains a special place today to every visitor, whatever their reason for coming.

'Length of time has so decayed them that not only most of the cross-stones which lay on the top are fallen down, but many of the upright also, notwithstanding the weight of them is so prodigious great. How they came thither, or from whence ... is still the mystery, for they are of such immense bulk that no engines or carriages which we have in use in this age could stir them.'

DANIEL DEFOE – *A TOUR THRO' THE WHOLE ISLAND OF GREAT BRITAIN* (1724–7)

A HISTORY OF NEGLECT

Stonehenge was built, used and abandoned long before literacy came to Britain and as such every generation who has seen and written about it since has struggled to explain its meaning.

The first intimation we have of earlier peoples wondering about the monument is from the name itself – Stonehenge – which derives from the Anglo-Saxon for 'stone' and 'hanging' or 'gallows', implying they perhaps regarded it as a place of execution. In his *History of the Kings of Britain* (*c.*1136), the Welsh chronicler Geoffrey of Monmouth claims that the stone circle was brought from a mountain in Ireland to Salisbury Plain by Merlin with the help of 15,000 knights to form a memorial to Britons who had perished in a battle against the Saxons.

By the 16th century many legends had grown up around the site, including one stating that it was impossible to accurately count the stones and that anyone who did would instantly die, as the Elizabethan courtier Sir Philip Sidney noted. Charles II disproved this in 1651 on his way into exile in France, when he spent a day there counting them to while away the time and came to the same number each time. As Colonel Phelips of the king's retinue put it: '*... the King's Arithmetike gave the lye to that fabulous tale.*'

Seventy-three years later the author Daniel Defoe (1661–1731) agreed that the only reason the stones could not easily be counted was because they were tumbled down and in part buried. He also added that the antiquarians of his day, such as John Aubrey were still disputing whether it was a heathen temple, a place of sacrifice or a monument to the dead. Equally, Defoe noted, no-one could agree as to whether it was built by the British, Danes, Saxons, Romans or even the Phoenicians.

Throughout this period the stones were continuing to topple over and be quarried away. In an area with very little good building stone this is perhaps hardly surprising. In some cases fires were even lit on the lintel stones to break them up and bring them crashing down. Superstition also played a part in the monument's erosion. Visitors, possibly aware of the legendary associations with Merlin, would chip pieces off the stones and throw them down wells to remove toads or try to heal wounds with them. Perhaps some simply wanted a memento, and the blacksmith in nearby Amesbury was happy to hire out a hammer for the purpose. It is largely due to this 'erosion' that Stonehenge today is only about half the monument it once was.

An 18th-century print of Stonehenge. The accompanying text eulogizes the site as 'a great huddle of ancient stones, esteemed one of the wonders of England'.

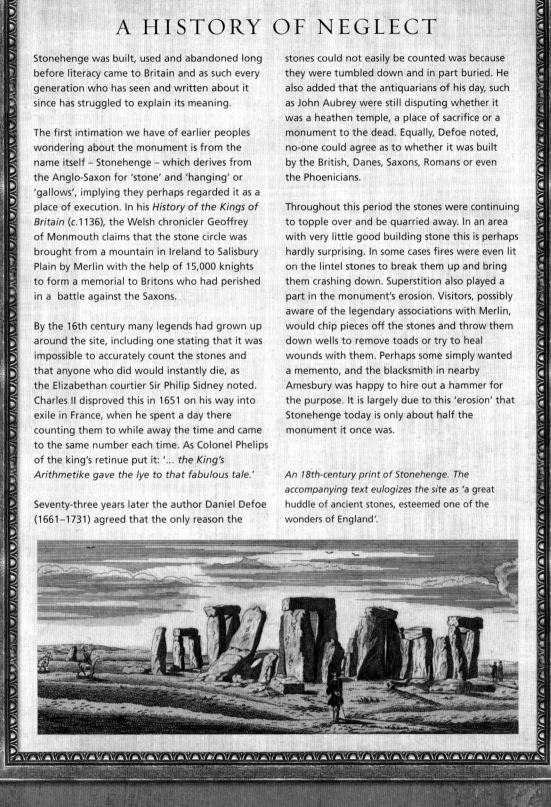

The Great Pyramid of Khufu and The Sphinx

Enigmatic wonders of the desert

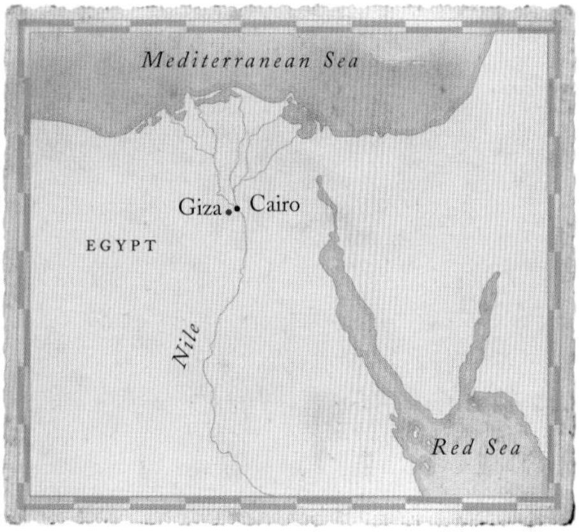

Of the seven wonders on Antipater's original list, only one today bears any resemblance to the sight that the ancients once saw. Earthquakes, war and theft have left no trace of some of the wonders, and made mere ruins of others, but the oldest one – and certainly the most magnificent – still stands relatively unchanged, 4500 years after it was built as the last resting place for the body of the Egyptian pharaoh Khufu.

The pharaoh Khufu, known to the Greeks as Cheops, ruled in the earliest dynastic era of Egyptian history – known as the 'Old Kingdom' – between around 2589 and 2566 BC, as the second pharaoh of the fourth dynasty. Coming from so distant a period, it is perhaps not surprising that precious little is known about him. There are faint inscriptions in Sinai indicating that his troops had been sent to secure the area. His name also appears on an inscription at Aswan, where the red granite for his sarcophagus and the valley temple associated with his pyramid was quarried. Other than that, his likeness has been preserved in a single, diminutive ivory statue that bears his name – at just 7.5-centimetres (3-in) tall, this is the smallest surviving statue of an Egyptian pharaoh. Beyond this scant legacy, however, what Khufu will forever be remembered for is his monumental pyramid at Giza.

A Monumental Achievement

Virtually everything about Khufu's pyramid is a superlative. Aligned almost exactly with the compass, its base deviates from the absolute horizontal by only a couple of centimetres across its entire 230-metre- (755-ft-) square ground plan (which covers a a total area of 5.3 hectares, or 13 acres). This remarkable engineering feat was achieved with only the most basic hand tools. When it was originally finished and clad in a smooth, polished limestone casing, now long since collapsed, it stood 146.7 metres (481 ft) high, making it the tallest building in the world for nearly four millennia, until the completion of the spire of Lincoln Cathedral in England in around AD 1300. Apart from the corridors and chambers within it, the pyramid is made of solid limestone, using a total of 2.3 million blocks with an average weight of 2.5 tons each. With a total weight of 5,700,000 tons, the Great Pyramid is probably still the most massive building ever constructed.

The largest of some 60 pyramids built by the ancient Egyptians on the west bank of the Nile, the Great Pyramid of Khufu remains a truly imposing sight 4500 years after its construction.

'Think of it, soldiers; from the summit of these pyramids, forty centuries look down upon you.'

Napoleon I Bonaparte – Speech to his troops on 21 July, 1798 before the Battle of the Pyramids

When Napoleon Bonaparte first set eyes on it, he calculated that there was enough stone in it to build a wall ten feet high and one foot wide around the whole of France.

The site Khufu chose for his last resting place was not the traditional pyramid field at Saqqara where previous pharaohs had been buried but a rocky plateau on the west bank of the Nile, just outside what is today the capital city of Cairo. Why he chose to move here is not recorded but considering the sheer scale of the pyramid he had in mind, it is probable that simple geological necessity brought him to a site near the Nile, where there was enough local stone to build on this unprecedented scale. Originally his pyramid formed part of a larger complex of buildings that included a valley temple by the Nile, where the pharaoh's body arrived for burial, a causeway leading from this to a mortuary temple sited against the pyramid itself, other smaller pyramids housing the remains of queens, a number of enigmatic 'boat pits' containing the disassembled parts of cedar wood ships and a finely cut limestone wall around the entire complex.

Puzzles of the Pyramid

The entrance to the pyramid is on the north face, 18 metres (59 ft) above its base. From here, one sloping corridor of finely joined limestone descends below ground level to an underground chamber, while another rises to meet the 'Great Gallery', a tall passageway with a coffered ceiling. A passage off here leads to what is known as the 'Queen's Chamber', while the main gallery continues up to the 'King's Chamber' with its huge multi-layered granite roof, designed to prevent the weight of the pyramid above from crushing the room. Above this room are the mysterious 'ventilation holes'; these may simply have allowed fresh air into the room, although their precise alignment has given rise to speculation that they may have also had a ritual and perhaps structural function that is now lost. One such notion is that the ventilation shafts were aligned precisely with the constellation of Orion, which for the ancient Egyptians represented the soul of Osiris, the god of death, the afterlife and rebirth.

This is the chamber where, we must suppose, Khufu was buried. Whether or not he did ever rest in this granite-lined vault must remain a matter of speculation, however, as no trace of his burial has been found inside the pyramid except his unfinished red granite sarcophagus. As for the pharaoh's body, or the magnificent grave goods we might expect to find in what is perhaps the most lavish tomb ever constructed, nothing has ever been recovered. If any of his funerary goods have survived the ravages of time and tomb raiders, they still await discovery.

Whatever Khufu's fate, his successors continued to build at Giza. His son, the pharaoh Khafre, built the second largest pyramid nearby. As it is built on slightly higher ground and still retains at its summit the limestone facing stones that once graced all the pyramids, it is often mistaken for the Great Pyramid. The third main pyramid at Giza is the smaller tomb of Menkaure, who was probably either the son or grandson of Khafre. Astonishingly, this whole complex was probably completed within a 100-year period, although precise dating for these pharaohs' reigns is uncertain.

Just how these rulers managed to commandeer and organize the quantity of labour needed for this feat remains a mystery. Originally it was thought that the pyramids were built by slaves, but modern Egyptologists suggest that they may in fact have been built by the ordinary people of Egypt, seconded to work on the monuments during the annual flooding of the Nile when the fields were submerged and no agricultural activity could take place. Estimates of the number of labourers required and the time taken to build Khufu's pyramid vary wildly. The fifth-century BC Greek historian Herodotus claimed that it took 100,000

TIMELINE

***c*.2589–2566 BC** Reign of Fourth Dynasty ruler Khufu

***c*.2480 BC** Probable completion date of Great Pyramid of Khufu

***c*.1425 BC** Thutmose IV places the Dream Stela between the Sphinx's paws

AD 1301 Massive earthquake loosens many of the casing stones, which are later used on other building projects in Cairo

1798 Napoleon Bonaparte visits the pyramids during his first Egyptian campaign

1880–2 First precise survey of the pyramids is undertaken by the British archaeologist Sir Flinders Petrie

1925–36 French engineer Emile Baraize clears the Sphinx site

1954 Egyptian archaeologist Kamal el Mallakh discovers the boat pits at the Giza temple complex

SOLE SURVIVOR

Khufu's pyramid is perhaps the most fortunate of the ancient wonders; its sheer scale and monumentality has ensured that it has survived remarkably intact, considering it is over four and a half millennia old. But even so its history down the centuries has not been an uneventful one.

Even in antiquity, the pyramid was not simply a wonder to foreign travellers such as Herodotus; the ancient Egyptians themselves also marvelled at it. It was nearly 1200 years old by the time Tutankhamun became pharaoh and more distant in time from Cleopatra than she is from us today. Yet for all the reverence the ancient Egyptians held towards the dead, the pyramids (like most of the later tombs in the Valley of the Kings) were almost certainly robbed of their treasures in ancient times.

This print of 1801, entitled Passage from the second to the third gallery *shows Caliph al-Ma'moun's incursion into Khufu's pyramid.*

From the Middle Ages onwards travellers to the Holy Land and later Renaissance scholars were drawn to Giza to measure and speculate on what was by then the only surviving Wonder of the Ancient World. Despite further internal explorations using al-Ma'moun's tunnels, no visitor had any more luck in finding the legendary cache. At some point in the medieval period the pyramid lost its smooth outer casing of limestone. This was probably caused by an earthquake, since many early visitors report seeing piles of rubble around its base. Over time, much of this limestone was carried off for building projects in the rapidly expanding city of Cairo.

By the time of the first recorded entrance into the pyramid in the modern era, the Egyptian religion was long dead, though stories of the great wealth hidden in tombs there endured. These inspired Caliph al-Ma'moun, who ruled Egypt from AD 831 to 832, to attempt to break in. Unable to find an obvious entrance he ordered his men to tunnel directly into the middle of the north side of the monument, lighting and quenching fires against the stones to shatter them into moveable pieces. After digging deep into the pyramid they finally broke into the descending passage leading to the underground chamber and from there went on to explore most of the interior. Sadly for the caliph, the promise of treasure proved false.

Modern archaeological work at the Great Pyramid began in the late 18th century, with attempts to measure and draw cross-sections of the internal structure. Many of the most illustrious names in Egyptology, from Flinders Petrie to Ludwig Borchardt and Karl Lepsius, have investigated the site.

Today it remains one of the world's foremost tourist attractions, although modern visitors are no longer allowed to climb it. Yet the Giza Plateau and Khufu's pyramid probably still hold many secrets. It was only in 1954 that Egyptian archaeologist Kamal el Mallakh discovered the boat pits with their intact wooden ships from the days of Khufu, only one of which has been excavated and reconstructed. Other parts of Khufu's funerary complex, the greatest wonder of the ancient world, may still lie buried in the sand.

labourers 20 years to build, but modern estimates vary from 50,000 men to over 300,000 taking anything from 10 to 20 years – all of whom would have had to be housed and fed.

The American writer Mark Twain neatly summarized the enigmatic lure of the Sphinx when he wrote in 1869 that: 'The Sphinx is grand in its loneliness; it is imposing in its magnitude; it is impressive in the mystery that hangs over its story.'

A simple calculation helps put into perspective the extraordinary effort expended in building the Great Pyramid. Let us assume it took 20 years to complete. We know from the number of stones used that to build the pyramid in that time, just over one stone would have to have been set in place every two minutes throughout a ten-hour day, 365 days a year. This does not take into account the time taken to quarry, dress and ship the stones, some of which weigh 80 tons, without the use of pulleys, wheels or iron tools. Assuming no delays, a single modern American limestone quarry using up-to-date technology and working at the standard rate would take 2673 years to cut, dress and transport that quantity of stone.

Whatever the actual statistics, there is no denying that, 4500 years ago, Khufu created what is still one of the most magnificent and imposing buildings on Earth.

The Pyramid's Mysterious Guardian

Close by the Great Pyramid stands the Sphinx, one of the largest effigies ever carved in the round by man, which has become a symbol of Egypt. Yet its history is filled with uncertainties stretching back to the time of the first pharaohs.

The concept of the sphinx seems to have originated in Egypt around 5000 years ago and the image of a lion with a pharaoh's head, symbolizing the power of the ruler, remained a common motif throughout the dynastic period. During this time other types of sphinx also emerged, often carved in figures lining processional routes, including the criosphinx, with the body of a lion and the head of a ram, and the hierocosphinx, with the body of a lion and the head of a hawk.

Exactly when the Sphinx at Giza was constructed is still hotly debated. The monument would appear to be contemporary with the great pyramids of Khufu, Khafre and Menkaure but no inscription survives to tell us which, if any, of these pharaohs may have ordered its construction. It is traditionally associated with the pharaoh Khafre (*c.*2575–*c.*2465 BC), builder of the second largest pyramid at Giza, which it stands directly to the south of. However, an inscription found in 1857 on the Giza plateau and known as the 'Inventory stela' claims that Khufu (Khafre's father) repaired the Sphinx's tail and headdress, which would date the statue even earlier. Yet since this inscription dates from around 600 BC, some 2000 years after the Sphinx was built, it may represent no more than folklore.

Most scholars believe that the monument certainly dates from the earliest dynastic period of Egyptian history, known as the Old Kingdom (2613–2498 BC), as it is stylistically very similar to other statues of this period. It shows a creature with a lion's body and a human head, which is wearing one of the traditional headdresses of the pharaohs, known as the nemes head cloth. In the centre of this is another pharaonic symbol, the *uraeus* – a stylized rearing cobra, which represented the god Wadjet and was a symbol of divinity and royal authority in Egypt. As such the monument is usually seen as an embodiment of the pharaoh's power.

Associated with the Sphinx are two temples, one of which is contemporaneous with the statue and stands on a terrace between the creature's paws. Sadly no inscriptions have been found to tell us what this building was for, indeed it has been suggested that it may never have been finished, but its alignment, like the Sphinx's itself, facing due east into the rising sun, would suggest that it was a site of solar worship. The construction of the monument was itself unique. The main body of the Sphinx is not built from cut stone blocks but instead carved from the living bedrock. To build it, a huge 'U'-shaped trench was dug into the rock of the plateau leaving a large central block, which was then carved into the shape of a lion's body. The limestone removed for the trench and in carving the body was then cut into blocks and used to construct the temple. The result was the largest single stone block statue ever built, standing nearly 80 metres (262 ft) long and over 20 metres (65 ft) high.

The Sphinx has weathered very unevenly, with weaker strata of rock crumbling and undermining other layers above them. The site of the Sphinx may originally have been a quarry and when the quarrymen reached a mass of rock that was faulted and unsuitable for building they worked around it and later carved it into the Sphinx. Certainly, its complex geological origins have not helped its survival, and it is perhaps only thanks to the fact that it has spent much of the last 3000 or more years buried in sand that it has survived at all.

MAINTAINING THE SPHINX

Even during the pharaonic period the Sphinx was almost swallowed by the desert. A stela placed between the Sphinx's paws by Thutmose IV (1425–1412 BC) relates how that pharaoh, when still a prince, was out riding when he became sleepy and decided to rest in the shade of the partly buried monument. As he slept a dream came to him in which the sun god, in the form of the Sphinx, told him that if he dug the sand away from the statue then he would become pharaoh. When he awoke Thuthmose promptly ordered the site cleared and duly, as prophesied, became pharaoh. This story may be little more than propaganda by Thutmose to legitimize his dubious claim to the throne but he certainly did restore the Sphinx. A second phase of restoration was undertaken in the 26th dynasty, in the seventh and sixth centuries BC, followed by a third in the Roman period. After this the Sphinx slipped from view again. Around the eighth century AD the nose was removed, possibly hacked off in an attempt to deface a statue that was by then considered blasphemous and pagan. In 1380 further attacks by religious fanatics damaged the face.

By the time Napoleon arrived in Egypt in 1798, bringing with him the 167 artists and scholars who would be largely responsible for rediscovering ancient Egypt, the Sphinx was buried up to its neck. Their drawings of the colossal head inspired a Genoese merchant in 1816 to attempt to dig the monument out, discovering in the process what may be a piece of its beard (now in the British Museum), but he was overwhelmed by the scale of the task. The whole site was only fully cleared between 1925 and 1936.

Today, freed from the sand that has protected it for so many millennia, the Sphinx is once again at risk from pollution and erosion and a fifth restoration programme is underway to ensure that this ancient masterpiece continues to greet the rising sun on the Giza plateau each morning.

Mohenjo Daro

Jewel of the Indus Valley civilization

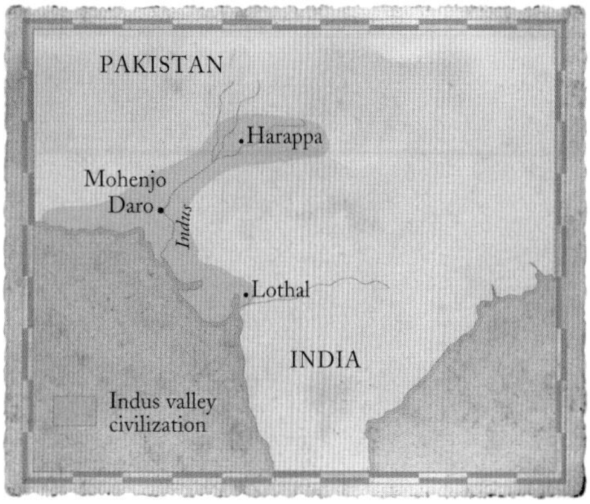

Before the 20th century it was widely believed that the Indian subcontinent had played little or no role in the growth of the earliest civilizations, simply because no evidence for this had been found. Then, in 1921–2, excavations uncovered two ancient settlements on the Indus river, one at Harappa in what is now northeast Pakistan and the other in the southern Pakistani province of Sindh. Locals thought the latter site was an old cemetery and so called it 'The Mound of the Dead' – or in Sindhi, Mohenjo Daro.

What was extraordinary about the site discovered at Mohenjo Daro was that it was not a burial mound or an old fort but one of the most sophisticated cities in the ancient world and the heart of the Indus Valley civilization, a culture that had disappeared without trace for nearly 4000 years. Today we know of over 100 Indus Valley civilization sites, covering an area from the Himalayas to the Arabian Sea, which were home to perhaps five million people. Among these sites, Mohenjo Daro was undoubtedly the greatest city.

A Planned Settlement

The centre of Mohenjo Daro covered an area of around 100 hectares (247 acres) on the banks of the Indus river. Together with its suburbs, which remain largely unexcavated, the city may have extended over a total area of more than 400 hectares (1000 acres) and been home to as many as 40,000 people. The central area consists of 12 mounds, each of which appears to have been a specific 'quarter' or 'block' of the city laid out on a grid pattern similar to many modern US cities. This probably makes Mohenjo Daro the first city ever to be planned. The central block on the western side of the city, known today as the 'Citadel', consisted of an area built up some 12 metres (38 ft) above the level of the flood plain. This mound was fortified with baked brick towers, protecting a group of structures including a massive central bath, 12 metres long by 7 metres wide by 2.4 metres deep (38 x 23 x 8 ft), which stood in a large colonnaded building. The floor of the bath was sealed with two layers of 'sawed' bricks set on edge in a gypsum mortar, sandwiching a sealer of bitumen between them. There was a large well in a room next door, which probably provided the water, and a huge drain, large enough to walk through, to empty it. Exactly what this structure was used for is unknown, as the writing system used by the Indus

Valley peoples has yet to be deciphered, but it has been suggested that it served some ritual use or was, perhaps, just the first public baths in world history. Also on the Citadel are three other peculiar structures. The first is a large residential area, although it is not clear if this is the home of one important family or group or just another residential block. Nearby is what excavators have called a 'granary', due to the presence of structures assumed to be flues for drying grain and a loading bay. Finally there are the colonnaded 'assembly halls', whose true use is still a mystery. The other part of the Citadel remains unexcavated as it is covered by a second-century Buddhist stupa.

'Thus India must henceforth be recognised, along with Persia, Mesopotamia and Egypt, as one of the most important areas where the civilising processes of society were initiated and developed.'

JOHN MARSHALL – *MOHENJO DARO AND THE INDUS CIVILISATION* (1931)

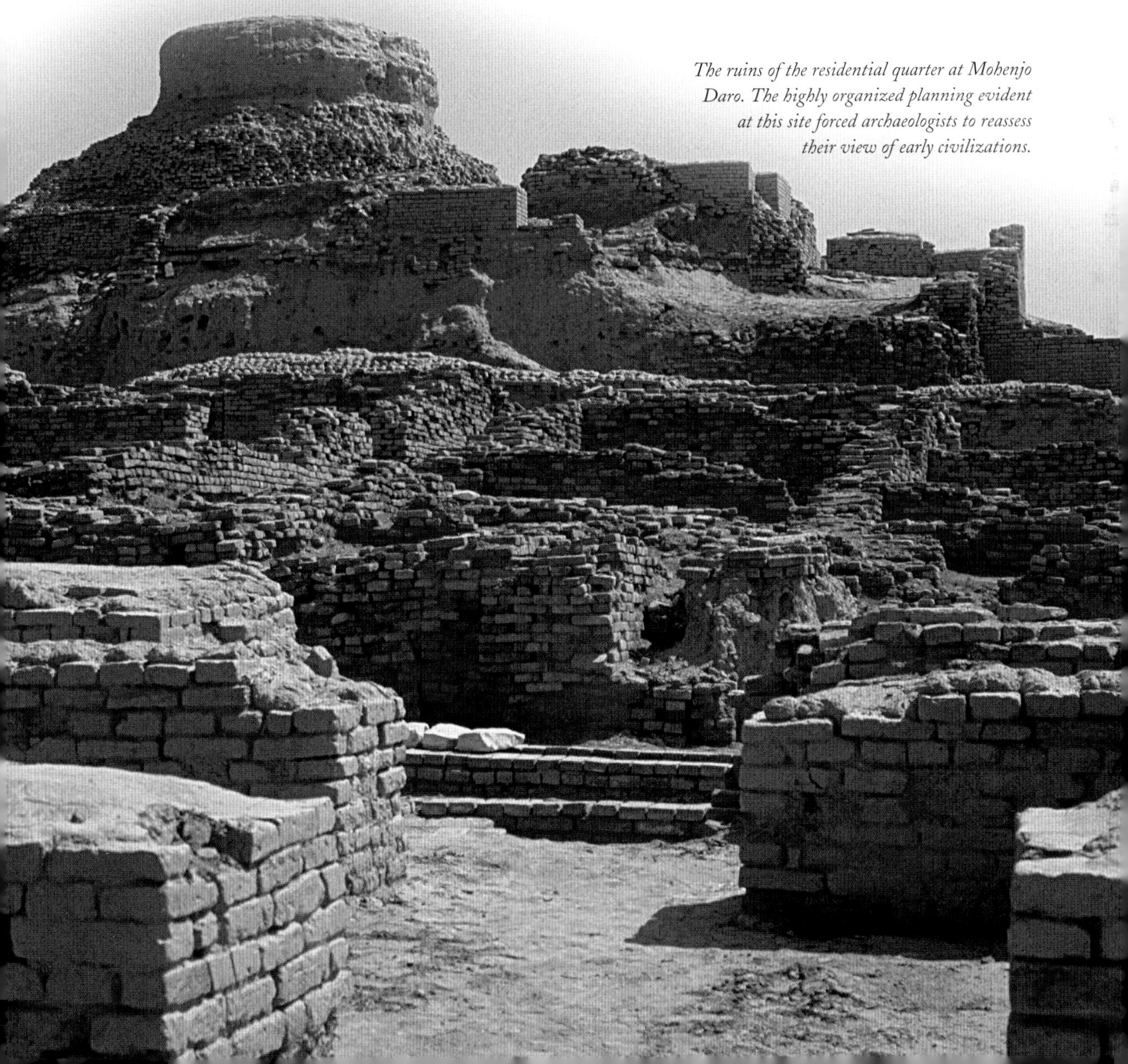

The ruins of the residential quarter at Mohenjo Daro. The highly organized planning evident at this site forced archaeologists to reassess their view of early civilizations.

TIMELINE

c.5000 BC First settled communities appear in the Indus Valley

c.2000 BC The Indus Valley civilization reaches its height, with over 100 settlements on the plain

c.1700 BC The Indus Valley civilization collapses and its cities and script are abandoned

c.AD 1921 Indian archaeologist R.D. Banerji uncovers the major Indus Valley city of Mohenjo Daro

1924 First publication of finds at Mohenjo Daro and Harappa, in Sir John Marshall's article 'First Light on a Long-Forgotten Civilisation' for *The Illustrated London News*

1925–31 Under Marshall's direction, extensive excavations are conducted at Mohenjo Daro, revealing that catastrophic floods brought about the downfall of the Indus Valley civilization

In the lower town, with its straight grid of roads stood rows of windowless brick houses, their blank walls protecting the inhabitants from the burning summer sun. The size of houses varied a great deal from single-room dwellings with a partition to screen off the cooking and bathing areas to large residences laid out around courtyards. Within these were living and dining areas and a bathroom plumbed in to the city's sewage system – the earliest such system known.

Yet despite the discovery of an entire ruined city at Mohenjo Daro, the Indus Valley civilization remains a mystery. There are no buildings that can be definitely identified as temples or palaces, and the dead were apparently not buried with grave goods, so we cannot discover what class system (if any) existed here. Moreover, there are no monuments or tombs to the élite as there are in Egypt and Mesopotamia. The little booths on the corners of the main boulevards have been identified as 'police offices', but there is no other evidence for a police force or even an army; indeed, there is very little evidence of any weaponry for such forces to use.

From the artefacts they left behind, we do know these people were farmers and traders. It is clear that they grew barley, wheat, rice, dates and cotton and kept domesticated cattle, sheep, buffalo, pigs, dogs, camels and elephants. Metal finds show they had bronze and stone tools and made ornaments of gold, silver, ivory and precious stones such as cornelian, much of which must have been brought from great distances, since they do not occur locally.

Although over 4000 objects bearing the Indus Valley script have been discovered and at least 400 major symbols identified, this civilization's language still defies translation. No bilingual text has ever been found (such as the Rosetta Stone, which held the key to the deciphering of Egyptian hieroglyphics), and neither the language that the script encodes nor even the language group it might belong to have been identified. Attempts at translation are further hampered by the fact that most inscriptions are less than five symbols long, with the longest being only 26 symbols, leading some scholars to suggest that this was never a full written language in the first place.

One of the most remarkable finds from Mohenjo Daro is the so-called 'priest-king', a delicately carved soapstone torso depicting a bearded man wearing a cloak decorated with trefoil (cloverleaf) motifs.

A Mercantile People

One thing we do know for certain about the people of the Indus Valley civilization is that they were great travellers. At the coastal city of Lothal, archaeologists have uncovered a huge dredged canal and docks for sea-going ships. In addition, Indus Valley artefacts, including examples of their mysterious writing, have been found as far afield as Mesopotamia. And while we may be

DESTROYED BY THE DELUGE

The Indus Valley civilization at Mohenjo Daro flourished for around 500 years before finally collapsing in around 1700 BC. As much of the site is below the modern water table, we cannot be sure that the city was entirely abandoned at that time, but there can be little doubt that the way of life that its inhabitants had come to enjoy came to an abrupt end.

The reason for this may lie in the fields surrounding the ruins. Nowadays the city lies some 2 miles (3 km) west of the Indus, but at the time of the Indus Valley civilization, the river lay hard by to the east. All of this area is a flood plain filled with a deep layer of silt; indeed, the archaeological layers of the city reach down 9 metres (30 ft) below the modern ground level, leaving only the top 12 metres (38 ft) of the 'mounds' protruding. The Indus flooded seasonally across this plain, irrigating the fields of the Mohenjo Daro farmers, much like the Tigris and Euphrates in Mesopotamia and the Nile in Egypt, providing the lifeblood of civilization there. But the river could be unpredictable. The Indus is what hydrologists call an 'exotic' river – that is, one that rises in a well-watered area but then flows through a very arid landscape. While irrigating the land, the Indus brought life to the dry valley floor, but it could also bring death.

A heavy season's rain in the distant Himalayas could have a catastrophic effect on the cities downstream. Excavations have revealed several metres' depth of silt in some areas, which must have washed through the streets in minutes, suffocating everything in its path. By 1700 BC these floods were becoming ever more frequent, and were made worse by earthquakes caused by the slow but inexorable collision of the Indian subcontinent with Asia. Around this time, it appears that the area was prone to particularly heavy rains. As the billions of tonnes of water hurtled through the Himalayan foothills, a series of earth tremors disrupted the course of the Indus, effectively damming it. The flood water built up, inundating the valley and drowning everything in it until it finally burst through.

For a people who had lived in the valley for over 3000 years, this was the final catastrophe. Their fields were choked, their cities engulfed. Stories of the tragedy may have reached Sumeria, where the legend of Gilgamesh records a terrible flood that destroyed the world. This myth was later incorporated into the Bible as Noah's flood. For at least some of the people of the Indus Valley, however, this was not simply a legend but a very real ecological disaster.

unable to read their script, we can read the cuneiform texts of old Sumeria, which tell of the people of Meluhha (probably the Indus Valley) who dealt in precious turquoise from India and lapis lazuli from Afghanistan and traded jade with distant China. Their ships were a familiar sight at Dilmun – modern Bahrain – where they traded peacocks, monkeys, incense, ivory, precious stones and rare spices with the Sumerians. Perhaps unsurprisingly, such compulsive traders are also thought to have developed the earliest accurate system of weights and measures.

What became of the Indus Valley people is the final mystery in their story. The social structures that held them together were collapsing by 1700 BC, by which time most of their cities had been abandoned and their script had fallen into disuse. Elements of their culture reappear later, suggesting that they adapted to the new world they found themselves in. However, the heyday of their civilization was long past and the ruins of Mohenjo Daro fell silent.

The Great Ziggurat at Ur

Mighty temple to the Sumerian moon-god

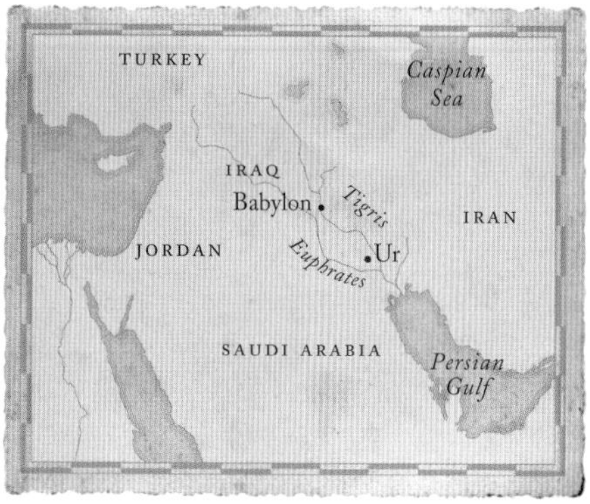

OVER 5000 YEARS AGO, THE CITY of Ur was a thriving settlement in one of the earliest civilizations of ancient Mesopotamia. Tradition claimed it as the birthplace of the biblical patriarch Abraham. The stepped pyramid there known as the Great Ziggurat is the largest and the best preserved of all the buildings to survive from this period.

Ur – which is known today as Tell el-Mukayyar (meaning 'the mound built of bitumen') and stands close to Nasiriyah in southern Iraq – was one of the most important cities of the Sumerian civilization that flourished between the Tigris and Euphrates rivers between the mid-fourth millennium BC and the late 3rd millennium BC. The city reached its height under the rule of the Third dynasty at Ur (known as Ur III) when it was home of a powerful series of kings and it was under one of these, Ur-Nammu (*c.*2122–2094 BC) that work on the great ziggurat began.

Temple Pyramids

Unlike the pyramids of Egypt – some of which come from the same period as the Great Ziggurat, and to which they bear some similarity – ziggurats were not tombs but temples for the worship of the patron gods of each of the dozen or so city-states of Sumer. The Great Ziggurat at Ur is easily the best preserved of the 25 known examples, all of which share a common structure: a series of stepped levels surmounted by a temple and approached by a grand staircase.
The Great Ziggurat stands at the high point of an extraordinary architectural achievement that saw Sumerian builders incorporate such sophisticated elements as columns, arches, vaults and domes into their structures more than 1000 years before Mediterranean cultures used these same features. The temple mound at Ur is built on three progressively smaller levels, each with walls that slope inwards, reminiscent of the old stepped pyramids of Egypt. The bottom stage was constructed from seven million sun-dried mud bricks – the main construction material in a land without stone – which were built up in courses six bricks high. Each sixth level was then capped with a

layer of reed matting and sandy soil to level out the course and improve drainage as the friable mud bricks were prone to waterlogging, caused either by rainy weather or the flooding of the Tigris and Euphrates, whose mouths were located close to the city at that time.

To further ensure that the whole structure did not slump down, window-like evaporation channels known as 'weeping holes' were cut into each level.This mud-brick core was then encased in 720,000 15-kg (33-lb) baked bricks joined together at the lower levels with waterproof bitumen (to protect against flooding) and with mortar higher up. The kiln firing of these bricks, which was expensive in a land where fuel for fires was rare, ensured they were waterproof and hence protected the core. The weeping holes were also lined with these waterproof bricks to improve drainage. So that no-one would forget who was responsible for this gargantuan task, the ruler of the day, Ur-Nammu, had his name embossed on nearly every baked brick.

On top of this 12-metre (38-ft) high, 42,000-ton mud structure another similar, but smaller, level was built and on top of this a third on which stood the actual shrine to Ur's patron deity Nanna. To reach this, three grand staircases were built to the top of the lowest level – two against the wall and one at 90 degrees to it. Here, all three met at a gateway which led to another single staircase up to the top of the second level and a third up to the shrine itself.

The Great Ziggurat at Ur. Today, only the first platform remains of what was originally a three-stepped pyramid.

TIMELINE

c.4300 BC The world's first city-states emerge in the 'Fertile Crescent' of Mesopotamia, between the Tigris and Euphrates rivers

c.2900 BC During the Early Dynastic Period, the main rival powers in Sumeria are the cities of Kish, Uruk and Ur

c.2112 BC The Third Dynasty of Ur (Ur III) is founded by Ur-Nammu

c.2095 BC Shulgi succeeds Ur-Nammu as ruler of Ur

c.1950 BC End of Ur III, as the city is overthrown by the Elamites

AD 1625 Italian traveller Pietro della Valle visits and describes the site of Ur at Tell el-Mukayyar

1854 The British Consul at Basra, J.E. Taylor, begins excavation of the Ziggurat at Ur dedicated to the moon god Nanna

1922 Excavations funded by the British Museum and the University of Pennsylvania are led by Leonard Woolley; the work, which lasts until 1934, unearths many major artefacts from the Royal Cemetery

2003 Concern over potential damage to Ur is raised during the US invasion of Iraq, due to the presence nearby of a major military base established by Saddam Hussein

To further increase the effect of height, the architects curved every wall inwards slightly towards the top; indeed, there are no right angles to be found anywhere in the ziggurat. This technique, known as 'entasis,' would be taken up by Greek architects over 1500 years later. The finished result was a mountain-like structure that draws the eye ever upwards. The Great Ziggurat measures around 60 metres by 45 metres (197 x 148 ft) at its base and rises 21 metres (69 ft) above the flat alluvial plain of the Tigris-Euphrates Valley, making it easily the largest building in the city. It is hence hardly surprising that the Sumerian term for ziggurat – *Etemennigur* – means 'a house whose foundation creates thunder'.

Sadly, due to the destruction of the uppermost levels of the ziggurat we are unsure as to exactly what the temple there looked like or what rites may have been performed inside it. We do know that the temple was dedicated to the moon-god Nanna (known as Sin in Akkadian), whose name means 'the illuminator' in Sumerian. Nanna's symbol was a crescent, representing the moon but sometimes shown as the horns of a bull, as the god was also associated with cattle herds.

Ur-Nammu's Demise

Despite Ur-Nammu's dedication of this enormous temple complex to him, it seems that Nanna did not smile on the Sumerian king. Ur-Nammu had enjoyed some spectacular successes during his reign, conquering the city of Lagash and presiding over an empire that included the major cities of Uruk and Eridu. As well as building the ziggurat, he made major improvements to the irrigation system in the city fields and is credited with producing the oldest surviving law code known, which deals with matters as diverse as witchcraft, slavery and personal injury. Finally, however, he found himself once more confronting his old enemy the Guti (who had ruled Sumer before his dynasty). During the ensuing battle, it appears that his troops deserted him and he was cut down. In the fragmentary Sumerian text *The Death of Ur-Nammu*, we hear of the king arriving in the gloomy netherworld and lamenting the loss of his still unfinished city, his new palace and his family:

> *'After five days, ten days had passed, lamenting for Sumer overwhelmed my king, lamenting for Sumer overwhelmed Ur-Nammu. As he could not complete the wall of Urim; as he could no longer enjoy the new palace he had built; as he, the shepherd, could no longer protect (?) his household; as he could no longer bring pleasure to his wife with his embrace; as he could not bring up his sons on his knees; as he would never see in their prime the beauty of their little sisters, who are yet to grow up, the trustworthy shepherd uttered a heart-rending lament for himself.'*

Ur-Nammu's son Shulgi proved more fortunate, completing much of his father's work during his 48-year reign, which saw the city grow to become probably the largest in the world at that time.

> *'Then did Ur-Nammu the mighty warrior, king of Ur, king of Sumer and Akkad, by the might of Nanna, Lord of the City, and in accordance with the true word of Utu, establish equity in the land.'*

PROLOGUE TO THE CODE OF UR-NAMMU

DECLINE AND FALL

The writings and architecture that have survived from Ur III have earned this period the title 'the Sumerian Renaissance'. This age of cultural flowering was eventually brought to an end around 2000 BC by an Elamite invasion, during which the city was sacked. A surviving text – the *Lament for Ur* – records this tragedy and suggests that the shrine on the top of the ziggurat, if not more, was destroyed at this time:

> *'The good house of the lofty untouchable mountain, E-kic-nu-jal, was entirely devoured by large axes. The people of Cimacki and Elam, the destroyers, counted its worth as only 30 shekels. They broke up the good house with pickaxes. They reduced the city to ruin mounds. Its queen cried, "Alas, my city". Ningal [the wife of the God Nanna] cried, "Alas, my house". As for me, the woman, both my city has been destroyed and my house has been destroyed. O Nanna, the shrine Ur has been destroyed and its people have been killed.'*

Leonard Woolley undertaking excavations at the Ziggurat of Ur in 1925.

Ur was rebuilt, but never regained its former importance. During the Neo-Babylonian period, Nebuchadrezzar II (605–562 BC) largely rebuilt the city, while the last king of Babylon, Nabonidas (556–539 BC) increased the height of the ziggurat to seven levels. However, the city began to decline shortly thereafter, perhaps due to a shift in the course of the Tigris and Euphrates rivers, which would have hindered irrigation and reduced the city's access to the sea and hence trade. By 500 BC it seems to have been abandoned. The mudbrick houses and palaces soon crumbled into a shallow mound, sand built up around the lower levels of the Great Ziggurat and Ur sank into obscurity.

The decaying remains of Ur survived into the modern period in the form of a mound known as Tell el-Mukayyar. The great antiquity of this site had been known about since the early 17th century, when the Italian traveller Pietro della Valle (1586–1652) visited Tell el-Mukayyar and noted piles of ancient brickwork printed with undecipherable writing. In 1854 the British consul carried out small-scale excavations there to reveal that the central mound was a huge ziggurat and concluded that the site was rich in antiquities and a prime candidate for full excavation. In 1922 the British scholar Leonard Woolley (1880–1960) began 12 years of excavation at Ur.

By the time Woolley arrived in Mesopotamia, monumental gateways, dramatic reliefs and clay tablets with cuneiform writing from Babylon, Nineveh and Nimrud already filled the museums of the West. But Ur was still relatively untouched. Woolley was a new breed of archaeologist, trained in stratigraphic excavation and with the patience to glean every scrap of information he could from each layer of earth rather than digging recklessly in search of treasure.

His groundbreaking work revealed the remains of a city whose origins dated back nearly 7000 years. Each phase of construction built on the ruins of its predecessor, from the earliest reed houses through the era when this city was the home to Abraham to its remodelling at the time of Nebuchadnezzar and its final decline in the years before the birth of Christ.

In modern times, although a military base was sited nearby, Ur survived the 2003 invasion of Iraq relatively unscathed. It is now once again attracting a trickle of tourists and academics, although insurgency in the region makes archaeological work there precarious. Much of the site has still to be excavated, and many of the secrets of one of the world's first cities may yet be brought to light.

The Temple of Solomon

The great shrine of ancient Judaism

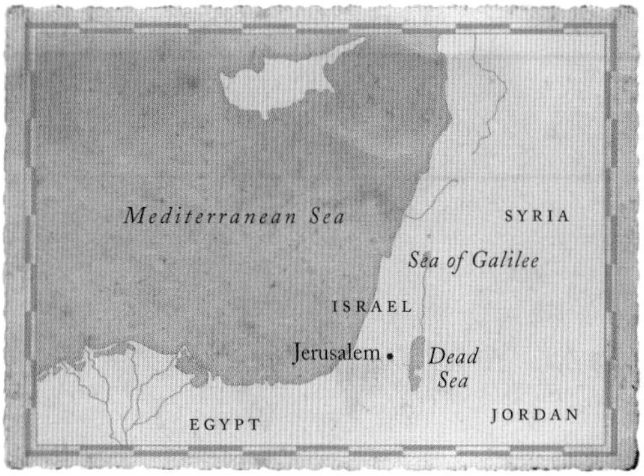

King Solomon's reputation has come down to us through nearly three millennia of history. The fact that his name is still recalled today is certainly due in part to his appearance in the Hebrew Bible (Old Testament), a text sacred to both Judaism and Christianity. But stories of his fabled mines, the visit of the queen of Sheba and, above all, the magnificent temple he built in Jerusalem have also enthralled successive generations.

Solomon (r. 967–931 BC) was the son of David (r. 1007–967 BC), the founder of the Judaean dynasty, who had established an empire stretching from the borders of Egypt in Sinai to the banks of the Euphrates river in Mesopotamia. How Solomon came to the throne is not entirely clear, since his mother Bathsheba was one of a large number of wives of David, many of whom had sons they wished to see on the throne. In the Old Testament it is God who decides, but historically – and not unusually for the period – Solomon probably achieved power through a coup d'état, organized with the help of his mother and an influential court prophet known as Nathan.

Solomon was an expert player in the game of Bronze Age Near Eastern politics. Having eliminated his enemies and promoted his friends to the most senior positions at court, he set about consolidating his international position through diplomatic marriages (the Bible says he had 700 wives and 300 concubines, although this is bound to be an exaggeration), the marrying off of his own children to foreign potentates and the exchange of gifts with friendly states. He also went to great lengths to secure and control the trade routes passing through his country, as reflected in the story of the visit to Jerusalem of the queen of Sheba, whose land (thought to be Saba, in present-day Yemen) was a major source of gold, frankincense and myrrh. This trade made Solomon wealthy and with this he fulfilled another vital role of a Bronze Age king – building.

In his capital, Jerusalem, Solomon built a new defensive city wall (known as the 'millo') and an extensive complex of royal palaces. These included the 'House of the Forest of Lebanon', which probably served as an armoury, and a private palace for his Egyptian wife (the Egyptians were one of the foremost powers of the day and hence worth pampering). Most important of all, however, he invested in a shrine that would serve as a single focus for the Jewish religion – the temple.

Jews praying at the Western Wall, in an 1873 painting by the English artist Charles Robertson. The Western Wall is sacred in Judaism as the nearest location to the former site of the First and Second Temples.

TIMELINE

c.967 BC King Solomon orders construction of the First Temple

c.957 BC Completion of the First Temple

10th–7th centuries BC Repeated raids on Jerusalem and the Temple by Judah, Egypt and other surrounding kingdoms

607–586 BC Three waves of attacks by the Babylonians leave Jerusalem and the First Temple in ruins; King Nebuchadrezzar II deports Jews into the Babylonian Captivity

537 BC Cyrus II (the great) of Persia allows the Jews to return to Jerusalem and rebuild the Temple

c.516 BC Second Temple completed

175–165 BC Antiochus Epiphanes of the Seleucid empire sacks Jerusalem and defiles the Second Temple

c.20–18 BC Herod the Great undertakes a massive renovation and expansion of the Second Temple

AD 70 During the Jewish revolt, Roman commander Titus captures Jerusalem and destroys the Second Temple, supposedly on the same day as the destruction of the First Temple (Tisha b'Av)

A Shrine to House the Ark

Before Solomon's reign, the focus of Judaism shifted with its most sacred relic, the Ark of the Covenant, which moved from sanctuary to sanctuary. The Ark contained the tablets of the Law (Ten Commandments) given by God to Moses and brought down from Mount Sinai during the Israelites' wanderings in the wilderness. Solomon resolved to give the Ark a permanent home by building a magnificent temple in his capital, Jerusalem.

The exact site of the temple is still disputed but tradition states that Solomon chose the hill where Abraham, the founding patriarch of the Jewish people, had offered to sacrifice his son Isaac to God. This is also the place where, in Islam, Mohammed rose to heaven to receive prayers from God. As a result, the Temple Mount is today sacred to Jews, Muslims and Christians alike. There is no unequivocal sign of Solomon's temple here today and the man-made plateau on top of Abraham's hill is now the home to the Muslim holy site of the Dome of the Rock and Al-Aqsa mosques, making archaeological investigation impossible. Yet the presence of the Western Wall (or Wailing Wall), which is the last surviving remnant of the Second Temple, strongly suggests that the First – Solomon's temple – was also here.

The descriptions we have of Solomon's temple come from the Hebrew Bible, or *Tanakh,* and are surprisingly consistent. Completed in 957 BC, the building faced east and was approached through two large courtyards, the outer of which was designed to be large enough to hold assemblies of all the city's people. This led to an inner courtyard, where a large bronze altar stood before the entrance porch. Near this was a huge bronze bowl, sometimes known as the 'brazen sea' or 'molten sea', supported by four bronze oxen and filled with water in which the priests performed their ablutions. The Bible is not consistent in giving the size of this, claiming that it held anything from 24,000 to 36,000 US gallons. Another ten smaller bowls on stands were laid out, five to the north and five to the south, around the courtyard. Approaching the main door, a visitor would come to two huge columns, the one on the left called Boaz and on the right called Jachin. These stood 8 metres (27 ft) high and 2 metres (6 ft) across and were surmounted with capitals decorated with lily and pomegranate designs. The Book of Kings claims that these, along with much of the wood for the temple, were supplied by Solomon's ally, King Hiram of Tyre, in exchange for a large quantity of food.

Past the porch lay the Holy Place or 'Greater House', which formed the main body of the temple used for services. All the interior space was panelled from floor to ceiling in pine and cedar, both rare commodities in Judaea, particularly cedar which had to be imported via Tyre from the Lebanon. Carved and gilded flower and palm-tree motifs adorned the panelling.

The Holy of Holies

Beyond this stood the most important part of the whole building, the Holy of Holies (*Kadosh Kadoshim*). This was a perfectly square room whose sides measured 20 cubits (around 8.5 metres/28 ft) and in which stood the Ark of the Covenant, concealed behind a veil of blue, purple and crimson cloth. It was flanked by two olive-wood cherubim (angels), whose outstretched wings touched the walls behind them and met over the ark itself. Into this gilded, windowless room, in what was believed to be the divine presence of God, just one man could enter – the High Priest and then only on the Day of Atonement (*Yom Kippur*).

What happened to the contents of this room is one of world's greatest mysteries. Not only did Solomon decorate his temple lavishly, but a series of chambers in it were also used as the royal treasury. As a result, every successive invader of Jerusalem would sack the temple in search of riches, leaving no trace of one of the most iconic buildings of all time.

CYCLE OF DESTRUCTION

A Roman bas-relief carving showing Titus's troops looting the Temple menorah during their sack of Jerusalem in AD 70.

Almost everything we know of Solomon's temple comes from the Bible, since not a single surviving stone or fragment of wood can unequivocally be identified as coming from it. Why there is so little remaining evidence of such a great building is bound up in the turbulent history of the ancient Near East.

Solomon completed his temple in 957 BC and lived another 24 years (or 35 years, depending on which chronology for his life is used). Despite factional wars under his son Rehoboam (r. 922–915 BC), the site survived and thrived until the reign of Josiah (r. 640–609 BC) who further increased its importance by abolishing all other sanctuaries. The wealth of this institution was not lost on neighbouring kings, however, and its treasury was frequently raided by the rulers of Egypt, Israel and Judah, according to biblical sources. These incursions peaked in 607 BC, when the Babylonian king Nebuchadrezzar II (*c*.630–562 BC), builder of the Hanging Gardens of Babylon (see pages 44–47), captured Jerusalem and destroyed both the city and its temple. He then deported many of its leading citizens back to Babylon, where they remained for 70 years, in the episode known as the Babylonian Captivity.

Nebuchadrezzar, an aggressive and expansionist king, almost certainly stripped the treasury and the decorations from the temple before destroying it. If the Ark of the Covenant had survived previous raids, it seems unlikely that it survived this. It was 538 BC before the Persian ruler Cyrus II (r. *c*.576–530 BC) allowed the Jews to return to their city and rebuild their temple. Work on this Second Temple, which was probably built on the site of the first, was completed around 516 or 515 BC, and although we have scant details of what it looked like we know that the Ark was no longer contained within it. During the Persian and Hellenistic period the temple thrived but was finally plundered in 169 BC by Antiochus IV Epiphanes in a raid that sparked a Jewish revolt but did not lead to the total destruction of the building. The success of the revolt and the rededication of the temple after Antiochus's soldiers had defiled it is the origin of the Jewish festival of *Hanukkah*.

With the expansion of Roman influence in the Near East the temple again came under threat. The Republican general and ally of Julius Caesar, Pompey the Great, entered the Holy of Holies in 63 BC during his suppression of a civil war in Judaea, and Marcus Crassus looted the treasury there in 54 BC. Under the Roman client king Herod the Great (74–4 BC), however, the temple was demolished and rebuilt on a grander scale, being completed around 18 BC. Work on the outbuildings continued until AD 64. It was this temple that the young Jesus visited to dispute with the Elders, according to the New Testament.

Yet just two years after the complex was finally finished, the Jewish Revolt against Roman rule began. Four years later, in AD 70, the future emperor Titus and his legions broke into Jerusalem and sacked the city. The temple, as a symbol of Jewish religious opposition to Roman rule, was razed to the ground. All that survived was a section of the western retaining wall of the complex, known today as the Wailing Wall – the last reminder of the site of the Temple of Solomon.

The Palace of Ashurnasirpal II

Magnificent seat of a merciless ruler

The story of the palace of King Ashurnasirpal II of Assyria at Nimrud is one of staggering artistic virtuosity built on the back of savage brutality. This vast edifice, one of the finest palaces the world has ever seen, was designed both as a luxurious dwelling for the ruler and his court and as a permanent monument to the martial prowess of his reign. Once completed, the Nimrud royal palace represented the most spectacular and intimidating expression of imperial majesty ever seen.

When Ashurnasirpal (r. 883–859 BC) inherited the throne of Assyria from his father, he immediately set about consolidating and expanding the military gains of the previous generation. For six years, the king moved around his empire continuously, reorganizing provinces and appointing legions of officials and administrators to take direct control of kingdoms previously held by unreliable client kings. Where there was dissent, he was ruthless in suppressing it; for example, the governor of Nishtun at Arbela (modern Irbil in Iraq) was publicly flayed alive when he dared to question his master. Needless to say, there were no further rebellions in that quarter.

In warfare too, Ashurnasirpal was a ruthless but innovative campaigner. He was the first Middle Eastern ruler to introduce the mobile battering ram and siege engines for breaking down the mud-brick walls of hostile cities and the first to make large-scale use of cavalry, which helped him to expand his empire across Mesopotamia and into the Lebanon.

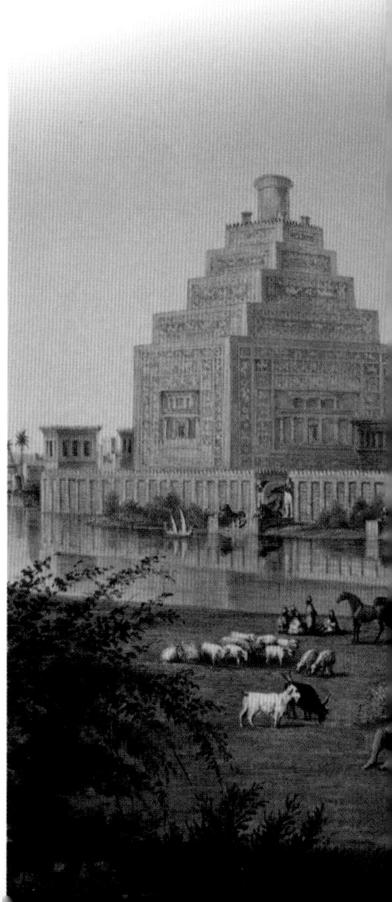

A Capital Fit for a King

In 879 BC, with his empire secure and having grown fabulously wealthy from the proceeds of his wars, Ashurnasirpal II embarked upon the construction of his lavish palace. The location for this wonder was the old city of Nimrud, known at the time, and in the Bible, as Calah (or Kalhu). The city, which lay on the east bank of the River Tigris about 20 miles (32 km) south of modern-day Mosul in Iraq, had been founded by King Shalmaneser I (r. 1263–1245 BC) over 300 years earlier but was little more than a ruin when Ashurnasirpal arrived there. On this relatively blank

'I built thereon [a palace with] halls of cedar, cypress, juniper, boxwood, teak, terebinth, and tamarisk as my royal dwelling and for the enduring leisure life of my lordship. Beasts of the mountains and the seas, which I had fashioned out of white limestone and alabaster, I had set up in its gates. I made [the palace] fittingly imposing. I bordered them all around with bronze studs. I mounted doors of cedar, cypress, juniper, and terebinth in its gates. Silver, gold, tin, bronze, iron, my own booty from the lands over which I ruled, as much as possible, I brought [to the palace]; I placed it all therein.'

THE STANDARD INSCRIPTION, NORTHWEST PALACE OF ASHURNASIRPAL AT NIMRUD

This artist's impression, created by the Scot James Fergusson in 1853, fully conveys the splendour of Ashurnasirpal II's palace in its heyday.

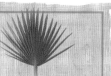

TIMELINE

*c.*879 BC Ashurnasirpal II begins contruction of his new capital city at Nimrud on the River Tigris

614 BC Median invaders from northwestern Persia sack the city of Nimrud, which declines into obscurity

AD 1820 British resident in Baghdad Claudius Rich investigates mounds near Kounyunjik near Mosul in his hunt for the ancient city of Nineveh

1842 Austen Henry Layard begins excavations at the site, which he also at first mistakenly believes to be Nineveh

1845–51 Ashurnasirpal's palace unearthed at Nimrud

1988 Iraqi archaeologist Muzahim Mahmud discovers tombs of the Assyrian queens below the floor of the Nimrud palace harem

This statue, carved from magnesite, of Ashurnasirpal II, dates from c.*880* BC. *In his left hand, the king holds a mace, symbol of his authority as vice-regent of the supreme Assyrian god Ashur.*

canvas, the king decided to put to use the wealth and the large supply of slave labour that his wars had brought him in building a new capital to replace Nineveh.

The site was surrounded by a mud-brick wall 5 miles (8 km) long and 36 metres (118 ft) thick, inside which he built a new temple to the city's own god Ninurta, the god of war and hunting, and another for Enlil, the chief deity of the already ancient Sumerian religion. In the southwestern corner the raised acropolis contained temples and the administrative offices for running the empire, while the area between the official and domestic settlements was filled with botanical and zoological gardens. Water was brought in from the Great Zab river via a huge canal, which provided for the 100,000 people who called Nimrud home.

But it was Ashurnasirpal's own palace that was the jewel in the crown. Built in the northwest section of the acropolis, it was constructed in sun-dried mud brick around three courtyards. The first courtyard was lined with the official state apartments and contained the throne room where visitors could meet Ashurnasirpal in all his magnificence. Behind this lay a second courtyard where the internal administration of the palace was managed and finally a third courtyard containing the king's private world – the harem. Here his queens and concubines both lived and died, for the burial place of Assyrian queens was beneath its floor. With a total ground plan covering some 25,000 square metres (269,000 sq ft), the palace was one of the largest ever built.

Testament to a Ruthless Reign

However, it was not its vast size alone that inspired awe in visitors. What was so striking was its decoration. Beyond the huge *lamassu* – carvings of human-headed, winged bulls and lions – that guarded the entrance, the walls of the staterooms and living quarters were everywhere lined with 2-metre- (6-ft-) high limestone murals, carved in low relief and vividly painted in a manner never before seen in Assyria. The delicate modelling and painting of the scenes often contrasted dramatically with their content. A major theme was Ashurnasirpal's ruthlessness and invincibility, expressed in violent images of his military campaigns, the defeat of enemies and the cruel fate awaiting captives. Here could be seen the full might and ingenuity of the Assyrian army at work, crossing rivers using inflated sheep hides as floats, running down enemy units with chariots and besieging cities. Inscriptions boast further of the king's savage majesty:

> *'I burnt many captives from them. I captured many troops alive: from some I cut off their arms (and) hands; from others I cut off their noses, ears, (and) extremities. I gouged out the eyes of many troops. I made one pile of the living (and) one of heads. I hung their heads on trees around the city.'*

Other scenes showed the king's personal physical prowess as a hunter, taking on bulls and lions from his chariot. If this were not sufficient to dazzle a visitor to Nimrud, more reliefs down the long hallways reminded them that this king was divinely favoured and protected by

AN ASTONISHING FIND

Ashurnasirpal's great city was built to celebrate the power of one man on the proceeds of his own conquests; it would in turn be eclipsed by the cities of later rulers and then destroyed by new conquerors.

In 710 BC the Assyrian king Sargon II (r. 722–705 BC), another great warlord keen to leave his mark in the annals of history, ordered the building of a new capital at Dur-Sharrukin (modern Khorsabad). Yet Nimrud and its palace complex remained a major royal residence until 614 BC when the Medes sacked the city. Two years later, with their southern Mesopotamian allies, they returned and razed Nimrud to the ground, stripping it of everything of value, even scraping the gold from ivory figurines. Similar fates befell Assur, the ancient Assyrian religious capital and Nineveh, which was then the current capital. These attacks spelt the end of the Assyrian empire.

No new city arose from the ruins of Nimrud and, other than some evidence of squatter settlements, no one seems to have lived there until the mid-third century BC, when a small Hellenistic settlement arose in the southeastern corner of the citadel. When even this was abandoned the site fell further into disuse, with the mud bricks of the buildings crumbling until the city resembled nothing more than a natural hill.

And so Nimrud lay forgotten until 1820, when the British 'resident' (a state official) at Baghdad, Claudius Rich, came across a huge mound near Mosul, covered with broken pottery. His report of the site came to the attention of a young civil servant in London named Austen Henry Layard (1817–94), who was just about to take up a post in Ceylon (Sri Lanka). As he journeyed across Iraq, Layard surveyed Rich's site and recognized it as an ancient city, which he believed to be Nineveh.

Layard abandoned everything and began (at first in secret) to excavate the site. In no time, he came across a stone panel protruding from the ground and tried to pull it free. When he could not he ordered it dug out, only to discover that this was one of the relief panels from Ashurnasirpal's palace. He was not standing in Nineveh, but the remains of Nimrud, the biblical – some had even thought mythical – city of Calah, unseen for over 2500 years.

Layard's descriptions of his excavations became the first archaeological bestsellers, as a previously lost civilization emerged from the sands of Iraq. Even today much of the Assyrian capital remains unexplored. As recently as 1988, Iraqi archaeologist Muzahim Mahmud noticed an unusual patch of relaid tiles on the floor of the harem. Removing these, he revealed a series of untouched royal tombs belonging to the Assyrian queens. This was a treasure trove unparalleled in scope and importance since the discovery of Tutankhamun's tomb in the 1920s.

the spirits. If any further clarification was needed, across nearly all of these panels was written the same long text, known as the 'Standard Inscription', which described in detail the king and his achievements in the Akkadian language of the court, repeating time after time that he: '*granted to his dominion their fierce weapons (and) made him more marvelous than (any of) the kings of the four quarters with respect to the splendour of his weapons (and) the radiance of his dominion*'.

When the building was complete, the king ordered a great feast there to celebrate the creation of his new capital and new home. The festivities turned out to be no less magnificent than the palace in which they were held. The party lasted for ten days and nights and, according to a contemporary inscription, provided entertainment for 69,574 guests.

La Venta

Long-lost city of the Olmecs

In a swamp in the Tonalá river basin on the border between the Mexican states of Tabasco and Veracruz stand the remains of one of the earliest and most mysterious settlements in the Americas. The city of La Venta was built by the Olmec civilization in the early part of the first millennium BC, on what was then an isolated island surrounded by humid rainforest. Between 800 and 400 BC it grew to become the most important city in Mesoamerica.

The La Venta site is dominated by a large civic-ceremonial area divided up into four complexes, which archaeologists call a, b, c and d. Complex 'a' appears to have been a ceremonial area consisting of two courtyards surrounded by symmetrically arranged low mounds, the whole area being enclosed by a series of basalt columns. Within this area have been found the burials of 'important' people together with a large number of offerings, although exactly who these people were and what role they played in Olmec society is still unknown. Of the 50 caches of artefacts, deposited over the four centuries in which the complex was built, five are of a type unique to this site and known as 'massive offerings'. These consist of large pits up to 15 metres (49 ft) by 19 metres (62 ft) wide and 7 metres (23 ft) deep, filled with the mineral serpentine and other metamorphic rocks, which had to be transported to the site from an outcrop over 60 miles (96 km) to the south. The tops of these vast stone caches were then capped with clay and in some cases had stone pavements made of serpentine blocks set over them. To date only one massive offering has been fully excavated and this produced approximately 1000 tons of serpentine in 28 layers, which later had a mud-brick building constructed over it surrounded by basalt columns. This complex has also yielded a relief sculpture of the 'feathered serpent' – the earliest known representation of this major pre-Colombian South American deity, known most commonly by the Aztec name Quetzalcoatl.

A Site of Ritual Significance?

To the south of complex 'a' lies complex 'c'. Like all the other main structures on the site, this is oriented exactly 8 degrees to the west of due north, probably on an astronomical alignment that has yet to be identified. This complex is dominated by the largest surviving structure at the site, the huge clay pyramid known as C-1, which rises 30 metres (98 ft) above the city on a 130-metre (426-ft) wide platform and contains, at a conservative estimate, over 100,000 cubic metres (3.5 million cu ft) of material. With its smooth sides, the mound was originally thought to represent a volcano (the Río Palma volcano visible from the site was active at the time La Venta was occupied) but modern research has shown that the pyramid was originally stepped. However, since it was constructed only of clay – there is no building stone in the immediate vicinity – over the intervening millennia it has slumped to take on its present form. The function of the pyramid is

still unknown and no excavation has been undertaken on it. A remote sensing magnetometer survey has located a large anomaly on its south side, which has been identified as a possible high-status burial, although without excavation this is impossible to determine.

The enigmatic stone figure on altar 5 from complex 'b' at the La Venta site, cradling in its arms a 'were-jaguar' baby.

Complex 'b' immediately to the south appears, unlike complex 'a', to have been a public area, as it contains a great plaza with a small platform in the middle and another much larger platform to the east, which is today known as the Stirling Acropolis after the first surveyor of the site. Precisely what happened in this plaza is, like so much at the site, still a mystery, but this area also yielded some of the most impressive stone monuments, which may have had a ritual purpose. These include the vast carved stone blocks known as 'altars', of which seven have been found at the site. Each 'altar', which is around 2 metres (6.5 ft) high and 4 metres (13 ft) wide, is carved with strange crouching figures beneath its front face. These may represent either kings or perhaps captives, and in some instances are cradling strange creatures described by archaeologists as 'infant supernaturals' or 'were-jaguar' babies. Although the significance of this symbolism is still unknown, these 'altars' are now thought actually to be thrones.

Also in the north part of complex 'b' stood perhaps the most iconic artefact from the Olmec era, known today as Monument 1 (although this has now been removed to the archaeological park at nearby Villahermosa). This comprises four huge carved heads of what are thought to be Olmec rulers of La Venta, each carved from a single massive basalt boulder. These blocks, which weigh up to 18 tons, were quarried over 80 miles (128 km) away to the west of the city at Cerro Cintepec in the Tuxtla mountains and there is still debate as to how they were brought to the site. They represent some of the earliest monumental work at La Venta and probably date from between 850 and 700 BC.

Complex 'd' further south forms the largest area of the ceremonial centre and consists of 20 mounds in three parallel lines arranged down the sides of long avenues making what may be a processional way. Another five complexes lie outside this central area.

Secrets Still Hidden

Other than the massive heads and 'altars' from the site numerous caches of jade and serpentine objects, sandstone figurines and polished stone mirrors have also been found, particularly in the tombs from complex 'a'. These demonstrate the sophistication of Olmec craftsmanship and the existence of an extensive trading network with other communities as none of these materials are local. Perhaps surprisingly, however, very few human remains have been located in the tombs, with only the bones of two (or perhaps three) young individuals being recovered from the complex. These had been stained with the red mineral cinnabar – the most common ore of mercury.

Despite the massive ceremonial complex at the centre of the site, which extends for over one mile (2 km), very little is known of the lives of the city's ordinary inhabitants. It has been estimated that at its height the city covered around 200 hectares (494 acres) and was home to as many as 18,000 people. To date, however, archaeologists have found none of the customary evidence, such as rubbish dumps, of how these people led their lives. Such finds might prove far more illuminating than the curious objects, such as magnetite mirrors and stingray spines, that have so far come to light. The vast majority of La Venta's buildings were constructed of clay, wood and palm leaves and so have disintegrated back into the silty soil of the swamp. As most of the site has yet to be excavated, further secrets of this enigmatic civilization may still be lying just beneath the surface.

TIMELINE

***c*.1600 BC** Possible earliest appearance of Olmec civilization on the lowlands of the Gulf of Mexico

***c*.1200 BC** Emergence of San Lorenzo as the principal Olmec settlement

***c*.900 BC** La Venta begins to gain preeminence

early 4th century BC La Venta abandoned

AD 1926 First detailed archaeological descriptions of La Venta by Frans Blom and Oliver La Farge

1939–42 American ethnologist and archaeologist Matthew Stirling carries out extensive investigations at the La Venta site

'After an hour's brisk walking from Blasillo, we at last turned off from the trail and stood in front of the first idol. This was a huge stone block, 2.25 meters high, 86 cm broad, and 72 cm thick. It had fallen on its back and showed us a human figure ...'

FRANS BLOM AND OLIVER LA FARGE – *TRIBES AND TEMPLES* (1926)

A SEMINAL CIVILIZATION

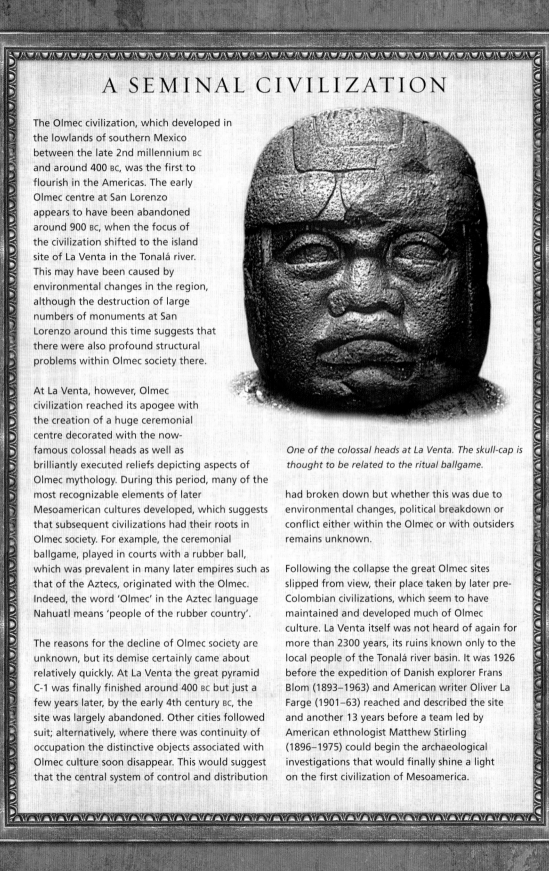

One of the colossal heads at La Venta. The skull-cap is thought to be related to the ritual ballgame.

The Olmec civilization, which developed in the lowlands of southern Mexico between the late 2nd millennium BC and around 400 BC, was the first to flourish in the Americas. The early Olmec centre at San Lorenzo appears to have been abandoned around 900 BC, when the focus of the civilization shifted to the island site of La Venta in the Tonalá river. This may have been caused by environmental changes in the region, although the destruction of large numbers of monuments at San Lorenzo around this time suggests that there were also profound structural problems within Olmec society there.

At La Venta, however, Olmec civilization reached its apogee with the creation of a huge ceremonial centre decorated with the now-famous colossal heads as well as brilliantly executed reliefs depicting aspects of Olmec mythology. During this period, many of the most recognizable elements of later Mesoamerican cultures developed, which suggests that subsequent civilizations had their roots in Olmec society. For example, the ceremonial ballgame, played in courts with a rubber ball, which was prevalent in many later empires such as that of the Aztecs, originated with the Olmec. Indeed, the word 'Olmec' in the Aztec language Nahuatl means 'people of the rubber country'.

The reasons for the decline of Olmec society are unknown, but its demise certainly came about relatively quickly. At La Venta the great pyramid C-1 was finally finished around 400 BC but just a few years later, by the early 4th century BC, the site was largely abandoned. Other cities followed suit; alternatively, where there was continuity of occupation the distinctive objects associated with Olmec culture soon disappear. This would suggest that the central system of control and distribution had broken down but whether this was due to environmental changes, political breakdown or conflict either within the Olmec or with outsiders remains unknown.

Following the collapse the great Olmec sites slipped from view, their place taken by later pre-Colombian civilizations, which seem to have maintained and developed much of Olmec culture. La Venta itself was not heard of again for more than 2300 years, its ruins known only to the local people of the Tonalá river basin. It was 1926 before the expedition of Danish explorer Frans Blom (1893–1963) and American writer Oliver La Farge (1901–63) reached and described the site and another 13 years before a team led by American ethnologist Matthew Stirling (1896–1975) could begin the archaeological investigations that would finally shine a light on the first civilization of Mesoamerica.

The Hanging Gardens of Babylon

Pleasure park for a homesick queen?

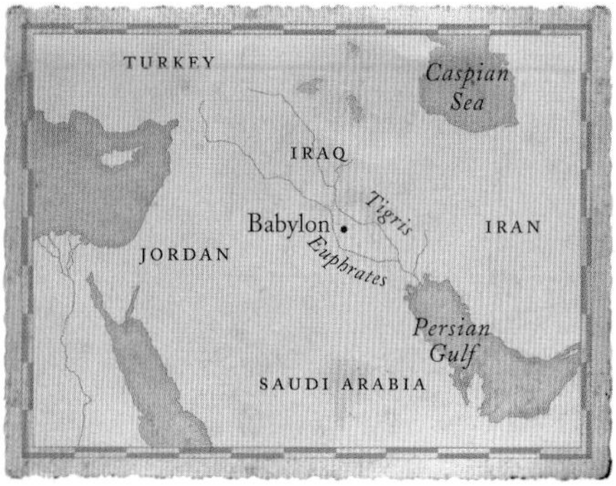

The Hanging Gardens of Babylon are the most enigmatic of all the original seven wonders of the world listed by Antipater of Sidon: not only has no trace of them survived, but we still cannot be sure exactly where or even what they were.

Gardens were a common feature in Assyria, Persia and especially Mesopotamia – the land around the floodplains of the Tigris and Euphrates rivers in what is today Iraq – where Babylon is situated. They usually took one of three forms. The first was the game reserve, not unlike the biblical descriptions of Eden, the second was a pleasure garden, planted with trees for shade and criss-crossed with cooling streams, and the third was the mysterious 'hanging' garden. From what the ancient sources say about this latter type of garden, it would appear that they were somehow arranged into a series of terraces, and that their somewhat baffling name may derive simply from a mistranslation of the Greek *kremastos,* which means 'overhanging' rather than 'hanging'.

What Were the Hanging Gardens?

What hanging gardens actually looked like is a matter of conjecture, since we cannot be sure that any of the descriptions we have of the gardens are by people who had actually seen them at first hand. The Greek historian Diodorus Siculus, writing in the first century BC, describes such a garden in the following terms:

> *'The garden was 100 feet long by 100 feet wide and built up in tiers so that it resembled a theatre. Vaults had been constructed under the ascending terraces, which carried the entire weight of the planted garden; the uppermost vault, which was 75 feet high, was the highest part of the garden, which, at this point, was on the same level as the city walls.'*

Writing a century later, the Greek geographer Strabo seems to describe a similar structure of:

> *'... arched vaults, which are situated, one after another, on checkered, cube-like foundations. The checkered foundations, which are hollowed out, are covered so deep with earth that they admit of the largest of trees ... .'*

What we do not know is whether the second account is based on the first, whether they are both based on a third lost account or if the two are genuinely completely independent. If we assume that there is at least some first-hand evidence preserved in these accounts, it would appear that the gardens formed a series of terraces, rising like the traditional Mesopotamian stepped pyramid, the ziggurat, planted with trees and shrubs that hung down over the edge of each level. Water would then have been introduced at the highest point and cascaded down to the bottom, irrigating each level of plants as it went.

Building gardens on any form of terrace would certainly have been impressive, but would also have created numerous engineering problems. Babylon was situated in a drought-prone region, where farming relied on irrigation. A terraced garden would therefore have to have been artificially watered, and involved some mechanism for pumping thousands of gallons of water up to the top of the structure. Strabo hints at how this might have been achieved:

> *'The ascent to the uppermost terrace-roofs is made by a stairway; and alongside these stairs there were screws, through which the water was continually conducted up into the garden from the Euphrates by those appointed for this purpose.'*

Once again Diodorus Siculus appears to concur:

> *'And since the galleries projected one beyond the other, where they were sunlit, they contained conduits for the water which was raised by pumps in great abundance from the river, though no one outside could see it being done.'*

This suggests that the garden was irrigated by an Archimedean screw, a spiral screw housed within a pipe which, when the screw was turned, raised water up the tube. This ancient but effective method of drawing water is still used in many locations today.

A highly speculative illustration of what the Hanging Gardens of Babylon might once have looked like. There is no archaeological evidence of these structures.

TIMELINE

c.605–562 BC Hanging Gardens of Babylon created

5th century BC Herodotus describes the walls and gates of Babylon (and probably also compiled a list of wonders, now lost)

1st century BC Diodorus Siculus describes the Hanging Gardens in his *Bibliotheca Historica*; Antipater of Sidon draws up his list of the Seven Wonders of the World

7 BC–AD 23 Strabo's 17-volume *Geographica* contains information on hanging gardens and their construction

1st century AD Historian Flavius Josephus describes the Hanging Gardens in *Contra Apion*

However, getting the water up to the terrace of the garden was only a part of the problem. The usual building material in Mesopotamia – a land with virtually no building stone and precious little wood – was sun-baked clay bricks, which would have disintegrated if soaked. To overcome this, Diodorus states that a foundation of massive stone slabs (presumably hugely expensive to import) was laid and then covered with layers of reed and asphalt between the clay bricks. This construction method is quite feasible, since the use of asphalt and reeds is exactly the building technique used for the well-preserved ziggurat at Ur (see pages 28–31).

Abiding Mysteries

Who ordered the construction of such an elaborate and expensive scheme is also uncertain. The most famous story is related by the Romano-Jewish historian Josephus (AD 37–*c.*100) in his book *Contra Apion* ('Against Apion'), who describes the 'pensile paradises' the Babylonian king built to resemble the mountains far to the north. Josephus claims that the gardens were built by the Chaldean king Nebuchadrezzar II (*c.*630–562 BC), who is recorded in the biblical books of Daniel and Jeremiah as the conqueror of Judah and Jerusalem. Nebuchadrezzar married Amytis, the daughter of King Cyaxares of Medea, who wished to forge an alliance between his people and the Babylonians. Coming from the lush Medean homelands in what is today northwestern Iran to the flat and dusty plains of the Euphrates Valley, Amytis was homesick for the Zagros Mountians where she had grown up and so Nebuchadrezzar ordered his own green mountain to be built for her in his city – the hanging gardens.

However, there is not a single mention of this extraordinary garden among the extensive surviving cuneiform chronicles from Babylon. Critics have pointed out that if the city really had housed a sight so spectacular that the Greeks considered it a wonder of the world, then surely some contemporary Babylonian sources would at least mention it in passing. The fact that they do not has led some scholars to suggest that ancient authors may have confused Babylon with another Mesopotamian city – Nineveh – where tablets have been recovered indicating that there were once extensive gardens. If this is the case, then the builder is more likely to have been the Assyrian king Sennacherib (r. 706–681 BC).

The problem with this interpretation is that the oldest reference to the Hanging Gardens being in Babylon comes from a Babylonian writer, Berossus, whose work *The History of the Babylonians* appeared around the mid-third century BC. Sadly, this book does not survive but was summarized in another book in the first century BC (which also does not survive but was in turn quoted by Josephus in a work that is still extant). According to Josephus, Berossus wrote his book using the archive in the Esaglia temple in Babylon, so if we are to believe that the gardens were actually in Nineveh, we must assume that a local priest in Babylon using the Babylonian archive made a fundamental mistake about a wonder of the world being in his own town. Moreover, since all the other six entries on this well-known list of ancient wonders most definitely did exist in the place claimed, there is no reason to suppose that the gardens should be an exception.

Whatever the truth behind the location of the gardens, no physical evidence has ever been found for them at either site. The German archaeologist Robert Koldewey (1855–1925), who first relocated the then-lost site of Babylon in the late 19th century, did discover a series of vaults and foundation chambers, including a well, which he believed to be the foundations of the garden, but they are not in the location suggested by Strabo and tablets found in the area indicate that these were actually store rooms. In the absence of any further written information, it may prove impossible to positively identify any one set of ruins as being of the gardens, leaving them as the most elusive entry on Antipater's list.

THE LOST WONDER

Antipater of Sidon's list did not include the Pharos lighthouse at Alexandria. Instead, the first wonder he mentions is 'the wall of lofty Babylon on which is a road for chariots,' which he claims to have seen for himself and which had been built on the orders of Nebuchadrezzar II. We know from other authors that the walls of this city were certainly deemed extraordinary. The Greek historian Herodotus (*c.*484–425 BC), whose own list of wonders does not survive, recorded them in detail elsewhere in his writings:

> *'Such is the size of the city of Babylon, and it has a magnificence greater than all other cities of which we have knowledge. First there runs round it a deep and broad trench, full of water; then a wall fifty metres in thickness and hundred metres in height [...]. At the top of the wall along the edges they built chambers of one story facing one another; and between the rows of chambers they left space to drive a four-horse chariot. In the circuit of the wall there are set a hundred gates made of bronze.'*

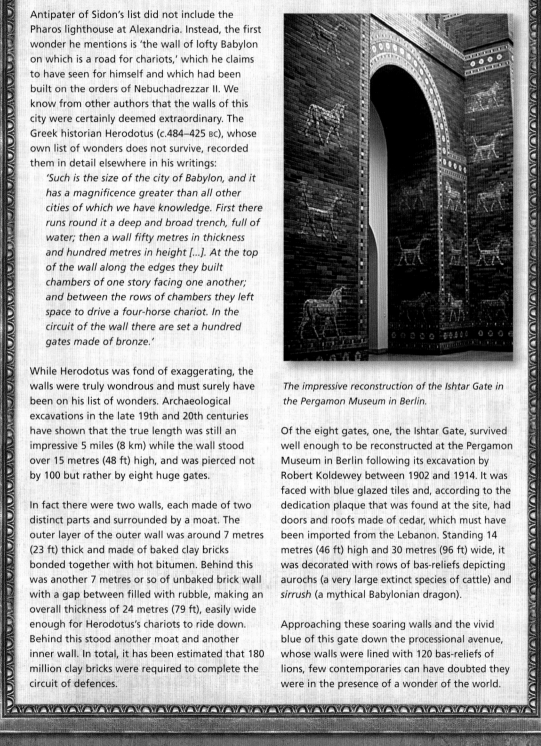

The impressive reconstruction of the Ishtar Gate in the Pergamon Museum in Berlin.

While Herodotus was fond of exaggerating, the walls were truly wondrous and must surely have been on his list of wonders. Archaeological excavations in the late 19th and 20th centuries have shown that the true length was still an impressive 5 miles (8 km) while the wall stood over 15 metres (48 ft) high, and was pierced not by 100 but rather by eight huge gates.

In fact there were two walls, each made of two distinct parts and surrounded by a moat. The outer layer of the outer wall was around 7 metres (23 ft) thick and made of baked clay bricks bonded together with hot bitumen. Behind this was another 7 metres or so of unbaked brick wall with a gap between filled with rubble, making an overall thickness of 24 metres (79 ft), easily wide enough for Herodotus's chariots to ride down. Behind this stood another moat and another inner wall. In total, it has been estimated that 180 million clay bricks were required to complete the circuit of defences.

Of the eight gates, one, the Ishtar Gate, survived well enough to be reconstructed at the Pergamon Museum in Berlin following its excavation by Robert Koldewey between 1902 and 1914. It was faced with blue glazed tiles and, according to the dedication plaque that was found at the site, had doors and roofs made of cedar, which must have been imported from the Lebanon. Standing 14 metres (46 ft) high and 30 metres (96 ft) wide, it was decorated with rows of bas-reliefs depicting aurochs (a very large extinct species of cattle) and *sirrush* (a mythical Babylonian dragon).

Approaching these soaring walls and the vivid blue of this gate down the processional avenue, whose walls were lined with 120 bas-reliefs of lions, few contemporaries can have doubted they were in the presence of a wonder of the world.

The Temple of Artemis at Ephesus

Peerless wonder of the ancient world

When Antipater compiled his list of wonders, he did so not in order to grant them equal glory but to single out one as the most magnificent; the Temple of Artemis at Ephesus on the coast of Asia Minor. Today all that remains to mark the site of this extraordinary building is one solitary column erected by 20th-century archaeologists. Some 2500 years earlier, however, and for many centuries after, it was the talk of the ancient world, a structure so vast, so beautiful and so richly endowed that it put all others in the shade.

The oldest known temple of Artemis at Ephesus was constructed around 800 BC on marshy ground near to the River Selinus. It was, as far as we can tell, the first 'Greek' style temple in Asia Minor, with a central *cella* (the room housing a cult statue) surrounded by columns to the front and sides, one or two column-widths from the *cella* wall. This temple was the site of worship of a carved wooden image often known the 'Lady of Ephesus,' images of whom have been found elsewhere on the site and who probably represents an Anatolian fertility goddess. This temple was destroyed by a flood in the seventh century BC, which left a thick layer of sand, half a metre deep, over the site. Buried in this silt, archaeologists have recently discovered the remnants of the amber jewellery that once adorned the cult statue.

Building on a Grand Scale

The site seems to have been quickly put back into use, suggesting that the Ephesians believed the location to be an important one, despite the risk of flooding. However, in around 550 BC Ephesus was captured by the Lydian king Croesus (595–*c*.546 BC), whose name has become synonymous with fabulous wealth. He put this wealth to use in completely rebuilding the temple, which had been destroyed during the conquest. By now the Lady of Ephesus was associated by the Greeks with their deity Artemis (the Roman goddess Diana) and so this building became known as the Temple

'I have set eyes on the wall of lofty Babylon on which is a road for chariots, and the statue of Zeus by the Alpheus, and the hanging gardens, and the Colossus of the Sun, and the huge labour of the high pyramids, and the vast tomb of Mausolus; but when I saw the house of Artemis that mounted to the clouds, those other marvels lost their brilliancy, and I said, 'Lo, apart from Olympus, the Sun never looked on aught so grand'.'

ANTIPATER OF SIDON – *GREEK ANTHOLOGY* IX.58

The forlorn site of the Temple of Artemis at Ephesus. Archaeological evidence indicates that a sacred site existed here from as early as the Bronze Age.

AN ACT OF VANDALISM

The story of the destruction of the greatest wonder of the ancient world is a tragedy with surprisingly modern overtones. By the mid-fourth century BC the Temple of Artemis was one of the most famous buildings on earth, known across the Mediterranean and celebrated in classical literature. In an age before mass media, this was a spectacular achievement in itself but the temple's fame held within it the seeds of its own destruction.

On 21 July, 356 BC a local man, whom some claimed was mad, went to the great temple and set fire to it. He was quickly captured but not before the flames had taken hold and entirely consumed the building. When the man was asked why he had done such a terrible thing he replied that he wanted to be famous and in destroying the most famous building on earth he would achieve his dream. The Ephesians were horrified that anyone should try to achieve immortality through such wanton destruction and so immediately passed a decree forbidding mention of the perpetrator's name on pain of death, in the hope that his perverse ambition would be foiled and others would not try to emulate him.

Sadly for them, and perhaps for history, it proved impossible to keep his name secret, as the news of the crime spread throughout the world. So, thanks to Strabo among others, we know that the arsonist was Herostratus – and his fame, or rather infamy, was assured.

According to Plutarch, on the very night that the temple burnt down Alexander the Great was born, leading the Greek philosopher Hegesias of Magnesia to comment that the calamity occurred because Artemis herself was too busy bringing Alexander into the world to protect it.

Many years later, when Alexander was at the height of his powers he offered to rebuild the temple but the Ephesians refused. It seems that they did not wish a rebuilt temple to have Alexander's name writ large on it. (Prudently, they told him that it was because it would not be fitting for one god to build a temple to another.)

It seems that after Alexander's death, the temple was rebuilt (or at least its remains restored) by the architect Dinocrates. Yet the reconstruction could not match the original. This building was partly stripped by the Roman emperor Nero but survived until AD 262, when the Goths destroyed it; it is unclear if it was rebuilt after this. Certainly by the later, Christian, Roman empire period the building fell out of use and must have fallen victim to the Emperor Theodosius's edict in 391 that all pagan temples be closed. By the first half of the sixth century AD, the site had become a quarry and some of the great columns were cannibalized for reuse in the Hagia Sophia in Constantinople (see pages 164–167). The location of the greatest wonder of the ancient world was only rediscovered in 1869 by the English archaeologist John Turtle-Wood (1821–90).

of Artemis, or the *Artemision*. This is the edifice that would go down in history as an unsurpassed wonder of the ancient world.

At its most basic level, the Temple of Artemis was simply a Hellenic-style temple, but what made it so extraordinary was its gargantuan size and its lavish decoration. Croesus could afford to build on a grand scale, and so ordered his architects, the Cretan Chersiphron from Knossos and his son Metagenes, to build a structure measuring around 110 metres by 50 metres (360 x 164 ft), though ancient sources vary on its dimensions – in other words, around three times the area of the floor plan of the Parthenon in Athens (see pages 60–65). Ancient commentators claim that this monumental undertaking took 120 years to complete.

In this anonymous Renaissance engraving of the Temple of Artemis, its architects are shown admiring the finished structure. The building is more likely to have resembled the Parthenon.

The architects chose to build the entire structure in marble, making it one of the first such buildings ever constructed. Although Ephesus had its own marble quarry, this construction method was fraught with difficulties; the columns were so huge that they could not be hauled to the site on carts, since the wheels would sink into the soft riverine soil. So, according to the first-century BC Roman architect Vitruvius, Chersiphron devised an ingenious system whereby each drum was attached to a wooden frame, like a lawn roller, and rolled to the site by teams of oxen. On site the drums were piled up to form 18-metre (59-ft) high columns in two rows around the central *cella*, over 120 columns in all.

A Shrine of Beauty

But beyond the sheer scale of the temple, it was its decoration that made it famous. Thirty-six of the huge columns had their bases carved in relief by the great sculptors of the day, one apparently being executed by Scopas, who also carved the east side of another wonder, the Tomb of Mausolus (the Mausoleum at Halicarnassus; see pages 70–73). Other columns were covered in gold and silver leaf, while the best artists in the Greek world produced paintings for the interior. As well as the new wooden cult statue, created by Endoios (supposedly a pupil of the legendary Daedalus, builder of the Minotaur's labyrinth on Crete), there were other statues by the finest sculptors. Polycletus, famed for his statues of athletes at Olympia, took part in, and won, one of the longest-running sculptural competitions of all time, in which the greatest artists of each generation attempted to create the finest image of an Amazon for the temple (the Greeks believed the Amazons had founded the city of Ephesus). In his *Natural History*, the Roman writer Pliny the Elder (AD 23–79), tells the story:

> *'The most celebrated of these artists, though born at different epochs, have joined in a trial of skill in the Amazons which they have respectively made. When these statues were dedicated in the Temple of Diana at Ephesus, it was agreed, in order to ascertain which was the best, that it should be left to the judgment of the artists themselves who were then present: upon which, it was evident that that was the best, which all the artists agreed in considering as the next best to his own. Accordingly, the first rank was assigned to Polycletus, the second to Phidias, the third to Cresilas, the fourth to Cydon, and the fifth to Phradmon.'*

One can only wonder at the quality of work in a sculptural competition where the legendary Phidias, creator of the statue of Zeus at Olympia and the cult statue of Athena in the Parthenon, only came second.

But Croesus's legacy was not to last. Despite the hoards of Lydian coins – some of the earliest coins known – that he ordered placed in the foundations of his temple as talismans to ensure its future, it was fated not to endure. Having taken well over a century to complete, it would survive as a wonder of the world for only another 75 years before tragedy struck.

TIMELINE

c.550 BC Croesus of Lydia orders work to start on constructing the *Artemesion* at Ephesus

c.430 BC Work completed on the Temple of Artemis

356 BC (21 July) Herostratus deliberately sets fire to the temple, which is completely destroyed in the conflagration

323 BC Temple restored (though not to its former glory) after death of Alexander the Great

c.140 BC Antipater of Sidon exalts the original temple above all other buildings on his list of the Seven Wonders of the World

AD 262 Partially restored *Artemesion* is destroyed by invading Goths

391 Emperor Theodosius orders all pagan temples to be closed

401 Remains of the temple torn down by a mob led by the Christian zealot St John Chrysostom

1869 After an eight-year search on an expedition sponsored by the British Museum, archae-ologist John Turtle-Wood discovers the site of the *Artemesion*

Persepolis

Home of the richest rulers on Earth

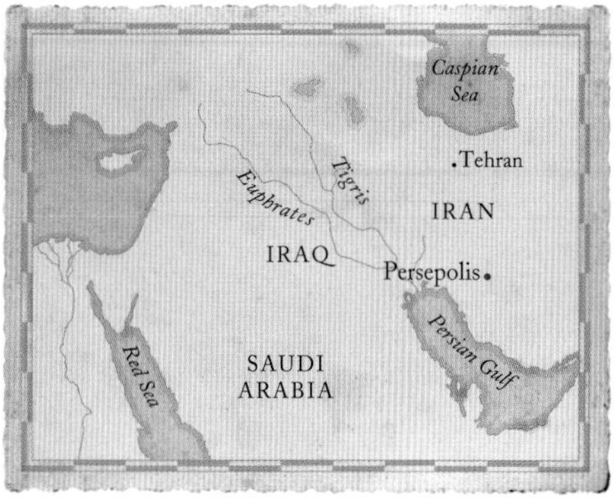

In 330 BC Alexander the Great, then at the height of his powers, was storming through the Near East when – near where the Pulvar and Rud-e Kor rivers join in the Fars region of what was then Persia and is today Iran – he came upon the city of Persepolis. Astonishingly, until that moment this place had been unknown in the Greek world. Thanks to its inaccessible location, the capital of Greece's great enemy had avoided detection – a beautiful jewel hidden deep in the heart of the Persian empire.

What Alexander found was a city fit for the richest and most powerful rulers on earth. The city was begun by Darius the Great (550–486 BC), who had been a bodyguard to King Cambyses II (d.522 BC) but had seized control of the empire after his master's death. To consolidate his position on this notoriously unstable throne, Darius had ordered the construction of a new capital, well away from older cities associated with other claimants, which he wished to become a 'showcase' for Persia.

A City Built into a Mountain

The city he built was certainly designed for show. The whole structure was built on a man-made terrace 400 metres (1312 ft) wide and 350 metres (1148 ft) deep, which is cut into the base of a mountain known as the Mount of Mercy (Kuh-e Rahmat) and approached by two staircases of 111 steps. On this platform stood the imposing halls and palaces with which the king intended to inspire his people and overawe his enemies. Greatest of these was the Apadana, or audience hall. In common with all the main buildings on the site, this was constructed from the local grey stone, polished to look like marble, and built without the use of mortar, relying instead simply on the massive weight of each element to bind the structure together. Those approaching this chamber would first walk up a grand staircase, lined with bas-reliefs of the Persian New Year's festival depicting the 23 subject nations of the empire parading past in their native dress. By now thoroughly intimidated, visitors would then enter the audience chamber itself, whose roof soared above them, supported on 72 columns, each 25 metres (82 ft) tall. Lest there be any doubt about who was responsible for this wonder, there was also an inscription reading: *'Darius the Great King, king of kings, king of countries, son of Hytaspes, an Achaemenian, built this palace.'*

Nearby, Darius also built his great treasury, the building designed to hold the booty from Persia's wars of conquest and the tribute from the subject nations who depended upon the empire's goodwill. According to the 'Fortification Tablets' (one of the two cuneiform libraries discovered on the site), in 467 BC this one building alone employed 1348 people to count, clean and protect Persia's treasure. Many other details concerning the administration of what must have been the largest state treasury in the world at that time still remain to be discovered, since only around 2000 of the 30,000 Fortification Tablets have been published to date.

'The approach to Persepolis, as the traveller crosses the vast plain of Merdusht, is described by every one who has had the good fortune to visit it, as magnificent in the extreme.'

WILLIAM SANDYS – *NINEVEH AND PERSEPOLIS* (1850)

Persepolis Expands

The work at Persepolis was continued by Darius's son Xerxes I (r. 485–465 BC), who further increased the sense of awestruck wonder in those approaching the site by adding the Gate of All Nations. This monumental entranceway, guarded by two giant stone bulls on the western side and two equally massive *lamassu* (bulls with the heads of bearded men) to the east, contained the great bronze doors that gave access to the Apadana courtyard and was itself approached by a magnificent staircase built with shallow, wide steps to ensure those

The Tachara, or winter palace, at Persepolis was begun by Darius and completed by his son Xerxes. The relief on the front of the building shows dignitaries carrying tributes.

ascending had to move slowly. On the gate, in three languages (Persian, Elamite and Babylonian) to make sure everyone understood, Xerxes had written:

> *'This Gate of All Nations I built. Much else that is beautiful was built in this Persepolis, which I built and which my father built. Whatever has been built and seems beautiful – all that we built with the favour of [the God] Ahuramazda.'*

Not to be outdone by his father, Xerxes also added his own palace, twice the size of Darius's, and converted part of the treasury into a harem for the daughters of kings and nobles who also formed a part of his treasure. As a result of his own military campaigns, the treasury itself also had to be extended. The last great building phase was completed under Xerxes' son, Artaxerxes I (r. 465–424 BC) who built the Hall of a Hundred Columns, a square throne room with sides measuring 70 metres (21 ft), which shortly thereafter was converted into another store room, as further wars brought yet more booty to the city.

Alexander Loots the 'Richest City Under the Sun'

With a few minor additions, this is the city that Alexander discovered when he arrived in 330 BC. The effect on the Greek and Macedonian army was extraordinary. None of them knew of the city's existence, tucked away in the mountains; indeed, its inconvenient location meant that the Persian kings only spent the summers here. The business of the Persian empire had always been conducted in Susa, Ecbatana and Babylon, but Persepolis was the showcase where the Persian monarchs could entertain and dazzle their subjects and guests, where the greatest single treasure then known, the wealth of all the great ancient nations of the Near East, was gathered together in an overwhelming display of magnificence.

The 1st-century BC writer Diodorus Siculus claimed that Persepolis was *'the richest city under the sun'*. All this was now Alexander's. That year he had defeated the last Achaemenid king, Darius III (r. 336–330 BC), who was subsequently deposed and assassinated by his own court. Diodorus adds that when the contents of the treasury were added up, it came to 120 thousand talents of silver. We do not know exactly how much a talent of silver weighed or was worth, but it has been conservatively estimated at around US $300,000 per talent in modern money, making the Persepolis treasury worth around $36 billion. Certainly it was bulky enough for Alexander to have to send for what Diodorus calls *'vast numbers'* of pack mules and 3000 camels to transport just a part of the treasure to Susa. The rest was used to pay his army.

The wealth and luxury that Alexander the Great and his army found at Persepolis was dazzling even to men who had set out to conquer the world. According to Diodorus Siculus, the sight of this great opulence, together with their long-held hatred of the Persians, brought on an orgy of looting and destruction in the city, which reduced one of the wonders of the world to a smouldering wreck.

Diodorus claims that so massive was the quantity of treasure, in gold, silver, rich fabrics and jewels that Alexander's men gave themselves up to an entire day of unbridled looting. All the private houses as well as the palaces were ransacked and any Persian man found in the city killed while all the women were taken off into slavery. In their greed, the invaders simply sliced great works of art in half with their swords to divide up their bullion value. Some of Alexander's troops even cut off the hands of their fellow soldiers as they tried to drag away booty in order to take it for themselves. Diodorus's final comment on this terrible spectacle was: *'As Persepolis had exceeded all other cities in prosperity, so in the same measure it now exceeded all others in misery'.*

TIMELINE

***c*.518 BC** Darius the Great of the Persian (Achaemenid) empire begins construction of the Apadana, the Debating Hall and the treasury at his new capital of Persepolis

485–465 BC Xerxes I continues construction work at the site, adding the Gate of All Nations

***c*.450 BC** Artaxerxes I builds the Hall of a Hundred Columns at Persepolis

330 BC During his conquest of the Persian empire, Alexander the Great captures the city; his troops sack the treasury and private homes

AD 200 Seat of government relocated to Istakhr 2 miles (5 km) to the north; Persepolis falls into disuse

1602 Arrival of Portuguese missionary Antonio de Gouveia, the first modern western traveller to visit Persepolis

1931–4 First archaeological investigation of Persepolis is undertaken by the German scholar Ernst Herzfeld, under the auspices of the University of Chicago

1979 Persepolis is declared a UNESCO World Heritage Site

CONSUMED IN FLAMES

An artist's impression of Persepolis in its heyday. The city remained the ceremonial capital of the empire for almost 200 years until its destruction.

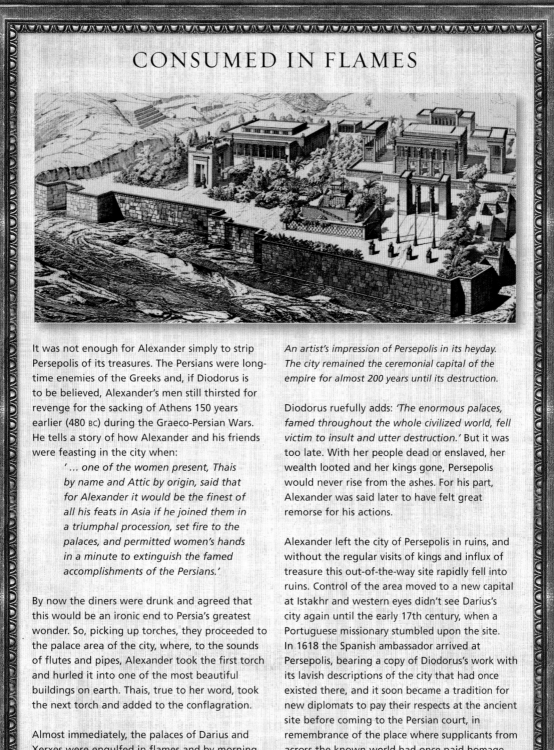

It was not enough for Alexander simply to strip Persepolis of its treasures. The Persians were long-time enemies of the Greeks and, if Diodorus is to be believed, Alexander's men still thirsted for revenge for the sacking of Athens 150 years earlier (480 BC) during the Graeco-Persian Wars. He tells a story of how Alexander and his friends were feasting in the city when:

> *'... one of the women present, Thais by name and Attic by origin, said that for Alexander it would be the finest of all his feats in Asia if he joined them in a triumphal procession, set fire to the palaces, and permitted women's hands in a minute to extinguish the famed accomplishments of the Persians.'*

By now the diners were drunk and agreed that this would be an ironic end to Persia's greatest wonder. So, picking up torches, they proceeded to the palace area of the city, where, to the sounds of flutes and pipes, Alexander took the first torch and hurled it into one of the most beautiful buildings on earth. Thais, true to her word, took the next torch and added to the conflagration.

Almost immediately, the palaces of Darius and Xerxes were engulfed in flames and by morning the whole palace area had been consumed.

Diodorus ruefully adds: *'The enormous palaces, famed throughout the whole civilized world, fell victim to insult and utter destruction.'* But it was too late. With her people dead or enslaved, her wealth looted and her kings gone, Persepolis would never rise from the ashes. For his part, Alexander was said later to have felt great remorse for his actions.

Alexander left the city of Persepolis in ruins, and without the regular visits of kings and influx of treasure this out-of-the-way site rapidly fell into ruins. Control of the area moved to a new capital at Istakhr and western eyes didn't see Darius's city again until the early 17th century, when a Portuguese missionary stumbled upon the site. In 1618 the Spanish ambassador arrived at Persepolis, bearing a copy of Diodorus's work with its lavish descriptions of the city that had once existed there, and it soon became a tradition for new diplomats to pay their respects at the ancient site before coming to the Persian court, in remembrance of the place where supplicants from across the known world had once paid homage at the feet of the King of Kings.

The Grand Canal

A vital trade link for a growing nation

There is one monument in China which, above all others, is seen by the outside world as the supreme achievement of this ancient civilization – the Great Wall (see pages 92–97). Yet while this defensive barrier certainly helped set the boundaries of China and so define what was within and without its confines, another far less well-known structure actually played a much greater role in the development of Chinese civilization.

In its final form, the Grand Canal ran for a total length of 1115 miles (1795 km), forming a link between the two great rivers of China, the Yangtze and the Huang He (Yellow River), and joining the capital Beijing with the city of Hangzhou on the Yangtze Delta. It remains the longest artificial waterway in the world, longer than the next two largest (the Panama and Suez Canals) put together. Made up of hundreds of sections of natural waterway, canalized river and newly built canal it was – and still is – a vital transport artery in this vast country.

Vital Arteries

The need for canals in China was recognized from deep in antiquity. China's great rivers were its principal trade routes, but they generally flow from west to east. Providing transport from the southern grain-growing areas to the north therefore entailed linking these rivers with artificial waterways running north–south. As an indication of just how important these canals were to the development of China, the historian Sima Qin, writing in the second century BC, claimed that the origins of the Grand Canal lay with the legendary emperor Yu the Great in the 21st century BC. In fact, there is no substantial evidence for anything so ancient but the first main stretch of what would become the Grand Canal was certainly established long before Sima Qin's time.

Work on the first section of the Grand Canal began towards the end of the so-called 'Spring and Autumn Period' of Chinese history, which ran from the eighth to the fifth centuries BC. In 486 BC, Fuchai, duke of Wu, was in the middle of a military campaign against the Qi and needed to provide supplies for his troops as they moved north out of Wu and into the states of Song and Lu. In just three years, he managed to create the Han Gou Canal, a waterway linking the Yangtze and Huai rivers, using natural watercourses and marshes connected where necessary with new canals. The canal was a great success and Qi was conquered, although Duke Fuchai would not enjoy his victory for long, being forced to commit suicide after his state was annexed by another warring nation, the Yue. But his canal did survive, providing not only an excellent transport route for troops but increasingly becoming a source of wealth as grain was traded with the north. (Grain was not just a vital commodity in ancient China; taxes were often paid in this form.)

'... an inland navigation of such extent and magnitude as to stand unrivalled in the history of the world. I may safely say that, in point of magnitude, our most extensive inland navigation of England can no more be compared to the grand trunk that intersects China, than a park or garden fish-pond to the great lake of Windermere.'

JOHN BARROW – *TRAVELS IN CHINA* (1804)

The Sui Emperors' Great Leap Forward

China at this time was not a coherent country, and it would be over 1000 years before the next major part of the Grand Canal project could be completed. In AD 581, Emperor Wen (r. 581–604), the first ruler of the short-lived Sui dynasty, finally took control of China, unifying the northern and southern provinces after four centuries of separation. Having

Trading boats plying the Grand Canal in the mid-19th century. China's canal system linked the wheat-growing north and the rice-rich south.

defeated the Northern Zhou, and supposedly put to death all 59 princes of the Zhou dynasty, Wen needed to consolidate the links between the north and south of his new country, and so decided to expand massively the existing canal network. Accordingly, a new waterway known as the New Bian Canal was built parallel to an old sixth-century BC 'Canal of the Flying Geese', which had become silted and unusable in parts. Wen completed this project in 604, after which his son Yangdi (r. 604–18) proposed an ambitious new scheme, joining the New Bian Canal and Duke Fuchai's canal with hundreds of miles of new waterway that would, when complete, link Beijing with Hangzhou, over 1100 miles (1700 km) to the south. This monumental project was put into action between 604 and 609. Using somewhere between one and six million conscripted labourers (sources vary wildly), over 600 miles (1000 km) of new canal and canalized river were constructed to provide the backbone of China's trade and communication network. The technological achievement was astounding, as the emperor's engineers created a largely flat, navigable waterway, in places over 100 metres (320 ft) wide and incorporating 24 'flash' locks. These locks consisted of a single gate made of wooden boards that could be removed when a barge was above them, enabling it to shoot down the incline on the flash flood of water that was released. For barges travelling upstream the gate would be removed and the barge towed or winched through.

However, grain barges were not the only form of transport employed on the canal. Next to the waterway itself was built an imperial roadway, lined with willow trees and with guard houses set at regular intervals (determined as being the distance ridden in a day by the emperor's messengers). As well as facilitating trade and taxation, the Grand Canal and its infrastructure also therefore came to form the most important north–south communication route across China. By 609, with most of the major sections complete, the emperor was able to head a 65-mile (104-km) long flotilla from the north down to Yanzhou to celebrate the opening of the country's most economically important trade artery.

An Enduring Achievement

Despite this achievement, history would not be kind to the Sui dynasty. Their military conquests and administrative reform programme, which reintroduced Confucian ideals to government and education, bound the nation together again but their reforming zeal was considered excessive by many. Nowhere was this felt more than in the building of the Grand Canal, during which as many as half the workforce are believed to have perished from hunger, disease and exhaustion. Yangdi's huge expenditure of human and financial resources on the canal, his insistence on rebuilding the Great Wall, his lavish palace-building programme and an increasingly unsuccessful series of attempts to expand his empire into Korea bred discontent and brought China to the edge of bankruptcy. In the late spring of 618, he was strangled by one his own army officers, leaving his nephew to rule for one further year before the Sui dynasty collapsed.

Ironically, the successors to the Sui, the Tang (618–908), would benefit greatly from the hard reforms and expensive investment programme initiated by their unpopular predecessors. The canal made grain imports to Beijing not only much more plentiful but considerably cheaper and by 735 165,000 tons of grain were being shipped every year along the waterway. From the Tang to China's last ruling dynasty, the Qing (1644–1912), the Grand Canal would form the main artery between northern and southern China. At its height, 8000 boats carried 4–6 million *dan* (240,000–360,000 tons) of grain annually, generating the wealth for an unprecedented flourishing of Chinese art and culture. Nor has the canal's role faded in the modern world. According to the Chinese Ministry of Communication, 100,000 vessels carry 260 million tons of goods on the canal each year.

TIMELINE

c.486 BC Fuchai orders construction of the Han Gou Canal linking the Yangtze and the Huai rivers

AD 604 Emperor Wen of the Sui dynasty builds the New Bian Canal

604–9 Wen's son Yangdi undertakes a major construction project linking the New Bian and Han Gou canals; this combined waterway forms the basis of the Grand Canal

618–908 The Tang dynasty makes extensive improvements to the infrastructure of the Grand Canal

c.984 Under the Song dynasty, pound locks are introduced on the Grand Canal

1128 Transport on the Grand Canal south of the Huang He is severely disrupted after dams and dykes on the river are deliberately broken to hamper Jurchen invaders

1279 The Yuan restore and extend the Grand Canal

1411–15 Further renovation and improvements under the Ming

1855 The Huang He changes its course, severing the course of the canal in Shandong

EBBING AND FLOWING FORTUNES

The fortunes of the Grand Canal have swung violently throughout its 2500-year history, as geographical, political and economic factors have affected its importance. Yet as China enters the 21st century as a dynamic growth economy, the canal remains very much in use.

Following the collapse of the Sui dynasty, the importance of the canal was instantly recognized by the Tang, who set about making a number of improvements, installing more locks and constructing grain stores along its course in case natural disasters temporarily closed the waterway. Subsequently, in around 984 a new system of 'pound' locks with double gates was introduced, allowing ships to pass up and down stream without being winched or having to 'shoot' flash locks. This precarious earlier method of negotiating locks often led to vessels being wrecked and then plundered by bandits.

These improvements, along with the removal of the capital to Kaifeng, increased the importance of the canal and by the 11th century three times the quantity of traffic from Tang days was moving along it. However, man-made and natural disasters began to take their toll, and in the 12th century the canal fell into disuse as large areas of land around it were deliberately flooded to hold back invaders. Having finally been repaired, another even more implacable enemy reared its head in 1195 when the meandering Huang He river suddenly changed course, swamping the former mouth of the Huai river and disconnecting the canal from one of its major arteries.

After the Mongol conquest of China in the 13th century it was decided to build a new section of canal to link it up again with the new course of the Huang He. It is this section that forms the final part of the waterway known today as the Grand Canal. Economically the importance of the canal was waning, however, and the decline of the Mongol Yuan dynasty (1271–1368) is echoed in the decline in the canal, which lost out to cheaper seagoing transport.

With the advent of the Ming dynasty and the movement of their capital back to Beijing in 1403, fortunes revived and the whole canal was dredged and refitted, remaining in use until the 19th century when the Huang He again changed course. The canal now seemed a dangerously vulnerable artery, its course severed in places by flood waters. Rebellions against the Manchu emperors did little to help either, showing how vulnerable Beijing was if its main food supply route was the canal. As such, increasing emphasis was placed on sea transport and the new railways and so another period of decline began.

The 20th century proved kinder to the canal, as economic and political priorities again changed. In 1934 ship locks were added to one section to allow larger steamers to use the canal and, after the foundation of the People's Republic of China in 1949, a full-scale restoration project was begun to turn the canal into a major modern transport link for ships up to 600 tons.

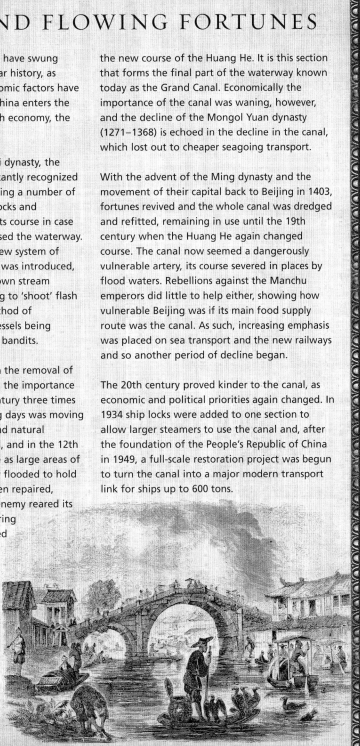

A 19th-century engraving showing a section of the Grand Canal near Beijing.

The Parthenon

A perfectly proportioned architectural gem

The Parthenon in Athens is undoubtedly the most iconic and well-known temple to survive from the classical Greek period and represents the apogee of the most elegantly simple of the Greek architectural orders – the Doric. Yet for all its apparent simplicity of form, it is one of the most complex buildings from that era, and the subtleties of its construction have inspired visitors for nearly 2500 years.

'Earth proudly wears the Parthenon as the best gem upon her zone.'

RALPH WALDO EMERSON – *THE PROBLEM* (1839)

The Parthenon was not the first temple to stand on the prominent hill of the Acropolis in Athens. Around the sixth century BC a limestone temple was constructed which is known as the 'Hekatompedon' or 'hundred footer'. This in turn was replaced by what is known as the 'Older Parthenon', an archaic temple dedicated to Athena Parthenos or Athena the Virgin which was hence the first to bear the name 'Parthenon' or 'Temple of the Maiden'. This marble building was begun shortly after the battle of Marathon, (490 BC) at which the Greeks held back the attempted Persian conquest of their country, but remained unfinished when the new Persian king Xerxes (r. 485–465 BC) invaded in 480 BC. During this invasion the temple was destroyed by the Persians and the site remained unoccupied for 33 years.

Just why no attempt was made to rebuild or restore this older Parthenon is uncertain, although Greek sources claim that, at the battle of Plataea in 479 BC, in which the Greek states decisively defeated the Persians, they made an oath never to rebuild any of their sanctuaries that were destroyed by their enemy. As part of the Peace of Callas in 450 BC, the Greeks were absolved from this oath, leaving the Athenians free to begin rebuilding their greatest temple. In truth the delay perhaps had as much to do with the crippling costs of the war as any oath, while the removal of the Treasury of the Delian League to Athens in 454 BC probably provided the financial impetus to undertake the project.

The Parthenon atop the rocky outcrop of the Acropolis in Athens. The building suffered severe damage in the late 17th century when it was used as a gunpowder store and was hit by a shell.

The Making of a Masterpiece

The Parthenon we see today was begun in 447 BC. Thanks to the survival of a number of stelae from the site that record the work, we know something of those who ordered its creation and those who actually built it. The Parthenon was constructed under the rule of Pericles (*c*.495–429 BC), the Athenian statesman and orator who came to epitomize his city's 'Golden Age'. He ordered the temple reconstructed using Pentelic marble from the quarries of Pentelicon northeast of the city, whose flawless brilliance made it the building material of choice for Athens' boldest public statements. A number of architects were chosen to work on the project, including Callicrates and Ictinus, who wrote an account of his work on the site and whose temple to Apollo at Bassae in the Peloponnese in southern Greece is today one of the best preserved of all ancient buildings. These men all came under the supervisory eye of one of the greatest Greek artists, Phidias (*c*.480–430 BC), who was responsible for creating one of the original Seven Wonders of the World – the statue of Zeus at Olympia (see pages 66–69).

This brightly painted group of pedimental sculptures, from the Philadelphia Museum of Art in the USA, gives a good impression of how the sculptures on the Parthenon would once have appeared.

The building was constructed on a rectangular plan, with eight fluted Doric columns on the east and west ends and 17 columns down the south and north sides, all baseless and standing on a platform of three steps (known as a stylobate). At the east and west ends, another six columns behind the first range then formed a portico to the building itself, known as the *cella*, which was a two-roomed windowless structure. The door at the east end of this led into the main sanctuary, where Athena was worshipped and which was lined with two rows of smaller Doric columns. Behind this was another room, probably the treasury, which was entered from the west portico and was supported on four large columns. The building's total ground plan measured nearly 31 metres (101 ft) by 70 metres (230 ft) and was topped with dazzling white marble roof tiles.

Peerless Decoration

Aside from the architectural virtuosity of the building, another factor that has ensured the Parthenon lasting fame is its decoration. This was carried out by Phidias's own workshop and many see the hand of the master himself in some of the surviving fragments. The decoration originally consisted of three parts. Above the plain architrave on top of the columns stood alternating 'triglyphs' (blocks carved with vertical grooves) and 92 'metopes' (blocks carved in high relief). The metope reliefs depicted four scenes, all demonstrating the triumph of the Greeks over 'barbarian' enemies – one on each side of the building. To the east was the battle between the gods and the giants known as the Gigantomachy, to the south was the battle between the Lapiths – a legendary pre-Hellenic people whose home was in Thessaly – and centaurs (the Centauromachy), to the west was the battle between the Greeks and Amazons (the Amazonomachy) and to the north was probably scenes from the sack of Troy, although these are largely destroyed, making the attribution uncertain.

On the outside of the *cella* was a more unusual decoration – a relief moulding of a current event rather than a mythological story. This evokes the Panathenaic procession in which the

A STUDY IN PERFECT FORM

The construction of the Parthenon is quite extraordinarily complex. Although the building appears to conform exactly to the Golden Ratio (where the ratio between the height and the length is the same as the ratio between the length and the sum of the height and the length), there are in actual fact almost no right angles in the building. Rather than simply build with mathematical precision, the architects of the Parthenon were aware that practical necessity and human perception also played a part in how buildings actually looked, and to accommodate this they made a number of practical deviations. The stylobate is not actually flat but imperceptibly curved to allow rainwater to run off more easily. This slight curvature has then been carried through the entire building to preserve its sense of symmetry, from floor to ceiling. Nor are the columns perfectly straight. When standing near to a very tall, vertical column, an optical illusion can cause the sides to appear concave, thus making the column look top-heavy. To counteract this impression, the columns of Parthenon employ a technique called entasis – in which the columns are made wider in the middle than at their base and then taper towards the top. Furthermore, a different optical illusion made the columns on the corners of the building, when seen head-on, appear thinner than their neighbours, since they did not have a column to either side of them. To 'correct' this illusion the corner columns were made very slightly wider than the rest. Like all great buildings down the ages, the end result of the painstaking exactitude and attention to aesthetic detail that went into the Parthenon's construction is an impression of effortless simplicity and perfect harmony of form.

The elegant lines and beautiful proportions of ancient Greek buildings such as the Parthenon inspired the growth of neoclassical architecture in the West from the 18th century onwards.

A TURBULENT HISTORY

The Parthenon remained almost intact surprisingly late into history and long after the classical period. Apart from the occasional looting of the gold from Phidias's statue and fires in 165 BC and AD 267 (the latter of which gutted the interior and led to the replacement of the statue) the building itself survived throughout antiquity and the Middle Ages.

A section of the east frieze from the Parthenon, showing (left to right) Poseidon, Apollo and Artemis.

In the fifth century AD the great statue of Athena was removed to Constantinople where it was later destroyed, possibly by the knights of the Fourth Crusade who sacked the city in 1204. By the end of the 13th century the Parthenon had been converted into a church, with some structural alterations. It survived as such in Greek Orthodox and Roman Catholic guises and always dedicated to the Virgin (in an interesting parallel to its original dedication to the 'maiden Athena') up to the Ottoman seizure of Athens in 1458.

In 1460 the building was converted into a mosque and a minaret was added, but the main structure was left remarkably intact. In 1674 a visiting French artist, Jacques Carrey, sketched much of the sculpture (although some of the central parts of the pediment had by this point already been destroyed). Carrey's timing was fortunate, for just 13 years later disaster struck.

In 1687 a Venetian force under Francesco Morosini (1618–94) attacked Athens and the defending Ottomans fortified the Acropolis, turning the Parthenon into a gunpowder store. On 26 September a Venetian mortar battery set up on the Hill of Philopapus opened fire on the Acropolis. One mortar scored a direct hit on the powder magazine in the Parthenon and the building exploded. All of its internal structures were destroyed, the tops were ripped from many of the pillars on the south side and the roof collapsed. As a result of this explosion, many of the famous sculptures on the building were hurled to the ground and broken.

Morosini, who was later elected doge, took some of the sculptures from the devastated building back to Venice but much remained scattered on the Acropolis. In 1801 this was how the British envoy to Constantinople, Thomas Bruce, 7th Earl of Elgin (1766–1841), found them and he agreed to purchase them from the Ottoman authorities. Elgin's acquisition of these 'marbles' led to one of the longest and most bitter arguments over the ownership of ancient artefacts in history. The sculptures and reliefs he removed from the site were eventually sold to the British Museum (although at a loss to himself) where they remain to this day.

When Greece finally achieved her independence in 1832, the minaret by the Parthenon was removed and the Ottoman buildings on the Acropolis cleared away, revealing the full ancient site for the first time in centuries. Since then the Acropolis has become one of the foremost tourist attractions in Europe and from 1975 onwards a continuous restoration project has been underway there.

citizens of Athens honoured their goddess and may possibly also be intended as a memorial to the young Athenians killed at the Battle of Marathon.

On the triangular pediments at the east and west ends stood the third group of statues, carved fully 'in the round'. On the east end was depicted the birth of Athena (who sprang from the head of Zeus) whilst the west showed Athena's battle with the sea god Poseidon for the land on which Athens was built. All of these sculptures were originally fitted out with bronze accoutrements, such as weapons and armour and, more strangely to modern tastes, vividly painted, although only the slightest traces of this paint now survives.

The final masterpiece in the Parthenon was Phidias's chryselephantine (gold and ivory) statue of Athena Parthenos herself. We have a good idea of what this looked like thanks to the survival of a small Roman copy of the original and representations on coins and votive objects. We also have an eyewitness account. According to the second-century AD Greek geographer Pausanias:

> *'The statue itself is made of ivory and gold. On the middle of her helmet is placed a likeness of the Sphinx ... and on either side of the helmet are griffins in relief ... The statue of Athena is upright, with a tunic reaching to the feet, and on her breast the head of Medusa is worked in ivory. She holds a statue of Victory about four cubits high, and in the other hand a spear; at her feet lies a shield and near the spear is a serpent. This serpent would be Erichthonius. On the pedestal is the birth of Pandora in relief.'*

Phidias constructed the statue on a wooden core, clad in gilded bronze plates, which formed the drapery, and with ivory panels for the skin. To ensure the ivory did not crack in the dry Athenian heat, the statue stood behind a shallow pool, probably filled with oil, which could be rubbed on the ivory sheets and which additionally provided a striking reflection of the monumental sculpture to those approaching it.

Work on the building itself finished in 438 BC, the year Phidias's statue was dedicated and just nine years after the whole project began, but the decoration took at least another six years. The end result however was a temple whose size, architectural innovation and lavish decoration would come to epitomize the greatest period in ancient Greek history.

'Dull is the eye that will not weep to see
Thy walls defaced, thy mouldering shrines removed
By British hands, which it had best behoved
To guard those relics ne'er to be restored.
Curst be the hour when from their isle they roved,
And once again thy hapless bosom gored,
And snatch'd thy shrinking gods to northern climes abhorred!'

LORD BYRON – *CHILDE HAROLD'S PILGRIMAGE* CANTO THE SECOND, VERSE XV (1818; ON THE REMOVAL OF THE 'ELGIN MARBLES').

TIMELINE

480 BC Earlier temple on the Acropolis is destroyed by King Xerxes of Persia

447 BC Pericles orders construction of the Parthenon under the supervision of the sculptor Phidias

438 BC The Parthenon is completed and dedicated to the goddess Athena

AD 267 A fire damages the interior of the Parthenon, destroying Phidias's renowned statue of Athene Parthenos, which is later replaced

5th century AD Statue of Athene Parthenos taken to Constantinople

13th–15th centuries The Parthenon is used first as a Greek Orthodox and then as a Roman Catholic church

1458 Ottoman troops take control of Athens; the Parthenon is converted into a mosque

1687 The Parthenon suffers massive damage while being used to store gunpowder by Ottoman troops during a siege of Athens by Venetian forces

1806 The earl of Elgin purchases some of the building's marble friezes and transports them to London

1975 The Greek government begins a major programme of preservation and restoration of the Parthenon, including lobbying for the return of the Elgin marbles

1987 The Parthenon is declared a World Heritage Site by UNESCO

The Statue of Zeus at Olympia

Monumental image of the supreme god

The statue of Zeus at Olympia was the masterpiece of perhaps the most famous Greek sculptor of all time – Phidias – and was considered a work of such accomplished virtuosity that it was included in Antipater's original list of the Seven Wonders of the World. Many ancient sources even maintained that it was the finest of them all.

Phidias was an Athenian who had already won international fame for the works he had completed in his home town during the rule of Pericles (*c.*495–429 BC). His workshop was responsible for the metope statues and pediment frieze around the newly built Parthenon (which are today sometimes known as the 'Elgin Marbles'; see pages 60–65), but it was the freestanding statue of the city patron goddess Athena within the shrine that assured him lasting renown. This was a colossal chryselephantine (gold and ivory) statue consisting of a wooden core onto which were attached carved panels of elephant ivory (for the exposed skin) and beaten gold (for the hair and drapery).

Driven into Exile

But while Athena Parthenos brought its creator fame it didn't bring good fortune; Phidias was accused of impiety by his enemies, who claimed he had included images of himself and Pericles, the sponsor of the work, on the shield held by Athena. They also alleged he had purloined gold originally intended for the statue. Phidias was now either exiled or fled to Elis, the ancient district of the Peloponnese that was home to the Olympic games, where he began his masterpiece.

The sanctuary at Olympia had been home to sacred games since at least the early eighth century BC. They had been reorganized into a four-yearly event in honour of Zeus by Kings Iphitos of Elis, Kleosthenes of Pisa and Lykourgos of Sparta in 776 BC. By the time Phidias arrived at the site around 430 BC, the games had grown into a national institution, accompanied by a nationwide truce and the Eleans required a new cult statue of the god in whose name the games were held.

In the sacred grove at Olympia, known as the Altis, there was already a temple of Zeus built by Libon of Elis around 30 years earlier. This was one of the largest Doric temples in Greece, constructed from a shelly limestone, covered with a fine white stucco and roofed in marble.

An artist's impression of the massive figure of Zeus that dominated the colonnaded hall in the temple dedicated to the supreme Greek deity at Olympia.

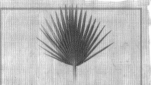

Its 38 10-metre- (33-ft-) high columns surrounded a central inner chamber or *naos*. This was to be the home of the new statue.

We know that Phidias assembled the statue nearby, as, astonishingly, his workshop has been discovered and excavated. The fact that this building is mentioned by later ancient authors such as Pausanias in the second century AD suggests that the statue made such a great impression on visitors that its creator's workplace was deliberately preserved in his honour. Like the rest of Olympia, however, it collapsed into ruins and was covered by landslides and river silt in the Middle Ages and only came back to light during excavations in the 1950s. In the course of these, archaeologists uncovered the terracotta moulds that were used as forms on which to hammer the gold sheets into shape, bone goldsmith's tools, pieces of ivory and even a small black painted *oinochoe* (wine jug) inscribed *Pheidio eimi* – 'I belong to Phidias'.

An Awesome Spectacle

Ancient sources claim the statue took eight years to build and from its dedication onwards all ancient writers agreed that it was Phidias's masterpiece. The wooden statue, plated in gold and ivory, was seated on a throne made from scented cedar wood, which had to be imported from the Lebanon, and was almost 12 metres (39 ft) high. Indeed, one visitor noted that, if anything, the statue was too big, for if it were to stand up, it would take the roof off the temple. The seated figure of Zeus, who was modelled on Homer's description of the god, held in his right hand an image of the winged goddess Nike, the bringer of victory, which was itself as tall as a man. In the other hand, he held a sceptre made of numerous precious metals and topped with an eagle. His feet rested on two golden lions, which sat on a black stone floor encircled with a Parian marble kerb. This formed a reservoir for the olive oil that was regularly rubbed into the statue to prevent the precious ivory plates from drying out and cracking in the heat. Everywhere the statue was wonderfully ornamented. The gold of the robes was figured with animals and flowers, jewels and ebony were inlaid into the throne and panels were painted with scenes from Greek mythology. The overall effect was awe-inspiring; the historian Polybius (*c.*203–120 BC) noted with satisfaction that:

> *'Lucius Aemilius visited the temple in Olympia, and when he saw the statue of Zeus was awestruck, and said simply that Phidias seemed to him to have been the only artist who had made a likeness of Homer's Zeus; for he himself had come to Olympia with high expectations but the reality had far surpassed his expectations.'*

Pausanias adds that even Zeus himself was impressed with the statue:

> *'... the god himself according to legend bore witness to the artistic skill of Phidias. For when the image was quite finished Phidias prayed the god to show by a sign whether the work was to his liking. Immediately, runs the legend, a thunderbolt fell on that part of the floor where down to the present day the bronze jar stood to cover the place.'*

What became of Phidias remains a mystery. There are two traditions concerning his death. According to Plutarch (AD 46–120) he became a victim of Pericles' enemies in Athens and died in prison; however, the excavations at Olympia have now shown beyond doubt that he was active there after his work on the Parthenon. The other legend states that he was put to death sometime later by the Eleans themselves, although no reason for this is given. Whatever happened, his Olympian Zeus made him feted throughout the ancient world as the greatest of sculptors and the originator of the idealistic, classical style. Despite this, not a single surviving piece of sculpture today can be definitively identified as being by him. Our knowledge of his astonishing works is based entirely on classical descriptions, crude images on coins and a few later copies of his work.

TIMELINE

438 BC The Parthenon is completed, housing Phidias's sculpture of the goddess Athena

***c.*432 BC** Phidias is driven from Athens by his enemies

***c.*430 BC** Phidias and his team of sculptors create the statue of Zeus at Olympia

***c.*AD 40** Roman emperor Caligula orders the face of the statue to be replaced with his own; Calilgula's assassination in 41 forestalls this plan

393 Emperor Theodosius I abolishes the Olympic Games as a pagan festival

5th century Statue of Zeus possibly destroyed *in situ*, as Emperor Theodosius II orders destruction of all pagan temples, or that they be taken to Constantinople

1766 Site of Olympia rediscovered by the English antiquarian Richard Chandler

1829 First archaeological investigation of Olympia, by a team of French scholars

1894 French aristocrat Baron Pierre de Coubertin revives the Olympic Games

1954–8 Phidias's workshop is discovered at Olympia

A VICTIM OF CHANGING TIMES

Statues from the west pediment of the temple of Zeus, showing the Lapiths' battle with the centaurs.

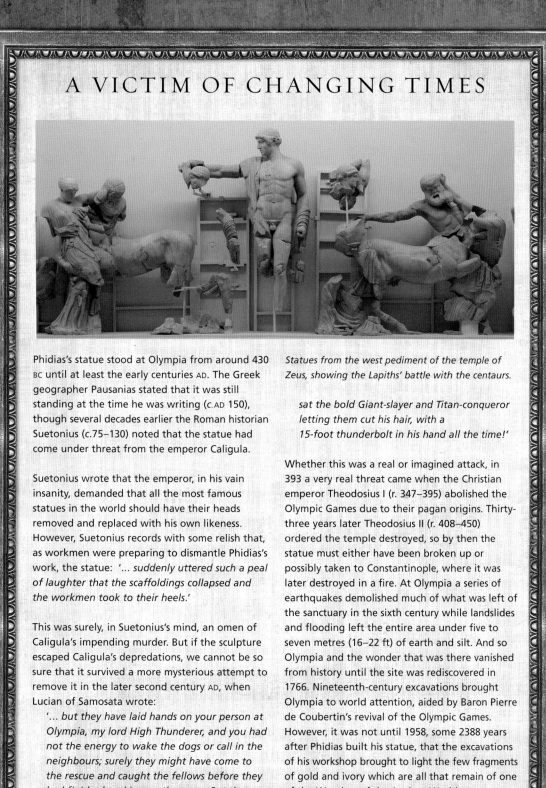

Phidias's statue stood at Olympia from around 430 BC until at least the early centuries AD. The Greek geographer Pausanias stated that it was still standing at the time he was writing (c. AD 150), though several decades earlier the Roman historian Suetonius (c.75–130) noted that the statue had come under threat from the emperor Caligula.

Suetonius wrote that the emperor, in his vain insanity, demanded that all the most famous statues in the world should have their heads removed and replaced with his own likeness. However, Suetonius records with some relish that, as workmen were preparing to dismantle Phidias's work, the statue: *'... suddenly uttered such a peal of laughter that the scaffoldings collapsed and the workmen took to their heels.'*

This was surely, in Suetonius's mind, an omen of Caligula's impending murder. But if the sculpture escaped Caligula's depredations, we cannot be so sure that it survived a more mysterious attempt to remove it in the later second century AD, when Lucian of Samosata wrote:

> *'... but they have laid hands on your person at Olympia, my lord High Thunderer, and you had not the energy to wake the dogs or call in the neighbours; surely they might have come to the rescue and caught the fellows before they had finished packing up the swag. But there sat the bold Giant-slayer and Titan-conqueror letting them cut his hair, with a 15-foot thunderbolt in his hand all the time!'*

Whether this was a real or imagined attack, in 393 a very real threat came when the Christian emperor Theodosius I (r. 347–395) abolished the Olympic Games due to their pagan origins. Thirty-three years later Theodosius II (r. 408–450) ordered the temple destroyed, so by then the statue must either have been broken up or possibly taken to Constantinople, where it was later destroyed in a fire. At Olympia a series of earthquakes demolished much of what was left of the sanctuary in the sixth century while landslides and flooding left the entire area under five to seven metres (16–22 ft) of earth and silt. And so Olympia and the wonder that was there vanished from history until the site was rediscovered in 1766. Nineteenth-century excavations brought Olympia to world attention, aided by Baron Pierre de Coubertin's revival of the Olympic Games. However, it was not until 1958, some 2388 years after Phidias built his statue, that the excavations of his workshop brought to light the few fragments of gold and ivory which are all that remain of one of the Wonders of the Ancient World.

The Mausoleum at Halicarnassus

A mighty tomb for a minor ruler

The tomb of King Mausolus of Caria in Asia Minor made such a powerful impression on the minds of the people of the ancient Mediterranean that it was not only accorded a place on the list of Seven Ancient Wonders of the World, but also gave us the term for any grand tomb – a mausoleum – a word that originally meant simply 'dedicated to Mausolus'.

King Mausolus was the son of Hecatomnus (r. 377–353 BC), who ruled the land of Caria on the Mediterranean coast of Asia Minor (in what is now Turkey) as a vassal or 'satrap' of the Persian empire. Mausolus ascended the throne on his father's death in 377 BC and quickly set about remodelling and expanding his kingdom along Hellenic lines, adopting Greek culture and language and even attempting to foster a limited form of Greek democracy in his realm. He chose for his capital the city of Halicarnassus (modern Bodrum) which he refounded in 367 BC and immediately began rebuilding. The port was dredged, the material removed being used to form new breakwaters, and the channel between them was defended by stringing a row of ships across it. The city was paved and Mausolus ordered the construction of a large fortified palace for himself as well as a private harbour on an island in the bay, commanding views both out to sea and inland.

A Legacy in Stone

It was also at this time that Mausolus is thought to have begun work on his greatest monument, his own tomb. Much of what we know of this building comes from a description in the *Natural History* by the Roman historian Pliny the Elder (AD 23–79). Although there is no evidence that Pliny ever visited the site we do know that he possessed a copy of a book by the architect of the Mausoleum on the building

so his description, though limited, is probably quite accurate. The man called on to design this greatest of tombs was Pythius of Priene, who was also responsible for the temple of Athena Polias at Priene. According to the later Roman architect Vitruvius, he was assisted by another architect, Satyrus of Paros. Their plans were barely off the drawing board, however, when Mausolus died in 353 BC, leaving his grief-stricken widow Artemisia II (who was also his sister) to put his plans into action. In his *Attic Nights,* the Roman author Aulus Gellius (*c.*AD 125–80) relates that Artemesia was so devastated by her loss that after her husband's funeral she ground down his bones and mixed them with spices before putting them in a glass of water and drinking them. As a more lasting memorial, however, she determined to give Mausolus the finest tomb in Asia Minor, and it is thanks largely to her dedication that the grave of this minor ruler would go on to become a wonder of the world.

'Of all the examples of the wonderful arts of the Greeks, the remains or the memories of which have come down to us, no one has excited such curiosity as the far-famed Mausoleum at Halicarnassus.'

JAMES FERGUSSON – *THE MAUSOLEUM AT HALICARNASSUS RESTORED* (1862)

According to Pliny, the Mausoleum was constructed of brick faced with a dazzling

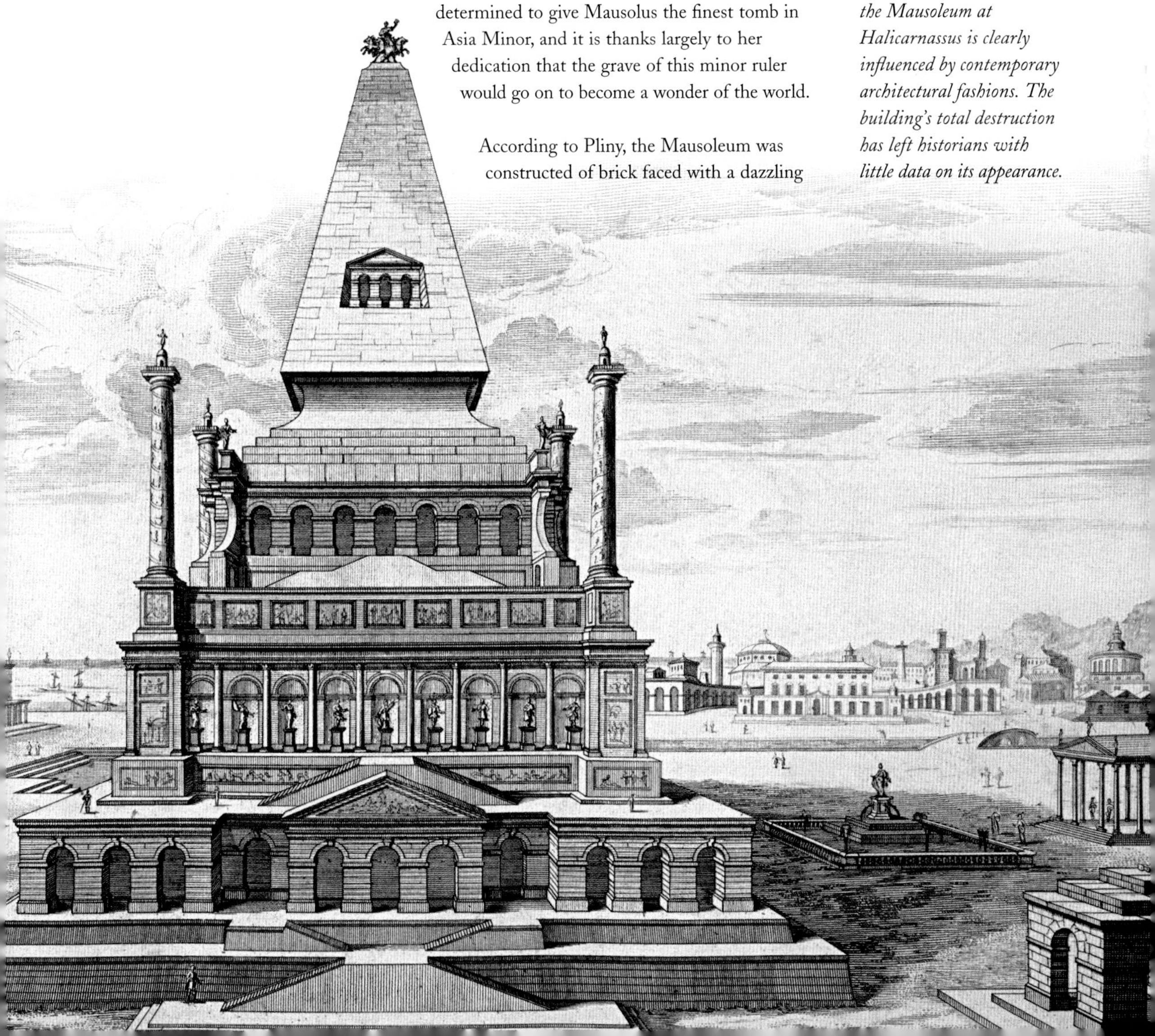

This 1721 engraving of the Mausoleum at Halicarnassus is clearly influenced by contemporary architectural fashions. The building's total destruction has left historians with little data on its appearance.

TIMELINE

367 BC Mausolus, Persian satrap of Caria, reconstructs Halicarnassus as his capital

353 BC Mausolus dies and is buried within his unfinished tomb

351 BC Death of Artemisia II and interment alongside her husband in the Mausoleum

334 BC Aleaxnder the Great captures Halicarnassus but leaves the Mausoleum intact

***c.*AD 77** Roman naturalist and philosopher Pliny the Elder writes about the Mausoleum in his *Naturalis Historia* (Natural History)

11th–14th centuries Mausoleum is destroyed probably by a series of earthquakes

1404 The Hospitallers build the Castle of St Peter (Bodrum Castle) on the former site of the Mausoleum, incorporating parts of its original decoration into the structure

1846 Sir Stratford Canning, British ambassador in Istanbul, purchases the Amazonomachy and dispatches it to London

1856 Charles Thomas Newton, vice-consul at Mytilene, begins to excavate the site of the Mausoleum; the artefacts he discovered are sent to the British Museum

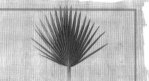

white marble from the mines on the island of Proconnesus in the Sea of Marmara. So famous were these mines that they have given their name to the entire sea – the Greek word for marble being *marmaros* – 'shining stone'. The tomb itself consisted of a stone platform with a high central podium 30 metres long by 36 metres wide (98 x 118 ft). On top of the podium was a colonnade of 36 columns and above this stood a roof in the form of a stepped pyramid of 24 steps, the whole structure reaching a height of around 43 metres (141 ft).

And yet it was not the structure itself that made the tomb of Mausolus a wonder, but rather the work of the artists and sculptors who decorated it. On the steps up to the podium were free-standing sculptures of battles, hunts and sacrifices, while the lover level of the tomb proper was decorated with reliefs of the battle between the Greeks and the Amazons (the 'Amazonomachy'). Between each of the columns of the colonnade were further classical statues, which stood beneath a carved and coffered ceiling. The cornice at the top of the colonnade was lined with marble lions and at the apex of the pyramid, just above a frieze of centaurs, stood a sculpture of four horses pulling a chariot driven by two figures that were probably Mausolus and Artemesia.

Nor was Artemisia satisfied with simply providing her husband with a legacy in stone. At the initial dedication of the building to the 'deified shades of Mausolus' she also instituted an *agon* – a contest offering large prizes for the orator who could produce the most magnificent eulogy to the dead king. This attracted some of the greatest Greek writers to Halicarnassus as well, making this capital of a minor Persian satrapy one of the great centres of Greek art.

Reunited in Death

Sadly Artemisia did not live long enough to see her work finished. She died in 351 BC while the sculptors were still at work and was probably buried beside her husband. Such was the fame already surrounding the Mausoleum, however, that the artists vowed to complete the work, even after their paymaster's death. When they finally finished, a year later, so high was the quality of their exertions that, according to Pliny, no visitor could decide which of them had excelled the most. Knowledge of this most perfect tomb resonated around the ancient world and through Greek and then Roman history. Five hundred years after it was finished, the satirist Lucian of Samosata (*c.*AD 125–180) was still putting words into the long-dead Mausolus's mouth as he describes his last resting place to the philosopher Diogenes as they converse in Hades:

> *'... a vast tomb lies over me in Halicarnassus, of such dimensions, of such exquisite beauty as no other shade can boast. Thereon are the perfect semblances of man and horse, carved in the fairest marble; scarcely may a temple be found to match it. These are the grounds of my pride: are they inadequate?'*

But Lucian then shows us that perhaps not every ancient was impressed with the Wonders of the World, as he has Diogenes reply:

> *'... as to the tomb and the costly marbles, I dare say such a fine erection gives the Halicarnassians something to brag about and show off to strangers: but I don't see, friend, that you are the better for it, unless it is that you claim to carry more weight than the rest of us, with all that marble on the top of you.'*

Yet, for all Lucian's dry wit, Artemisia did ensure that her dead husband's name would live on down the centuries and, unlike Lucian, still be regularly recalled more than 2350 years after his death.

SCANT REMINDERS

A section of the Amazonomachy frieze from the Mausoleum at Halicarnassus.

Almost nothing survives today at Halicarnassus to suggest the wonder that once stood there. Other than a small archaeological site strewn with broken fragments of Proconnesian marble we have only Pliny's description and the results of some excavations to hint at what impact the Mausoleum had on those who saw it.

The Mausoleum survived for much of the Classical period, no doubt due in part to its reputation. When Alexander the Great took Halicarnassus in 334 BC he left it untouched, as did later generations of Mediterranean pirates who raided the city in 62 and 58 BC. Indeed the building seems to have outlasted the fall of the Roman empire and survived well into the Middle Ages but at some point between the 11th and the 15th centuries it must have collapsed, probably due to earthquakes. In 1402 the site was captured from Rhodes by the crusading Knights Hospitaller, who found nothing left standing at the site other than the base. They quickly began fortifying their territory by constructing on the site of Mausolus's palace the Castle of St Peter, using local stone and whatever they could salvage from the ruins of the Mausoleum.

In 1494, to protect themselves against the growing threat from the Ottoman empire, the knights decided to further fortify their position, again using stone from the mausoleum to thicken the castle walls. Between 1505 and 1507 they also took away some surviving sculptures from the site to incorporate them into the castle's decoration. Smaller pieces were burnt to produce lime for mortar. Subsequent Ottoman aggression in the next decade led to the almost complete stripping of the site of the Mausoleum, as the knights scrambled to find stone to improve their defences. Their efforts were all to no avail, as the castle fell to Suleiman the Magnificent in 1522.

Under the new owners of the castle, the surviving fragments of the Mausoleum seem to have been left untouched until 1846. In that year the relief of the Amazonomachy, which had been removed to the castle came to the attention of the great collector and British ambassador to the Sublime Porte in Istanbul, Sir Stratford Canning. He managed to arrange for its purchase and removal to London. In London the arrival of pieces of one of the Wonders of the Ancient World ignited interest at the British Museum in excavating the site. In 1852 Charles Thomas Newton, a former museum employee, left to become vice-consul at Mytilene with the principal purpose of surveying the coast and locating the site. His attempts were hampered by the necessity of buying the land on which he wished to dig, something which his funds did not always permit. However, in 1856 he secured a small piece of land at the site and from there dug tunnels under other areas (which he did not own) allowing him to locate the foundations of the building. With a rough plan now in his possession he was able to secure the funds to buy just the land he needed. Newton's work revealed everything the medieval knights had left behind. As well as locating the corners of the site and a staircase, he recovered parts of the stepped roof, one large broken stone wheel from a carved chariot and several statues, including two that have been identified as Mausolus and Artemisia. These artefacts were all removed to the British Museum, where they remain to this day.

Delphi

Home of antiquity's most revered oracle

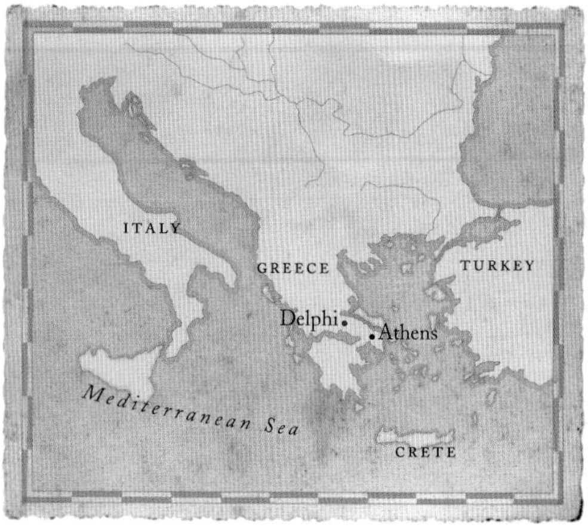

The Greek city of Delphi on the steep southern slopes of Mount Parnassus, 6 miles (10 km) from the Gulf of Corinth, was one of the most important sites in the ancient world, not because it was home to a powerful ruler but because of a famously accurate oracle there, which few world leaders would dare to ignore.

The foundation of Delphi is steeped in myth. Greek legend relates that Zeus, who wanted to find out where the centre of the universe lay, released two eagles, one from the west and one from the east. They collided over Delphi, and at the very spot where the eagles supposedly fell to earth, the Greeks placed a carved, conical marble stone known as the *omphalos*, or 'navel'. The *omphalos* gave Delphi a central position in ancient minds but it was the association of the site with Apollo that

brought it fame and wealth. Apollo, according to legend, went to the site when it was known as Pytho and was home to a serpent called the Python which he slew before setting up his own cult there based on an oracle who received visions of the future when breathing in the fumes of the decaying monster. Apollo now renamed the site Delphi, from the Greek *delphus* meaning 'womb' in honour of it being the womb or navel of the universe.

'They say that the seat of the oracle is a cave that is hollowed out deep down in the earth, with a rather narrow mouth, from which arises breath that inspires a divine frenzy, and that over the mouth is placed a high tripod, mounting which the Pythian priestess receives the breath and then utters oracles ...'

STRABO – *GEOGRAPHICA* BOOK IX, CHAPTER 3 (*c.*7 BC)

A Long-hallowed Site

Archaeologically we know that the site of Delphi was occupied from at least 1400 BC, in the Mycenean bronze age – the age in which Homer set the Trojan Wars – and there is a reference in Homer to Agamemnon consulting the oracle there. The first evidence we have for a temple to Apollo at the site, however, comes from around 600 BC, although local tradition had it that three previous temples, one of laurel branches, one of beeswax and feathers and one of bronze preceded this. This temple was, according to the Homeric hymn, built by Apollo himself, aided by the legendary architect brothers Trophonios and Agamedes.

Regardless of the legend this was a real structure which was destroyed by fire in 548 BC and replaced with a marble-clad building in around 510 BC, paid for by international subscription around Greece and beyond. This Doric temple was decorated by the famous sculptor Antenor and included scenes of Apollo's arrival at Delphi with his sister Artemis and mother Leto and the battle between the Greeks and the giants known as the Gigantomachy. This structure came crashing down in 373 BC during one of the many earthquakes that affect this area which lies on two geological faults.

The final temple, and the one which we know most about as it survives in ruins today, was completed in 330 BC and stood at the centre of the sanctuary of Apollo. This Doric peristyle

The ruins of the tholos, *a circular temple dedicated to Athena Pronaia, which was constructed at Delphi in 380 BC. Perched high above the Gulf of Corinth, Delphi occupies one of the most spectacular settings in Greece.*

building consisted of a colonnade of six columns at each end and 15 down each side, containing a central *cella* which was divided into three aisles. Inside here was the *adyton*, the sacred underground room less than 3 metres by 4 metres (10 ft x 12 ft), where the oracle made her pronouncements and the whole reason for the wealth and prestige of the site.

Power of the Pythia

The oracle was chosen from among local women and was required to have lived a 'blameless life' and give up her family and individual identity on appointment. On one day of each month between spring and autumn (the oracle never pronounced in winter when Apollo was said to leave the sanctuary) she would descend into the *adyton* and await petitioners. Each petitioner would then ask her their question and she would breathe in the 'fumes' which intoxicated her and gave her visions before giving her cryptic answer. Exactly what these fumes are is unknown although recent suggestions include the leaking of ethene gas from a fissure in the rock beneath the temple. Plutarch (AD 46–120), who as well as being one of ancient Greece's most famed historians and biographers was also the senior priest at Delphi, tells us much about how the oracle worked but when it comes to the mysteries of the Pythia's inspiration only says that the temple smelled nice when the deity was present.

The Pythia's answer would often be in poetic form but prose utterances could be translated by poets employed for the purpose. The answer given would then be interpreted by the two priests of Apollo in the temple before the petitioner went home. Getting to see the Pythia was no easy matter, however. First, the questioner or their representative had to get to Delphi, an arduous journey over mountainous terrain that was a pilgrimage in itself. Arriving there, they would then have to purify themselves in the Castalian spring before being briefed on how to approach the oracle and how to phrase their question. This process also served to weed out those petitioners whom the priests thought mad or dangerous and to identify citizens of Corinth, Naxos, Chios, Thebes and the rulers of states and kingdoms, all of whom were able to jump the queue.

Once approved the petitioner could ascend the sacred way, bearing laurel leaves. Along this path stood several lavishly decorated 'treasuries' housing votive gifts and important trophies from the victories of various Greek cities. Today only one (reconstructed) example remains, the Treasury of the Athenians, built in Parian marble and decorated with scenes from the lives of Hercules and Theseus. Inside, the walls are also covered in inscriptions detailing festivals and customs along with the only two examples of ancient Greek hymns with their musical notation to have survived. Petitioners from city-states might stop here to make an offering before continuing past the Stoa of the Athenians, where the booty from Athenian naval victories over the Persians was displayed, past the huge Cyclopean wall of closely fitted polygonal blocks, dating from a still earlier period, to the temple itself. Passing through the portico the visitor would then read the maxims '*Know Thyself*' and '*Everything in moderation*' written high above them, along with a large letter 'E' before passing into the *cella*, past the iron chair where Pindar was said to have sung his hymns to Apollo, past the bronze statue of Homer, past the *omphalos* itself and down into the *adyton* for their audience with the Pythia.

TIMELINE

c.1400 BC Earliest human occupation at the Delphi site

c.600 BC Delphi is established as an important oracle centre

582 BC The Pythian Games are reorganized and held every four years at Delphi

548 BC Temple of Apollo burnt down, then rebuilt

373 BC Second stone temple destroyed by earthquake and subsequently rebuilt

100 BC Delphi site in decline

AD 362 Last recorded oracular response to a question, from Emperor Julian the Apostate

393 Emperor Theodosius closes the oracle down

1892 French archaeologists begin their excavation of the site

1987 Delphi is designated by UNESCO as a World Heritage Site

This circular painting (c.440–430 BC) is the only surviving contemporary image of the Delphic Pythia. It depicts Aegeus, a mythical ruler of Athens, consulting the priestess, who is sitting on a tripod and is screened from the king by a curtain. Utterances of the famous oracle at Delphi are cited hundreds of times in ancient literature.

WHAT BECAME OF DELPHI?

The oracle at Delphi brought the site fame and wealth but also ultimately led to its destruction. The build up of war booty and offerings in the city's treasuries effectively made Delphi the 'central bank' of Greece and so frequently brought it to the attentions of looters who felt confident in ignoring the threat of Apollo's vengeance. Philip of Macedon, the father of Alexander the Great, helped finance the expansion of his empire and ensure the success of his son's by robbing Delphi of its treasure and later Celtic tribes and then the Roman dictator Sulla also helped themselves to the wealth of Greece, ever diminishing the role of its cities in the ancient world.

Throughout this time, however, the oracle remained, and as its popularity grew so the number of Pythias was increased from one to three. The advent of Rationalist philosophy in Greece temporarily dented the oracle's authority within the country but abroad its influence remained undiminished, due in no small part to the fact that leaders took the oracle so seriously that they often made its predictions happen. This was in fact in line with the philosophy of the oracle, which was meant to '*give advice to shape future action*'. Delphi was thus less of a fortune-telling operation than a diplomatic guidance system.

The end for the oracle came with the widespread adoption of Christianity in the later Roman empire. In AD 393 the emperor Theodosius's decree banning all pagan temples brought the closure of the sanctuary. The very next year, the site was sacked by Slavic tribes and after this the ruins became the setting for a small Byzantine monastic community.

Under the orthodox bishopric of Delphi in the sixth century it seemed as though the site might gain a new lease of life as a major Christian centre. The bishopric did not prove long-lasting however and was abandoned in the seventh century, after which the small village of Kastri slowly grew up in the ruins. It would be over 1000 years before the attention of Western scholars returned to this little village on the slopes of Mount Parnassus, but in 1880 German archaeologists received permission to begin excavating the site. Working among the houses of the village of Kastri proved difficult however and in 1891 the French School at Athens was given the go-ahead for its ambitious plan to move the whole modern village and reveal the complete ancient site. This 'Great Excavation', as it became known, proved to be one of the most spectacular archaeological investigations ever to take place on mainland Greece. As well as recovering the Treasury of the Athenians, which was rebuilt on the site, the team found over 3000 inscriptions, which added immensely to our knowledge of the political and religious life of ancient Greece, as well as filling in many gaps in extant histories. Since then the *tholos* has also been partly reconstructed and the whole site cleared of later buildings in what is now a UNESCO World Heritage Site. Excavations and conservation work continue there to this day.

The oracle's success made Delphi rich and over the centuries many new amenities were donated to the site. A stadium and gymnasium provided facilities for the Pythian Games which took place at Delphi two years to either side of each Olympic Games. Like other Panhellenic games they included artistic as well as sporting competitions. Accordingly, a large theatre was cut into the side of the hill directly above the temple.

But it was the oracle that made Delphi a unique wonder, predicting the rise and fall of ancient civilizations, success and defeat in battles and even causing wars in its own right. The one prediction to elude it, however, was its own destruction, which left Delphi today just a ruin.

The Colossus of Rhodes

A giant bestriding the ancient world

Of the seven original Wonders of the World, none had as profound an impact on the ancient psyche as the Colossus of Rhodes. For centuries after its completion, the Romans, Greeks and Egyptians referred to the people of the island of Rhodes simply as 'Colossians' and yet the gigantic statue that gave them this name stood for only just over half a century.

The decision to build the tallest statue in the ancient world was born out of the wreckage of the conquests of Alexander the Great. On his death in 323 BC at the age of just 32, his empire, which had stretched from Macedonia to India, quickly collapsed as his generals fought each other for a share of the spoils. In Egypt, the richest of his conquests, it was his friend Ptolemy who seized control but the regent who had been appointed to protect the interests of Alexander's son (who was born after his father's death) was soon preparing to invade. At the time, Egypt was the breadbasket of the Mediterranean, exporting grain across the ancient world, so the outcome of a war in the country was everyone's business, not least the wealthy trading islands of the Aegean such as Rhodes.

Genesis of a Giant

When the time came for the Rhodians to take sides, they threw their lot in with Ptolemy, which proved a wise choice. Ptolemy the general quickly secured Egypt and its new capital Alexandria and transformed himself into Ptolemy I Soter the pharaoh (r. 323–283 BC), but for Rhodes the war was not over. Antigonus Monophthalmus (382–301 BC), another of Alexander's generals, sent his son Demetrius (337–283 BC) to invade the island as punishment for supporting Ptolemy and laid siege there for a whole year. During this time Demetrius and his father poured huge resources into trying to take the island. In particular Demetrius became renowned for the innovative siege engines he invented to try to breach the city walls. These included a 46-metre (150-ft) siege tower known as the *helepolis* – the 'taker of cities' – and a 55-metre (180-ft) long battering ram that required 1000 men to operate it. While these attempts earned Demetrius the title Poliorcetes ('the

A Roman statue reputed to be a copy of Chares of Lindos's design for the Colossus. The original, however, would not have been constructed of solid stone, but was a bronze casting with a stone core.

TIMELINE

305–304 BC Antigonus Monophthalmus and his son Demetrius unsuccessfully lay siege to the island of Rhodes; the siege is lifted when Rhodes' ally Ptolemy I Soter of Egypt sends a relief fleet

***c.*292 BC** Chares of Lindos begins work on the Colossus of Rhodes

***c.*280 BC** Date of completion of the statue

***c.*226 BC** The Colossus is destroyed by an earthquake or series of tremors

1st century BC Antipater of Sidon includes the Colossus on his list of the Seven Wonders of the Ancient World

***c.*AD 77** Roman naturalist and philosopher Pliny the Elder writes about the Colossus in his *Naturalis Historia* (Natural History)

654 An Arab force under the Umayyad caliph Muawiyah I captures Rhodes from the Byzantines; the wreckage of the Colossus is broken up and sold to scrap merchants

besieger') they did not gain him entry to the city. As the Rhodians delayed, turning the land around the city walls into a quagmire to prevent the *helepolis* being wheeled close to them, Ptolemy remembered his old allies and sent a fleet to relieve them.

Demetrius was forced to raise the siege and flee, leaving behind huge amounts of siege equipment and materials. According to the first-century AD Roman writer Pliny the Elder, the Rhodians sold these for a magnificent 300 talents (around US$150 million today) and with the money decided to make a statement that the ancient world would never forget. They would build the largest statue on earth.

The man chosen to execute the plan to build this statue was Chares of Lindos, a local architect who had studied under the sculptor Lysippos of Sicyon, who was himself famed for building an 18-metre (59-ft) high statue of Zeus at Tarentum. Chares's job was to outmatch this statue and every other statue and he set to work around 292 BC. Exactly how the statue, which represented the patron god of Rhodes, Helios, was built is not known but Pliny the Elder, in describing the fallen statue says: '*Where the limbs are broken asunder, vast caverns are seen yawning in the interior.*'

Finally, after 12 years of work, the construction ramp used to erect the Colosssus was removed to reveal the bronze statue of Helios in all its glory. The fate of its architect is unknown, however; he may even have been dead by this time. The only surviving references to him are almost certainly later legends, one of which states that as the statue neared completion, a Rhodian pointed out a small mistake and, unable to accept that his work was not perfect, Chares committed suicide. Another tale suggests that during construction he was asked by the city elders to double the height of the statue. In accepting this he doubled his fee without realising that twice the height meant much more than twice the quantity of materials. Unable to pay for the work, he then killed himself.

> '*This statue, fifty-six years after it was erected, was thrown down by an earthquake; but even as it lies, it excites our wonder and admiration.*'
>
> PLINY THE ELDER – *NATURAL HISTORY* XXXIV.18 (*c.* AD 77)

Exactly what the Rhodians saw that morning, when the scaffolding and ramps were finally removed and the gigantic statue of Helios could be seen in all its glory will never now be known for certain. Although the Colossus is one of the most famous statues in the world, its short lifespan means that we have no clear sources to tell us what it looked like or even where it stood.

A False Impression

The most famous image of the Colossus we owe not to ancient sources but to the 16th-century French diplomat Blaise de Vigenère (1523–96) who described it as straddling the harbour entrance so that ships entering the port passed beneath it. This idea was taken up by the contemporary Dutch artist Maarten van Heemskerck (1498–1574) in his famous, if fanciful, series of engravings of the Seven Wonders, and by William Shakespeare who has a

CONSTRUCTING THE COLOSSUS

The Colossus of Rhodes – standing and fallen – from the famous series of engravings by the 16th-century Dutch artist Maarten van Heemskerck.

Pliny's description of the Colossus of Rhodes indicates that the figure was a hollow bronze casting, which would have been attached via an internal iron framework to a solid central pier, most likely made of stone, which rested, according to one source, on a 15-metre (49-ft) high marble pedestal. Pliny hints at this stone core when he describes 'large masses of rocks' lying in the broken interior. This construction technique would not have been dissimilar to that of the Statue of Liberty (built 1882–4 by the French sculptor Frédéric Auguste Bartholdi), another colossal icon of freedom, which consists of a steel framework to which are attached the thin copper sheets of the statue proper. Building the statue presented Chares with unique engineering problems, as the finished figure was over 30 metres (100 ft) high. To achieve this, Demetrius' abandoned siege tower, the *helepolis* – now hopelessly stuck in the mud – was, we are told, dismantled and reused as scaffolding for the lower levels. The higher levels were then reached by building a construction ramp that largely enclosed the structure, hiding it from view until it was finished and its creator was ready to unveil his masterpiece.

character in his play *Julius Caesar* (1599) describe the eponymous hero in the following terms:

'He doth bestride the narrow world like a Colossus, and we petty men walk under his huge legs and peep about to find ourselves dishonourable graves.'

More recent engineering studies have shown that the Colossus could never have stood on breakwaters at the harbour entrance, however, as this would have involved shutting the port, the island's life-blood, for the 12 years it took to build the statue. Even if the Rhodians had agreed to this suicidal plan, it would have proved beyond the technology and materials of the day. Furthermore, when the statue fell it would have landed in the sea, blocking the harbour mouth, whereas we know from ancient sources that its remains were visible on land for another 800 years. This, combined with the fact that no ancient author mentions what would surely have been an interesting aspect of the construction, suggests that it stood to one side of the harbour.

What we do know is that the statue was of Helios, the sun god who was usually depicted standing, naked, in the traditional Greek manner, with a crown with spiked rays, representing sun rays emanating from it. As no author mentions anything different this is perhaps the most likely form. It probably stood on a marble plinth, as some ancient sources suggest, either to one side of what is today the Mandraki harbour

Two statues of deer on top of columns now flank the entrance to the harbour at Rhodes. It is highly unlikely that Chares's huge statue ever stood in this precarious position.

A FALLEN IDOL

Chares' statue proved as tragic as its creator and, having stood for just over half a century, an earthquake in 224 BC caused it to shear off at the knees and crash to earth. Ptolemy III of Egypt (r. 246–222 BC) quickly offered to rebuild it for the Rhodians but they refused, as an oracle had suggested that the reason for the statue's collapse might have been that Helios was offended by it.

The Rhodians were now presented with something of a problem. The wreckage strewn around the statue's plinth was so enormous that it was not possible to simply break it up and remove it. Nor would that prove necessary, since it turned out that the statue had lost none of its pre-eminence. So imposing did the statue remain, even in this crumpled and broken condition, that it was still one of the most impressive objects that any ancient traveller could set eyes on. It was in this wrecked state that Antipater of Sidon saw the Colossus, and yet he still counted it among his Seven Wonders of the Ancient World. Pliny the Elder gives us an idea of just what so impressed ancient travellers when he noted that: *'Few men can clasp the thumb in their arms, and its fingers are larger than most statues.'*

Strangely, now that the huge elements of the statue could be seen close up, they had perhaps a more profound effect on visitors than if it had remained standing, with its gigantic fingers so far off the ground that no one could really appreciate just how enormous they were. No doubt the tragedy of the fallen idol also appealed to many an ancient mind.

And so the statue remained in pieces on the Rhodian shore for 878 years until the island was captured by an Arab force under Caliph Muawiyah I (602–80) in 654. At this juncture, according to the chronicler Theophanes the Confessor (*c.*758–818), the remaining parts of the statue were sold off to merchants from Edessa who cut up what remained and carried it away on the backs of 900 camels. While the story of the huge force of camels may be invention, pieces of what was believed to be the Colossus did turn up for many centuries on the caravan routes east, so it seems perfectly likely that the statue was broken up for scrap over time. No visible sign of the Colossus remains on Rhodes today but the term, which originally just meant a type of Egyptian statuary, has survived as a way of describing anything truly enormous, thanks to the Colossus of Rhodes.

or further inland. We also know that the outer shell of the statue was cast in bronze; indeed, the author of *De septem mundi miraculis* ('On the seven wonders of the world') sometimes attributed to Philo of Byzantium (c.280–220 BC) suggested that:

> *'... the artist expended as much bronze on it as seemed likely to create a dearth in the mines, for the casting of the statue was an operation in which the bronze industry of the whole world was concerned.'*

He also gives vague figures for the quantities of bronze (13,600 kg/15 tons) for the castings and iron (8160 kg/9 tons) for the framework, which, if Pliny's figure for the statue's height is correct, are probably conservative. At this size, the statue would be about two-thirds the size of the Statue of Liberty, which was partly inspired by its classical forerunner. Considering the impact Liberty has had on those approaching New York, the effect of this gargantuan image of Helios on passengers aboard the little ships of the ancient Mediterranean as they sailed into Rhodes can only be imagined. And those that did see this wonder were a fortunate few, as Chares' masterwork was to be the shortest-lived of all the wonders on Antipater's list.

The Pharos of Alexandria

For those in peril on the sea

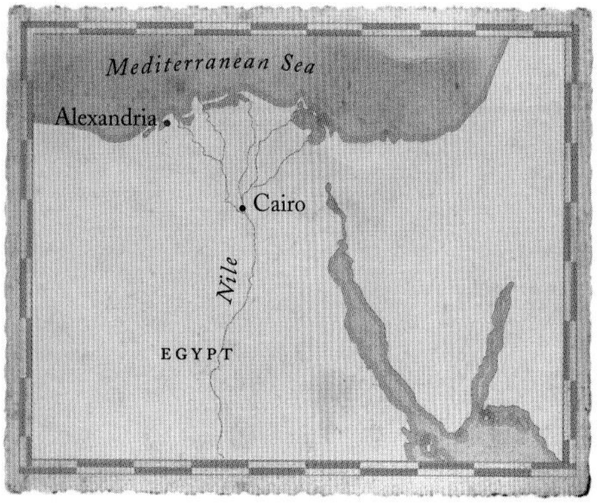

The lighthouse on the island of Pharos off the Alexandrian coast was the brainchild of one of the greatest rulers in Egyptian history. But he was not a native pharaoh, nor a descendant of the men who ordered the construction of that other Egyptian wonder, the Great Pyramid of Khufu. He was a new breed of ruler, a Greek and the son of one of the generals who had helped Alexander the Great conquer the world, and his name was Ptolemy II.

Ptolemy II Philadelphus (r. 281–246 BC) inherited Egypt from his father, also called Ptolemy (r. 323–283 BC), who, after the sudden death of the young Alexander the Great, had seized the country as his share of the great man's inheritance. In the third century BC, Egypt was the jewel of the ancient world, prosperous and peaceful, and the Ptolemies ruled it from another wonder in its own right, the new city of Alexandria, already famed for its unique museum and library, which played host to the greatest thinkers of antiquity, from Archimedes to Euclid.

Safe Passage for Seafarers

But Alexandria had one major problem. The city was built on an almost totally flat stretch of Mediterranean coastline, making its harbour hard to locate from ships several miles out at sea. And there was a further danger. Those vessels unwise enough to stray too close to the shore searching for the anchorage would find themselves in dangerous shoal waters, studded with reefs and sandbanks, where all but the most skilful captains might run into difficulties. Even with the harbour in sight, the most perilous reef lay hidden across the entrance itself. Ships that failed to take the correct bearing often ended up wrecked on the shores of the island of Pharos, where they were easy prey to the notorious inhabitants of the 'Port of Pirates'.

The thriving city of Alexandria was a principal port of call for any seaborne trader at that time, but gaining her harbour was a risky business. There was thus a pressing need to construct some sort of navigational mark that sailors approaching the city could use to ensure their safe passage, preferably both by day and by night. In short – a lighthouse.

'The extremity of the isle [Pharos] is a rock, which … has upon it a tower constructed of white marble with many stories and bears the same name as the island. This was an offering by Sostratus of Cnidus, a friend of the king's, for the safety of mariners, as the inscription says: for since the coast was harbourless and low on either side and also had reefs and shallows, those who were sailing from the open sea thither needed some lofty and conspicuous sign to enable them to direct their course aright to the mouth of the harbour.'

Strabo – *Geographica* Book XVII, Chapter 1 (*c.*7 BC)

For all its undoubted historical inaccuracies, this 1721 engraving of the Pharos, by the Austrian architect Fischer von Erlach (1656–1723), conveys the impressive scale of the lighthouse that guided ships safely into Alexandria harbour for many centuries.

TIMELINE

281 BC After assuming the throne of Egypt, Ptolemy II Philadelphus orders the construction of a lighthouse at Alexandria

***c*.280–247 BC** The Pharos is constructed by Sostratus on the island of Pharos in Alexandria harbour

1st century BC Antipater of Sidon includes the Pharos on his list of the Seven Wonders of the Ancient World

AD 642 Alexandria falls to Arab invaders

1303, 1323 The Pharos is severely damaged by two earthquakes

1480 Mamluke sultan of Egypt Al-Ashraf Sayt al-Din Qa'it Bey erects a fortress on the former site of the Pharos, reusing some of the stones from the collapsed building

1994 A French underwater archaeology team finds some pieces of masonry thought to have originally belonged to the lighthouse

The man credited with erecting the lighthouse was Sostratus the Cnidian, a famed architect and builder who is said to have constructed a 'hanging garden' in his home town of Cnidus in Caria on the Mediterranean coast of Asia Minor, as well as a clubhouse in Delphi where the inhabitants of that city could meet. Ptolemy expected great things – nothing less would do for the people of Egypt and the descendants of Alexander – but aided by the mathematicians of the city's museum and the books the architect could consult in the library, the structure Sostratus finally proposed was on a scale that dazzled even Ptolemy.

A Towering Achievement

The great lighthouse was to be constructed in granite and limestone blocks faced with white marble. Its total height would be at least 120 metres (394 ft) – that is, about the height of a modern 40-storey skyscraper. Erected on a solid base, it would have three levels. The first level would be square and would house all the workers needed to fuel and operate the great light. The second floor was to be octagonal in shape, decorated with exquisite statuary; this level, which commanded a sweeping panorama over both the sea and the city, would provide the people of Alexandria with a viewing platform from which they could enjoy the breath-taking views. The third level was circular, and was crowned with an enormous reflector, quite probably of parabolic shape (another first in scientific design) and made of polished brass. Finally, atop this stood a huge bronze statue of Poseidon, god of the sea, leaning on his trident. There was no question about the ideal location for the lighthouse, on a rock at the eastern extremity of the offshore island where so many ships had come to grief in the past. The name of this island – Pharos – once synonymous with wrecking and piracy, would eventually come to stand for 'lighthouse' in a wide variety of languages. The island was linked to the mainland by a newly-built causeway known as the *Heptastadion*.

The light of the Pharos was designed to shine both day and night. During the day the mirror could be used simply to reflect the rays of the sun out to sea, but at night something more was required. For this a circular shaft ran up the centre of the entire building, which enclosed the spiral staircase that gave access to the higher floors. Up the middle of this could be winched the bundles of resinous acacia and tamarisk wood that provided the fuel for a great bonfire whose light was reflected far out to sea each evening by the great mirror. Though wildly exaggerated claims have been made for both the height of the lighthouse (some have estimated 450 metres/1500 ft) and the distance from which the light was visible (500 miles/800 km) the general consensus is that it could be seen from about 30 miles (50 km) out to sea.

The building project took 12 years to complete and was said to have cost Ptolemy about 800 talents, approximately US$3 million at today's rates. An interesting story (which may be apocryphal) relating to the lighthouse's inauguration is told by the first-century AD writer Lucian of Samosata in his work *The Way to Write History*. Lucian recounts how, when the time came to place a dedicatory inscription at the building's entrance, Sostratus knew full well that this would have to be to Ptolemy II and his wife. Nevertheless, he was determined that he should not be forgotten. So, he had his inscription engraved in the stone, then had it plastered over and the dedication to the Ptolemies etched into the plaster. In time, and long after Ptolemy's death, Sostratus hoped that the plaster would then eventually crumble to reveal the words: '*Sostratus, son of Dexiphanes the Cnidian, dedicated this to the Saviour Gods, on behalf of all those who sail the seas.*'

Certainly this is the inscription that Strabo and other classical authors record as being carved into the lighthouse. Whether or not it was what Ptolemy saw at its dedication, however, will now forever remain a mystery.

THE REDOUBTABLE PHAROS

Sostratus certainly built the lighthouse to last. Surviving several tsunamis and a devastating succession of earthquakes, it was still working when the Arabs took the city in AD 642, though about 50 years later the reflector was damaged by a severe tremor. Around 1165 the Moorish traveller Yusuf Ibn al-Shaikh remarked that the building was still in use and confirmed its construction on three levels, adding that the base was made of massive red granite blocks, joined with molten lead rather than mortar to strengthen it against the pounding waves. He also affords us a rare glimpse inside the building, describing how at that time the first section housed government offices and a military barracks together with stabling for at least 300 horses. Above this, in the octagonal section, refreshment stalls sold fruit and roasted meats to tourists who had climbed the tower to marvel at the statues decorating the balconies. Above these a higher balcony gave visitors a panoramic view over the city and the sea beyond.

The third section had changed its use by al-Shaikh's day. The cylindrical tower no longer contained the cresset for the beacon fire, but had been replaced by a small mosque. Above this, and crowning the whole structure, the colossal statue of the sea god Poseidon, leaning on his trident, may still have gazed down on the tourists.

Yet by the time the renowned Arab voyager Ibn Battuta (1304–77) reached Alexandria in the 14th century, on his way to China, the Pharos was in its death throes. As he recorded in his account of his journey, *Travels in Asia and Africa*:

> *'At length we reached Alexandria (on 5 April, 1326) ... I went to see the lighthouse on this occasion and found one of its faces in ruins. It is a very high, square building ... It is situated on a mound and lies three miles from the city on a long tongue of land which juts out into the sea from close by the city wall, so that the lighthouse cannot be reached by land except from the city. On my return to the city in 1349 I visited the lighthouse again and found that it had fallen into so ruinous a condition that it was not possible to enter it.'*

A sad end for such an extraordinary monument, yet for a building of 40 storeys' height to have survived for more than 1500 years in an active seismic zone was little short of miraculous. Today, an Arab fortress stands on the spot where the Pharos once rose, its walls no doubt containing many of the original stones from that building. All trace of the lighthouse itself has gone, however, the majority of the stonework probably having tumbled into the waters of the harbour where they await rediscovery.

The sturdy Fort Qa'it Bey, built in 1480 by the Egyptian Mamluke ruler of the same name, now stands on the site of the Pharos.

The Library at Alexandria

The great seat of ancient learning

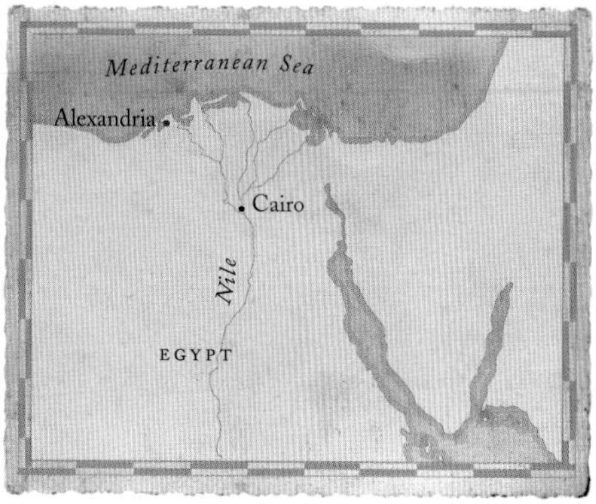

The city of Alexandria, on the Mediterranean coast of Egypt, was fortunate enough to be home to two ancient wonders. One was the Pharos, the lighthouse that would become one of the 'official' Seven Wonders, but it was the other that truly made the city's name and ensured its fame and fortune. Today we have only the faintest clues as to what this building (or rather buildings) looked like and only the tiniest fraction of what it once contained. But 2000 years ago, this was the intellectual centre of the ancient world and humankind's greatest repository of knowledge.

Along with many other ancient cities with this name, Alexandria in Egypt was founded by Alexander the Great (r. 336–323 BC), and within a few generations was the marvel of its age. Its main claim to fame, however, was not its size and beauty – the city boasted vast palaces, a safe harbour and a fabled lighthouse – nor even its market, the largest in the world. Rather, Alexandria's renown rested on knowledge, and at its heart stood the greatest library and museum of antiquity.

The idea for the library, if not the building itself, probably owes much to the exile of the tyrant Demetrius of Phaleron (*c*.350–280 BC) from Athens, where he had once been tutored by Aristotle. Demetrius ended up at the court of the first Hellenistic pharaoh of Egypt, Ptolemy I Soter (r. 323–283 BC), at Alexandria; Ptolemy had been a close confederate of Alexander, himself a former student of Aristotle. Both Demetrius and Ptolemy were greatly impressed by Aristotle's method of investigating the world through his two collections – one of objects and one of books – and their desire to emulate this formed the seed of the library and museum. And so they set about collecting both interesting artefacts and copies of any book they could find. Egypt, whose fertile, Nile-irrigated fields made the country the breadbasket of the Mediterranean, was the world's richest country at that time and so money was no object. Before long, not only books but also scholars were filling the new city.

Amassing Knowledge

Demetrius was appointed the first head of the library and museum. Over time, with the keen patronage of the ruling Ptolemaic dynasty, this institution became the meeting place and crucible of all the great cultures and minds of antiquity. For the Ptolemies and their librarians, the amassing of knowledge soon became an obsession; they impounded any books found in ships in the port and conspired in the outright theft of major works from other libraries. In an era when every book was

written out by hand, original editions were highly sought after and many libraries refused to loan them. When the Athenians were asked by Ptolemy II (r. 281–246 BC) if his library could borrow and copy original scripts by Aeschylus, Sophocles and Euripides, they agreed but demanded a huge sum as surety for their safe return. Ultimately, however, so wealthy was the Egyptian ruler that he simply retained the manuscripts and blithely told the Athenians to keep the money.

Ptolemy II Philadelphus Founds the Library of Alexandria *(1813) by the Italian painter Vincenzo Carnuccini.*

Ptolemy's purchasing power and his protection of academics brought the city the sort of fame that feats of arms or buildings alone could not. Nearly all of the greatest thinkers of the ancient world spent some time studying at Alexandria's 'university'. It was here in the anatomy school that the circulation of the blood was discovered 2000 years before the traditionally accepted date, and where the librarian Eratosthenes (276–194 BC) proved that the Earth was a sphere and measured its circumference. One Alexandrian scholar, the astronomer Aristarchus of Samos (310–*c.*230 BC), even went so far as to suggest that the sun was the centre of the solar system and that the earth orbited it, although the idea was not widely supported at the time.

The library was also the workplace of Euclid (*fl.* 300 BC), the father of geometry, whose books are still in print over 2000 years after his death, and of the polymath Archimedes (*c.*287–*c.*212 BC), one of the greatest mathematicians and engineers of all time. Here too was Galen (AD 129–*c.*200), the foremost doctor and physiologist of the age, Claudius Ptolemy

TIMELINE

331 BC Alexander the Great founds the city of Alexandria in Egypt

***c*.307 BC** Demetrius of Phaleron is exiled from Athens and arrives at the Alexandrian court of Ptolemy I

***c*.295 BC** Ptolemy I founds the Great Library of Alexandria and installs Demetrius as its first curator

***c*.281–246 BC** Ptolemy II greatly expands the library and museum

***c*.230 BC** The *Serapeum* is built by Ptolemy III

48 BC Many manuscripts are destroyed in a great fire started by Caesar's forces during the Alexandrine War

AD 391 The *Serapeum* is desecrated by a Christian mob during anti-pagan rioting

415 The last custodian of the Great Library, Hypatia, is lynched by Christian zealots

642 Alexandria falls to Arab invaders

2004 An archaeological team uncovers part of what may be the original library in the Brucheon district

(AD 83–161), the father of both astronomy and geography and Apollonius of Rhodes (b. *c*.295 BC), the author of the *Argonautica*, which contained the story of Jason and the Argonauts. Religious thinkers were also well represented at each period of the city's history. Plotinus (*c*. AD 240–70) the founder of Neo-Platonism, Clement of Alexandria (*c*. AD 150–211), creator of Christian theology, Arius (*c*. AD 250–336), the first great Christian heretic, and Philo the radical Jewish theologian (20 BC–AD 50).

A Haven of Scholarship

Although we know who worked here and the books they created, we have a very scant knowledge of the actual buildings. The initial library of Ptolemy I was probably an *ad hoc* affair in the royal palace, but as the collection grew his son Ptolemy II decided to commission a purpose-built complex. In place of the old dormitories and assembly halls, he built a magnificent range of buildings on the waterfront in the royal district known as the Brucheon, right alongside the palace, with expansive lecture theatres, laboratories, observatories, botanical gardens and even a zoo. At its centre was a shrine to the Muses – a *Museion* – from which we get the term 'museum'. Finished in marble and designed to harmonize with the royal palace, it was surrounded by gardens and waterways where philosophers could perambulate and great minds could ponder in peace.

From a relatively early date, the Great Library became known as the 'mother library'. Its 'daughter', founded by Ptolemy III (r. 246–222 BC), was located in the *Serapeum*, the temple dedicated to Serapis, a unique fusion of Greek and Egyptian gods created by the Ptolemies. Linked to the *Museion* by a white marble colonnade, the mother library comprised at least ten large interconnecting rooms or halls, each devoted to a specific area of learning, such as rhetoric, theatre, poetry, astronomy and mathematics, as defined by the great librarian Callimachus of Cyrene (*c*.305–240 BC) in 250 BC. Each hall had walls that were broken up into a series of alcoves where the papyrus scrolls were stored. Off the main rooms were smaller study rooms. The library was to be a sanctuary for thought in a violent age, and carved over its entrance was the simple inscription: *'A Sanatorium for the Mind'*.

Yet despite – or maybe precisely because of – its fame, the history of the library and museum at Alexandria is a troubled one. Ancient sources tell us that it held the largest collection of knowledge on earth and was probably both the first and the last place where everything ever known could be found. Such knowledge was often dangerous and throughout its history there are episodes of burning and destruction.

Exactly what became of the buildings and their contents is one of the great mysteries of all time, since there is no definitive account of their destruction. Egyptians, Greeks, Romans, Christians and Arabs have all lamented their loss and have, in turn, attempted to blame each other. In truth, the library probably did not disappear in a single catastrophe but was eroded away piecemeal. What has survived to this day probably represents no more than one percent of the original holdings. The remainder of the wisdom of the ancient world has simply vanished, along with the marble halls that once contained it.

'For Alexandria lies, as it were, at the conjunction of the whole world.'

GREEK WRITER DIO CHRYSOSTOM – *ORATIONS*, XXXII (*c*.AD 100)

LOST FOREVER

The first damage to the library and museum occurred in the Alexandrine War of 48 BC. In his attempt to restore Cleopatra VII to the throne, Julius Caesar (*c.*100–44 BC) besieged Alexandria and set light to ships in the harbour. With a strong wind blowing, the flames soon spread. It is unclear whether the great library in the Royal Quarter itself caught fire, or just the book repositories on the waterfront. The lack of explicit references to the great library after this date, however, suggest that this fire was far more serious than just a warehouse blaze. By the time the fire was out one source reports that some 400,000 papyrus scrolls had been lost.

A 19th-century print showing the fire that swept Alexandria during Caesar's siege in 47 BC.

This was not the end of the library, though, since we have records of visits to it from after this date. Even so, we cannot be certain if these refer to the Great Library itself or the 'daughter library' at the *Serapeum*. Either way, Alexandria was still a city of scholarship and remained so until at least AD 391, when the Christian Roman emperor Theodosius I (r. 379–95) ordered the closure of all pagan temples, which must have included both the *Serapeum* and the *Museion* (if it still existed). After priests at the *Serapeum* put up determined resistance, a Christian mob burst into the temple, destroying Bryaxis's 750-year-old statue of Serapis, a wonder of the world in its own right. This priceless artefact was dragged out into the street and smashed to pieces with a soldier's axe. There is no mention of the daughter library during this unrest but one Christian source is adamant that it was still housed in the temple at this time, so either it was removed and never heard of again or its destroyers were careful to erase all records of their vandalism.

Whether or not the books survived, the ethos of the library and museum was upheld by the city's last great pagan philosopher, Hypatia (*c.*370–415). Her teachings fell foul of the city's patriarch Cyril, who circulated a rumour that she was a practitioner of black magic. Naturally, this was a lie, but it still took root among Cyril's most fervent supporters. Searching her out, they stripped her naked and dragged her inside a church, where they set about her with broken pieces of pottery, flaying her alive. The last of the Alexandrian Hellenes was gone. By this time there was probably very little left of the original library. Indeed, one contemporary source claims the whole of the palace area was already in ruins, perhaps destroyed by a vengeful Roman emperor or just toppled in one of the city's frequent earthquakes.

One final story concerns the fate of the library's contents. Early Christian sources claim that when the Arabs took Alexandria in 642, their general found many thousands of books and, unsure what to do with them, wrote to the caliph for advice. The caliph replied that if their contents agreed with the *Qur'an* they were unnecessary and if they disagreed they were blasphemous, so the entire library should be destroyed.

This story is pure propaganda, since many of the surviving texts we have from the library have come to us from Arab copies; moreover, Aristotle only became known to medieval Europe through translations and commentaries by the Islamic scholars Avicenna (Ibn Sina) and Averroes (Ibn Rushd). What is beyond doubt is that by the time the city fell to the Arabs, it was a shadow of its former self, its library and museum in ruins.

The First Great Wall of China

The world's longest defensive barrier

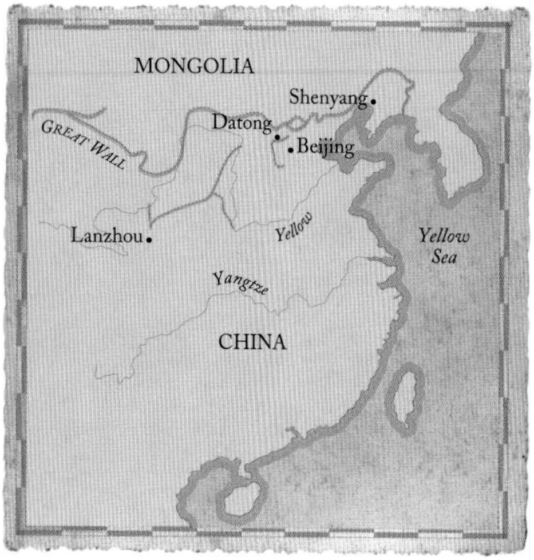

The Great Wall of China is one of the most spectacular and historically complex structures on earth. Dating in parts as far back as 700 BC it is, in terms of mass and surface area, the largest structure ever made by humans. Including all its subsidiary branches and secondary sections, the wall stretches for around 4540 miles (7300 km), equivalent to the distance between London, England and New Delhi, India.

The earliest attempt at a wall protecting a part of China dates from the so-called 'Spring and Autumn Period' of Chinese history (770–475 BC), with the construction of the 'Square Wall' by the Chu dynasty. In the ensuing period of intermittent warfare between the rival kingdoms that would one day make up China, other states soon also took to defending their territory with walls. The Qi state built a perimeter wall using the natural topography of river valleys and mountain ranges as well as earth and stone to mark its boundaries, while the Zhao state built two walls, one in the north and one in the south, to counter the threat from the Wei, who also built a wall to protect themselves from the Qin. Yan, Zheng and Zhongshan defended themselves in similar fashion during this period of warring states.

Unifying China

It was the Qin, however, who would build the first and perhaps the most famous Great Wall under the orders of Shi Huangdi (259–210 BC), the unifier of these fragmented states and the man who bears the title of China's First Emperor. Shi Huang, known in his youth as Zheng, was born into the ruling family of the state of Qin during the era of Chinese history known as the 'Warring States Period' (475–221 BC) and ascended to the throne when he was just 12 years old, being placed under the control of a regent. The young ruler was 21 by the time he managed to wrest personal power from his advisors in a palace coup. He immediately turned his attention to ending the incessant fighting by an audacious series of military campaigns that would eventually subdue all neighbouring Chinese states and bring them under his command.

This stretch of the Great Wall, at the Jiayuguan Pass in Gansu province in the far northwest of China, shows the rammed-earth mode of construction typical of early sections.

'There is nothing in the World equal to this Work, which is continued thro' three great Provinces, viz. Petcheli, Chan si, and Chen si, built often in Places which seem inaccessible, and strengthen'd with a Series of Forts.'

JEAN-BAPTISTE DU HALDE – *THE GENERAL HISTORY OF CHINA* (1741)

TIMELINE

***c*.700 BC** Earliest defensive wall built in China, in the Spring and Autumn Period

***c*.475–221 BC** During the Warring States Period, the states of Qi, Yan and Zhen and Zhongshan all build extensive fortifications to defend their territories

221 BC Shi Huangdi comes to power as the 'First Emperor' of China, instituting reforms and undertaking military action to unify the country

214 BC Construction of the defensive line now called the Great Wall of China, further north than the current line of the fortification, commences under the direction of the military commander Meng Tian

***c*.204 BC** First Great Wall of China is completed

AD 1487–1505 Construction of the stone and rubble core wall seen today begun by the Ming dynasty

1644 The Manchu breach the Great Wall and overrun China, assuming power as the Qin, China's last imperial dynasty (to 1912)

1987 Great Wall of China designated a World Heritage Site by UNESCO

Chinese defensive fortifications under attack from invading Manchus in the mid-17th century.

In 221 BC the 800-year-old state of Qi finally became the last to fall in the face of Zheng's huge and ruthless army. China was now his and in that same year, aged 38, he announced that from now on he would be known as Shi Huangdi – the 'First Emperor' – in what he claimed would be a line lasting ten thousand generations.

Unifying the previously warring states of China was an enormous task but one which the emperor and his prime minister Li Si set about with extraordinary daring. Abolishing centuries of feudalism, the empire was divided into regions, each commanded by a civilian governor and a subordinate military commander, both appointed and dismissed on the whim of the emperor. Dividing civilian and military control effectively prevented too much power falling into the hands of any one imperial servant while the appointment of independent inspectors in each region ensured that the emperor heard exactly how his nominees were behaving. To further prevent his governors becoming over-mighty, the emperor rotated each command, so no individual had enough time to build up a powerbase in any one area. He also set about creating an infrastructure for his new country, initiating an extensive programme of road and canal building, which both improved trade and provided his army with the ability to suppress trouble quickly in any quarter. To further integrate his government, he ordered all Chinese weights and measures to be standardized, along with the Chinese script, and also introduced a single codified legal system.

A New Threat

But a unified China faced a new threat – from those tribes and peoples who now lived beyond its borders, particularly the nomadic Xiongnu to the north. Accordingly, Shi Huangdi set about building the unified defence against them, which would over time become the first Great Wall of China.

This first Great Wall of China was not to last, however. The emperor died in September 210 BC in a provincial palace over two months' journey away from his capital. Fearing a rebellion, his prime minister Li Si concealed his death, entering the imperial wagon each day allegedly to speak with the emperor on the journey home. To prevent the imperial entourage from becoming suspicious, Li Si ordered that fish wagons should be placed in front of and behind the emperor's carriage to mask the dreadful stench of the rapidly decomposing body.

AN ENORMOUS UNDERTAKING

To secure his realm Shi Huangdi set in train, from 214 BC onwards, a building programme on an unprecedented scale. This Herculean task involved destroying those old sections of wall that were well within his territory and connecting up those useful sections that existed on what were now the borders of the new China. The emperor utilized the enormous quantity of labour that he had acquired from unifying the country, placing a total of two million soldiers, prisoners-of-war, conscripted labourers and convicts at the disposal of his general Meng Tian. In just ten years his wall, which was made of rammed earth and stone with wooden watchtowers at regular intervals, was completed. It stretched from the Gobi Desert to the Jieshishan Mountain near the Datongjiang river in Korea. The human toll for this monumental achievement is not recorded but Chinese sources estimate that perhaps up to one million people died in its construction. To ensure this vast boundary remained effective, the First Emperor then established 12 prefectures along its route, each of which was responsible for the maintenance and defence of the section of wall on its territory.

Li Si's fears were well founded. Zheng's empire was held together by his own extraordinary personality and within four years his son, the Second Emperor (Ershi Huangdi, r. 210–206 BC) was dead and a period of chaos returned to China. The First Emperor's dream of immortality in an eternal empire was over and only the thousands of miles of wall, now rapidly crumbling without a centralized state to administer it, survived as a testament to perhaps the most ambitious building plan in the ancient world.

Shifting Lines of Defence

The first Great Wall of China constructed by Qin Shi Huang is today barely visible on the ground. Having been constructed largely of rammed earth and wood, with stone only used in mountainous areas where there was a ready supply, the wall required constant maintenance and over the centuries has decayed away.

After the collapse of the Qin, subsequent dynasties continued to repair and reinforce Qin Shi Huang's wall. Under the Han dynasty (206 BC–AD 220) more strong points were added, with beacons, towers, forts and castles at regular intervals. Under the Northern and Eastern Wei (534–50) and the Northern Qi (550–77), new sections were added to counter new threats from China's northern and western borders. At times, these improvements involved a workforce of up to 1.8 million people.

With greater military success, however, the wall began to lose some importance and the expansion of the Tang dynasty's empire (618–907) beyond the line of the wall effectively rendered it useless. Yet the reversal of Chinese fortunes under the subsequent Song dynasty (960–1271) saw the wall not only become a front line again but actually fall into the hands of the northern tribes it was designed to protect against.

The Mongol (Yuan) period of (1271–1368) saw few developments on the wall, since the Mongols were themselves nomadic tribesmen from the north and so had little to fear from

their northern neighbours. However, under the Ming dynasty (1368–1644) the whole concept of the Great Wall was reborn. The wall we know today as the Great Wall is largely the one built by the Ming. Although this is a direct successor to the ancient Qin defence, it is slightly shorter and lies a little further to the south. What marks it out from the original wall, however, is its construction technique. This wall is largely built of dressed stone around a rubble core, and as such has survived the wear and tear of the centuries far better than Qin Shi Huang's defences. Between 1487 and 1505 the Ming, who were desperate to prevent another Mongol dynasty establishing itself within China, built a three-part system consisting of 'passes' (fortified bastions where trade routes passed through the wall); signal towers (which provided communication via smoke signals, banners, fires and clappers); and the wall itself (generally 6.5 metres (21 ft) wide at the base and between 7 and 8 metres (23–26 ft) tall).

For 150 years this wall kept the northern tribes out of China until in 1644 the Manchurians bribed a border general and swept through the boundary and into power as the Qing dynasty. With the wall now well inside Qing territory it was no longer a useful defence and quickly fell out of use, just as the original wall had done. The remote earth-built parts of the wall are again slowly eroding away leaving only the stone sections as one of China's greatest tourist attractions and the lasting memorial to the ancient world's greatest feat of engineering.

Many of the most strongly built (and hence now the best preserved) parts of the Great Wall, such as this section north of Beijing, were the work of the Ming.

The Tomb of the First Emperor

Necropolis for a totalitarian ruler

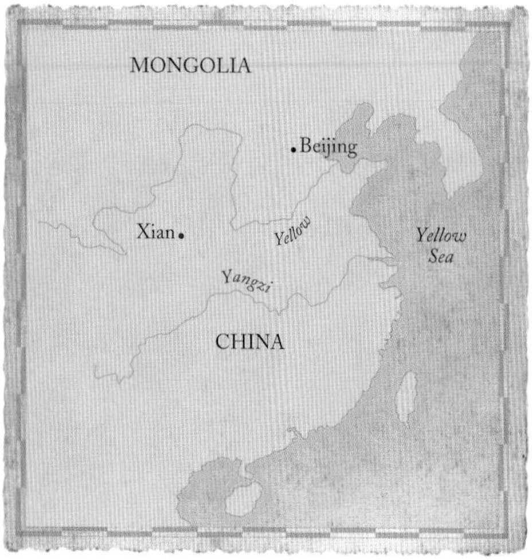

One of the most astonishing Wonders of the Ancient World lay hidden for over two millennia until its chance discovery in 1974. Under an artificial mound in Shaanxi province in central China, the country's First Emperor constructed a vast necropolis for his own burial. To accompany him into the afterlife was a huge bodyguard of over 8000 exquisitely modelled soldiers made from fired clay, now famous throughout the world as the 'Terracotta Army'.

The First Emperor was one of the most remarkable rulers in Chinese – and indeed world – history. Born into the ruling family of the state of Qin in the era known as the 'Warring States Period', he came to the throne in 247 BC under the name of Zheng when he was just 12 years old, and for the first years of his reign ruled through a regent. Eight years later he took power into his own hands and immediately launched an audacious series of military campaigns to subdue his neighbours. By 221 BC, Zheng proclaimed that he would henceforth be known as Shi Huangdi – the First Emperor – of a line he said would last ten thousand generations.

In the event the emperor died only 11 years later, in 210 BC and, lacking another dynamic leader, the Qin dynasty came to an end within four years. Yet, for all its brevity, the First Emperor's rule was truly revolutionary. He abolished feudalism, and divided his nation into regions ruled by personally appointed civil and military governors who were rotated around the country to prevent them acquiring a threatening powerbase. He also expanded the country's road and canal infrastructure and instituted vital administrative measures, including standard weights and measures, a unified Chinese script and a single, codified legal system. To safeguard China's borders, he also ordered the construction of the prototype of the Great Wall (see pages 92–97).

Bodyguard for the Afterlife

But it was in his tomb, probably begun when he ascended the throne, that the First Emperor really demonstrated his power. In the foothills of the Qiling Mountains in central China, near the modern city of Xi'an, the site today lies hidden under a huge man-made mound, which has yet to be excavated by archaeologists. Surrounding this site, however, is one of the most celebrated discoveries of modern archaeology – the Terracotta Army. Buried in pits around the mound, 8099 figures of warriors have been excavated, each one unique and slightly larger than life size.

'A man has only one death. That death may be as weighty as Mount Tai, or it may be as light as a goose feather. It all depends upon the way he uses it ...'

SIMA QIAN – *SHIJI* (*RECORDS OF THE GRAND HISTORIAN*; 109–91 BC)

The soldiers appear to have been made on a production line, with the same technology used in contemporary drain manufacture, individual parts being moulded and fired before being joined together. The finished figures were then lacquered and painted (although only traces of this paint now survive) to further increase their realism before being armed with various real weapons, some dating back to 228 BC, which may actually have been used in the emperor's wars to unify China. The army was then arranged in battle order in three huge trenches facing east, where traditionally the emperor's enemies had come from, and buried, never, as far as the emperor intended, to be seen again. Chinese archaeologists have estimated that the work would have taken 700,000 craftsmen and labourers 38 years to complete.

A section of the Terracotta Army. In their manufacture, great care was taken to ensure that no two soldiers were identical and each was moulded with the precise insignia and hairstyle appropriate to his rank.

TIMELINE

247 BC Zheng becomes ruler of kingdom of Qin; construction of his funerary complex near Xi'an begins around this time

221 BC Zheng assumes power as Shi Huangdi, the 'First Emperor' of China, instituting reforms and undertaking military action to unify the country

210 BC Death of Shi Huangdi

***c.*208 BC** Likely date of completion of the necropolis

AD 1974 Farmers digging wells accidentally unearth the first of the terracotta warriors surrounding the First Emperor's tomb

1987 Mausoleum of the First Qin Emperor designated a World Heritage Site by UNESCO

Pit 1, containing the emperor's main army, held 6000 horses and warriors; 204 of these infantrymen with light packs formed the vanguard of the army followed by 30 lines of chariots alternating with more infantry. To the right and left of this formation were two lines of infantrymen facing outwards, guarding the detachment. Pit 2 appears to have been modelled on the imperial bodyguard and contained 1400 archers, infantrymen and chariots, while Pit 3 apparently held the 68 high-ranking commanders of the army arranged around a spectacular war chariot, drawn by four horses. They had all stood guard there for well over 2000 years. Exactly what this army was for is still a matter of conjecture, although it seems most likely that they were a spirit army designed to protect the hugely superstitious emperor in the afterlife. Certainly he had invested a great deal of time and resources in preparing it, apparently in secret as no records from the period even make mention of it.

Aside from the army, archaeological work at the site has unearthed over 180 other pits, containing everything from terracotta dancers, acrobats and musicians (presumably placed there to entertain the emperor in the next life) to over 200 sets of stone armour (perhaps to placate the angry spirits of the soldiers who died in the emperor's army). There are also spectacular bronzes, including the 'secret chariot' – a half-size model of the two-compartment chariot probably used by the emperor himself. It is covered in a huge sunshade and drawn by four horses. This artefact and its associated guarding chariot were made up of 3400 pieces of bronze, all welded together so finely that the joints are only visible under magnification. The whole funerary complex is now thought to cover around 52 square kilometres (20 sq mi).

Riches Still in Store

The mound itself, however, has only been probed by some limited sampling and non-invasive radar and resistivity studies. The results of these are tantalizing. Remote sensing reveals that the entire mound is the weathered remains of a collapsed pyramid – larger than the Great Pyramid at Giza in its day – into which is set a tomb apparently containing large numbers of coins. Soil samples also show an unusually high level of mercury residue in the soil above the tomb. This tallies with the only known description of the contents of the tomb itself, written by the Grand Historian Sima Qian (145–90 BC) around a century after the emperor's death:

> *'As soon as the First Emperor became king of Qin, excavations and building had been started at Mount Li, while after he won the empire, more than 700,000 conscripts from all parts of the country worked there. They dug through three subterranean streams and poured molten copper for the outer coffin, and the tomb was filled with models of palaces, pavilions and offices as well as fine vessels, precious stones and rarities ... All the country's streams, the Yellow River and the Yangtze were reproduced in quicksilver and by some mechanical means made to flow into a miniature ocean. The heavenly constellations were above and the regions of the earth below.'*

The mausoleum was to be a jewelled model of the whole empire, set in a sea of mercury (which the emperor believed could instill immortality) under a celestial vault of gemstone stars.

Such a tomb would obviously have been a tempting target for any thieves who braved the mercury vapour-choked atmosphere, so the emperor took drastic security precautions. Just before the tomb was sealed, all those who knew its layout and contents were invited into its inner sanctum. The doors were then shut and bolted from the outside, forcing the tomb's architects, engineers and builders, plus hundreds of the emperor's concubines, to accompany him into the next world. Today there are still no immediate plans to open the tomb so whether Sima Qian's description is correct and, if so, how much of this wonder has survived the intervening centuries and the attentions of later tomb raiders still remains to be revealed.

THE SLEEPING ARMY

The First Emperor's prediction that he would found a dynasty that would rule for ten thousand generations proved hopelessly optimistic. His rule was highly autocratic and differences of opinion were not allowed. Books, including many of the earliest Chinese writings were systematically burnt and scholars who disagreed with his methods were executed. As the emperor grew older he also appears to have become more paranoid, developing an obsessive fear of death and spending his last years searching for the legendary 'Island of the Immortals' which was said to lie off China's eastern coast and which held the secret of eternal life. During this time historians record that the emperor also began taking mercury pills in the belief that these would prolong his life indefinitely; the poisonous effects of these may have further accelerated his deteriorating mental state.

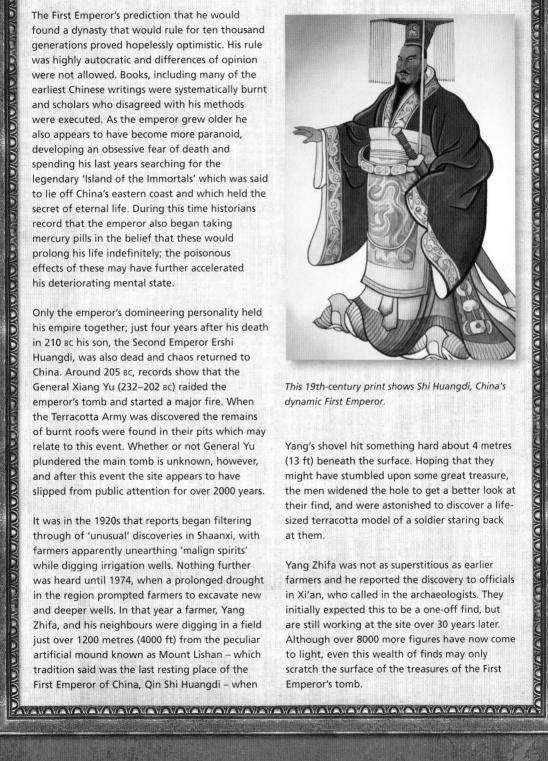

This 19th-century print shows Shi Huangdi, China's dynamic First Emperor.

Only the emperor's domineering personality held his empire together; just four years after his death in 210 BC his son, the Second Emperor Ershi Huangdi, was also dead and chaos returned to China. Around 205 BC, records show that the General Xiang Yu (232–202 BC) raided the emperor's tomb and started a major fire. When the Terracotta Army was discovered the remains of burnt roofs were found in their pits which may relate to this event. Whether or not General Yu plundered the main tomb is unknown, however, and after this event the site appears to have slipped from public attention for over 2000 years.

It was in the 1920s that reports began filtering through of 'unusual' discoveries in Shaanxi, with farmers apparently unearthing 'malign spirits' while digging irrigation wells. Nothing further was heard until 1974, when a prolonged drought in the region prompted farmers to excavate new and deeper wells. In that year a farmer, Yang Zhifa, and his neighbours were digging in a field just over 1200 metres (4000 ft) from the peculiar artificial mound known as Mount Lishan – which tradition said was the last resting place of the First Emperor of China, Qin Shi Huangdi – when Yang's shovel hit something hard about 4 metres (13 ft) beneath the surface. Hoping that they might have stumbled upon some great treasure, the men widened the hole to get a better look at their find, and were astonished to discover a life-sized terracotta model of a soldier staring back at them.

Yang Zhifa was not as superstitious as earlier farmers and he reported the discovery to officials in Xi'an, who called in the archaeologists. They initially expected this to be a one-off find, but are still working at the site over 30 years later. Although over 8000 more figures have now come to light, even this wealth of finds may only scratch the surface of the treasures of the First Emperor's tomb.

Petra

An eternal city hewn from the desert rock

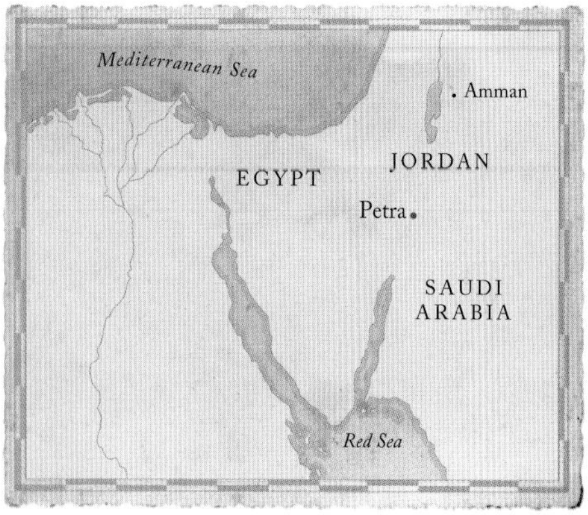

PETRA HAS GONE DOWN IN HISTORY as a 'lost' ancient city, thanks to its centuries of abandonment and its spectacular rediscovery by the Swiss explorer Jean Louis Burckhardt in 1812, yet in the ancient world this city cut from the red sandstone of the Wadi Musa (the Valley of Moses) in the Jordanian desert was a vital and well-known trading place.

The city of Petra lies on a terrace in the Wadi Musa, between the Dead Sea and the Gulf of Aqaba on the Red Sea. It is protected by high sandstone and limestone cliffs and fed, in this arid semi-desert, by its own perennial spring. This watercourse was reputed to be the one created when Moses struck a rock with his staff while he was leading the Israelites through the wilderness to the Promised Land. The city's protected position and its location at the crossroads of a number of trade routes running from ports on the Red Sea and the Persian Gulf to Gaza in the northwest and Damascus in the north made it a natural place for settlement. The earliest signs of habitation at the site come from the Old Stone Age (Palaeolithic), while the biblical Edomites made their capital here around 1200 BC, but the city that is famed today was built by the Nabataeans.

Built for Desert Survival

This still poorly understood culture first emerges into the dim light of early history in 312 BC, when it is mentioned in a Seleucid battle report. Arguments still rage as to whether various cities mentioned earlier, in the Bible, actually refer to Nabataean Petra. What we do know is that the Nabataeans were Arab traders operating in southern Jordan, Canaan and northern Arabia, who first arrived in the area as a nomadic tribe around the sixth century BC. This loose confederation was ruled from Petra, a city that offered a well-defended site secluded enough to avoid any hostile attention from jealous neighbours, at the centre of many lucrative caravan routes and, most importantly of all, a source of water in the vast desert. The Nabataeans were skilled hydraulic engineers and the flash floods to which the region was prone were controlled in the city by a series of aqueducts, canals, dams and cisterns, which gathered the excessive rainfall of the flood season and eked it out through the scorching drought of summer.

Exactly when the city was founded is uncertain, although the tombs that the Nabataeans cut for themselves in the cliff walls show the influence of Greek, Egyptian and Syrian culture. In the

The 'Treasury' (actually a tomb) cut from the cliff-face of the Wadi Musa is the best-known building in Petra, which was famously described by the 19th-century poet John William Burgon as a 'rose-red city half as old as time'.

second century BC, however, when both the Egyptian and Persian dynasties were weak, Petra really came to the fore as the heart of a thriving kingdom. It is from this period that many of the monuments that have made the city famous come.

Cliff-face Temples and Tombs

The city is approached along the Siq (Arabic for 'shaft'), a narrow gorge between 5 and 20 metres wide (16 and 66 ft) and over 200 metres (660 ft) deep, into whose walls are carved niches which originally held icons to the gods Dushara and al-Uzza who protected the place. Emerging from this the visitor comes face-to-face with one of the greatest wonders of the city – al-Khasneh, or the Treasury. This is actually a large royal tomb, over 40 metres (132 ft) high, cut into the living rock of the wadi. It was built sometime between the first century BC and the second century AD. The temple-like façade is carved with a two-tier colonnade of elegant Corinthian columns with a broken pediment, in the centre of which stands a solid sandstone urn. It was a later Bedouin rumour that this urn contained booty stashed there by bandits that led to the building becoming known as the 'Treasury'.

WATER MANAGEMENT AT PETRA – AN ENGINEERING TRIUMPH

Elements of Petra's complex water management system are still in evidence today. While this structure may lack the artistic splendour of the tombs, it is the reason behind the city's success. Petra's great natural advantage was its spring, but this only flowed for a few months a year. Otherwise, the desert landscape swung between periods of complete aridity and flash floods, which destroyed buildings before seeping away into the desert sands. The Nabataeans' engineering triumph was to control this erratic water supply and turn it into a sufficiently reliable source that a major city could be built at this vital trading crossroads. They achieved this by cutting channels and cisterns into every mountainside and piping water through every gully and wadi. Their hydraulic engineers utilized waterproof cement and ceramic piping as well as gravity-fed reservoirs and sophisticated siphons to bring water to all corners of the city. This essential supply was Petra's real great secret, enabling the Nabataeans to live and thrive in a region where no one else could.

The façade of the building is also carved with reliefs but these are poorly preserved; together with the fact that there are no inscriptions anywhere on the building, this weathering makes further identification of who this magnificent tomb was built for frustratingly difficult. Indeed, while we know the Nabataeans were literate, none of their literature has survived to tell us about their lives and beliefs. Instead all we have is some graffiti found at their sites. Beyond the Treasury, at the foot of the en-Neir Mountain, lies a classical amphitheatre, also cut into the hillside, which is surrounded by smaller tombs. This arena is thought to have been built in the first century AD and could hold 3000 people. But again with no inscriptions to help, it is still uncertain whether it was built by the Nabataeans themselves or their later Roman conquerors.

Amid the hundreds of smaller tombs cut into the cliffs several spectacular examples stand out. The Palace Tomb has a façade cut to resemble a three-storey Roman palace while the still more ambitious Corinthian Tomb is said to be a copy of the front of Nero's Golden House in Rome, which was built in AD 64–8 (see pages 124–127). The Urn Tomb has an open terrace on top of a double layer of vaults and was reused as a Byzantine church in the medieval period.

Constructed along the same lines as the Treasury, the Monastery is a far larger building, standing 220 metres (720 ft) above the main city of Petra.

At the very top of the site, about one hour's walk up from the base of the cliff, past the Urn Tomb, stands the largest tomb, known as the Monastery. This 50-metre (164 ft) wide and 45-metre (148 ft) high structure is again carved from the living rock and was certainly originally intended to outshine the Treasury in its architectural virtuosity. Sadly and for unknown reasons, it was never finished. Its misleading name may derive from crosses cut into the interior of the building during the Christian era.

What is surprisingly absent from this large city, which covers over one square mile (3 sq km), are ordinary dwellings. The reason for this lack of domestic building probably lies in the earthquake of 19 May, AD 363, which brought the freestanding houses of the Acropolis ('high city') crashing down, leaving only the rock-cut tombs of the Necropolis ('city of the dead') as reminders of the city that once was. At its height, the city of Petra is estimated to have had as many as 30,000 inhabitants.

The Demise of Petra

The final fate of the builders of Petra is almost as mysterious as their arrival. The city was conquered in the early second century AD and absorbed into the Roman empire. It continued to flourish under Roman rule until, in the early third century AD, the coinage, the building work and the production of pottery suddenly come to an end. It has been argued that a Persian invasion brought about its fall, that an earthquake destroyed the intricate water system or simply that the rise of the city of Palmyra in Syria and changes to trade routes drew the life-blood of trade away from the city.

The city of Petra was never lost to the Bedouin tribesmen who lived around the Wadi Musa but beyond those who still walked and rode the old trade routes, it slowly faded from memory in the centuries immediately following the collapse of the Roman empire.
It is thought to have been finally abandoned as a settlement after another devastating earthquake in 747.

In late antiquity, by the fourth century AD, we know that Petra was a Christian centre and the seat of a Byzantine bishop, much as Delphi briefly was. The city's Christian era came to an end with the Arab conquest of the entire Middle East region in 629–632. In 1096, during the First Crusade, a small garrison commanded by Baldwin I, ruler of the Latin kingdom of Jerusalem, occupied the city, although we have no records of what state the crusaders found it in. The Franks retained control of the area until 1189 but when Sultan Baibars of Egypt visited in the late 13th century he came as a tourist looking for ruins; by this stage, Petra had long since passed its heyday and was a dead city.

'It [the Treasury] is one of the most elegant remains of antiquity existing in Syria; its state of preservation resembles that of a building recently finished, and on a closer examination I found it to be a work of immense labour.'

JEAN LOUIS BURCKHARDT – *TRAVELS IN SYRIA AND THE HOLY LAND* (1822)

TIMELINE

6th century BC Nomadic Arab Nabataeans occupy the site and make it the capital of their trading kingdom

***c*.312 BC** First definite mention of Petra in a battle report by the Seleucid commander Antigonus Monophthalmus (quoted by first-century BC Greek writer Diodorus Siculus)

***c*.AD 77** Roman naturalist and philosopher Pliny the Elder mentions Petra in his *Naturalis Historia* (Natural History)

106 The Nabataeans are defeated by Roman forces of the emperor Trajan; Petra becomes part of the Roman province of Arabia Petraea

early 3rd century Petra declines in importance as Palmyra in Syria rises

363 Petra is hit by a major earthquake, which destroys many of the city's buildings

747 Petra is abandoned after another earthquake

1276 Mameluke Sultan Baibars visits Petra and gives the only account of the city between its abandonment and rediscovery

1812 Jean-Louis Burckhardt rediscovers the city of Petra during an expedition to find the source of the River Niger

1985 Petra is designated a UNESCO World Heritage Site

BURCKHARDT AND THE REDISCOVERY OF PETRA

The rediscovery of Petra is thanks to Jean Louis Burckhardt (1784–1817) a Swiss explorer in the pay of the African Association in London. He entered into a contract with this body to find the source of the Niger river in Africa. None of the men the Association had sent on this mission before had ever returned, so Burckhardt put forward a bold new plan. He intended to travel undercover, dressed as an Arab, first to Malta (where he would perfect his Arabic), and then to Aleppo in Syria. From there he planned to travel south down the coast and cross the Sinai Desert to Cairo. In Cairo he would wait for an Arab caravan travelling to Timbuktu and from there he would proceed down to the source of the Niger – wherever that might be.

Burckhardt, who taught himself Arabic, assumed the identity of 'Sheikh Ibrahim Ibn 'Abd Allah' to travel in Muslim lands.

And this was the route Burckhardt followed, journeying from Malta to Aleppo to Damascus before, following the trail of the annual Muslim *Hajj* (pilgrimage) to Mecca, he diverged east of the Dead Sea, to places nobody in the West had ever seen.

Travelling down to Kerek to the great Saracen castle of Shobak, which still bore the name of Saladin carved on its walls, Burckhardt then made the decision that would change his life and secure his reputation. Instead of pressing on to Cairo, he decided to take a small detour to Wadi Musa, where he had heard from locals that there were ancient wonders to be seen. Fabricating a story that he wanted to sacrifice a goat to the prophet Aaron, whose tomb lay at the head of the valley, Burckhardt persuaded his guides to take him as far as the mouth of the valley, where a local man, in return for two horseshoes, agreed to take him to the tomb. He was on the verge of entering a land unseen by Europeans for over 1000 years.

Passing some ancient tombs en route, the pair descended into a ravine, so steep and narrow that they could not see the sky above. After nearly half an hour winding though this *'gloomy and almost subterraneous passage'*, the path opened up and there before them: *'... a mausoleum came into view, the situation and beauty of which are calculated to make an extraordinary impression upon the traveller ... and heaps of hewn stones, foundations of buildings, fragments of columns and vestiges of paved streets; all clearly indicating that a large city once stood here.'*

But what was this place? Burckhardt had a shrewd idea. The Roman geographer Strabo (64/63 BC – after AD 23) had referred to a desert city protected by high cliffs on all sides, which was home to the Nabataeans. He also had a name for the city, from the Greek for 'rock' – Petra.

Burckhardt did not spend long at Petra, since his guide presently grew suspicious that he was a treasure hunter after the fabled bandit gold supposedly hidden in the buildings. After the briefest of surveys he left to continue his mission. Yet he would never fulfil his contract to find the source of the Niger. He died in Cairo in 1817, still waiting for a caravan to take him to Timbuktu, but not before he had committed to paper the discovery that would make his name.

The Tower of the Winds

Site of ancient scientific innovation

The Tower of the Winds stands in the shadow of the Acropolis in Athens and, in comparison to its famous neighbour, might not seem at first glance to be all that remarkable. But 2000 years ago, this modest building – which the Greeks called the *Horologion*, or 'timepiece' – was a very important edifice indeed, and a true wonder of the world that drew admiring comment from contemporary observers.

The tower is an octagonal structure, 12 metres (39 ft) high, made of Pentelic marble, one of the finest and most flawless marbles known in the ancient world, and the same stone that was used to build the Parthenon. On each of its faces is carved an image of the Greek personification of one of the eight winds. To the north is Boreas, the north wind that brought winter, portrayed as an old bearded and winged man, his cloak billowing behind him and a shell held to his lips. To the south is Notos, the hot, dry southerly wind that could ruin crops; he is depicted ready to unleash a torrent of showers. To the east is Euros, again winged and cloaked with water tumbling from his upturned vase, representing the warm, wet weather than often came from the east. In the west is carved the personification of the kindest of the winds, Zephyros, who brought the gentle spring and summer westerlies. As the messenger of spring, he is shown with his cloak full of flowers. Between these major winds are the minor gods of the winds. Kaikias, the bitter northeast wind, is shown pouring hailstones from his shield, while Apeliotes, the southeast wind that brought good rain for farmers, holds a cloak filled with fruit and grain. The northwest wind, Skiron, who represented the onset of winter, is shown holding a pot of hot ashes, while the southwest wind, Lips, favoured by sailors, is personified as a winged boy pushing the stern of a ship through the water.

The Heartbeat of Athens

For all the extraordinary quality of its carvings, however, the Tower of the Winds was not simply decorative, but intensely practical. Its architect, the Macedonian astronomer Andronicus of Cyrrhus, who built the tower in the first century BC, aligned the building precisely north – a remarkable feat in itself when one considers that the magnetic compass was unknown in Europe until the 13th century AD. He then placed on the roof a bronze weather vane (another Greek invention), in the shape of Triton – the son of Poseidon and the messenger of the deep – holding a pointer that spun round to point to the respective carving of the quarter from which the wind was blowing.

But the Tower of the Winds was far more than just a weather vane. Each of the eight faces also held a *gnomon* (the pointer of a sundial) and below the carving of the winds, lines were cut into the walls marking out time. In this way the entire building operated as both a sun- and moondial throughout the year. This involved some complex calculations, since the Greeks (and Romans) did not divide the day into equal hours as we do now, but divided daylight into 12 parts. During winter, therefore, a Greek 'hour' was much shorter than in the summer, as there were fewer hours of daylight.

Of course, the sundial could only tell Athenians the time when the weather was clear, while the moondial only operated when it was both clear and there was enough moonlight to cast a shadow. To provide the time when these conditions were not prevailing, Andronicus added another, yet more sophisticated device – a water clock. For centuries, the Greeks had measured the time allowed for each side in a legal case to put its argument using a *clepsydra* (literally 'water-thief'). This instrument consisted of a water container, usually a bronze sphere attached to a tube with one or more holes in the base through which water flowed. The amount of time allowed would be however long it took the water in the *clepsydra* to drain away. If the proceedings were interrupted, a bung could be placed in the tube, which would stem the flow of water until the case was resumed.

In around 270 BC, the son of an Alexandrian barber, Ctesibius,

The Tower of the Winds on the Roman agora *in Athens. The two personified winds shown in this view of the building are Zephyros (westerly; left) and Lips (southwesterly; right).*

TIMELINE

***c*.270 BC** Athenian inventor Ctesibius adapts the simple *clepsydra* to tell the time accurately, so creating the world's first true clock

***c*.50 BC** Architect Antigonus of Cyrrhus builds the Temple of the Winds in Athens

AD 1458 Ottoman forces overrun Athens but preserve the tower in the mistaken belief that it contains the tombs of Plato and Socrates

1837–45 The Tower of the Winds is excavated by the Archaeological Society of Athens

1902 The Antikythera mechanism is discovered in a shipwreck in the Ionian Sea

1951 Derek de Solla Price publishes a paper revealing the Antikythera mechanism to be an ancient form of analogue computer

was the first to adapt this simple timer into a water clock that actually measured time. He realized that if the *clepsydra* was kept full, the water pressure would always be the same and the water would flow out at a constant speed. To achieve this, he added another water tank on top that released water into the top of the *clepsydra* faster than it could flow out of the bottom (any excess simply overflowed). He then placed another tank below the outflow to catch the water draining out of the *clepsydra*. That tank now filled up at a constant rate, so if a scale was put on it and a pointer floated in it then it would mark time steadily. Ctesibius's designs proved so accurate that it was 1800 years before a better mechanical timepiece was invented.

Inside the Tower of the Winds, entered through a decorated Corinthian portico, Andronicus placed one of these water clocks, fed by a small tower on the south wall that acted as a cistern and which was, in turn, fed from a water supply up on the Acropolis. This ran day and night, ensuring that Athenians could tell the time regardless of the hour or the weather. This public clock and weather station provided the regular heartbeat for Athenian life and was celebrated by, among others, the first-century BC Roman architect Vitruvius in his great work *De Architectura*.

Home to an Early Computer?

Some scientists have recently suggested that Tower of the Winds may have been home to an instrument still more extraordinary than the water clock – indeed, Ctesibius's device may simply have provided the constant power for an even more groundbreaking and sophisticated ancient invention – the Antikythera mechanism.

During the salvage of an ancient shipwreck off the island of Antikythera in the Ionian Sea in 1902, divers recovered a thick lump of heavily corroded bronze, with traces of wooden panels clinging to the outside. Behind these panels were layers of carefully interlaced cogs and wheels. It would take another 50 years for the mystery of these cogs to be solved by an English physicist, Derek de Solla Price (1922–83). He had been fascinated by the Antikythera mechanism for years and in 1951 finally got the opportunity to travel to Athens and use recent advances in X-ray technology to look through the corrosion and see inside the mechanism. In 1959 DeSolla Price published his astonishing conclusions in *Scientific American* magazine: the device was indeed ancient – from the first century BC. And it was a computer.

The Antikythera mechanism appeared to be a hugely sophisticated analogue computer for calculating the movements of the planets, the rising and setting times of stars and constellations and the phases and movements of the moon. Its discovery entailed a root-and-branch reappraisal of our view of the classical world. On further investigation, scholars found that some ancient texts actually hinted at the existence of such machines. The poets Ovid and

'According to some, there are but four winds, namely Slanus, the east wind, Auster, the south wind, Favonius, the west wind and Septentrio, the north wind. But those who are more curious in these matters reckon eight winds; among such was Andronicus Cyrrhestes, who, to exemplify the theory, built at Athens an octagonal marble tower ...'

VITRUVIUS – *DE ARCHITECTURA*, BOOK I CHAPTER 6 (*c*.15 BC)

A TIMELESS TIMEPIECE

Whatever mechanical marvels once lay inside the Tower of the Winds, no trace remains of them today. Whether the mechanism broke, wore out, was stolen or sold is unrecorded and only the occasional asides in the works of Greek authors and the rusting cogs of the Antikythera mechanism hint tantalizingly at the former function of this little tower.

The structure itself, however, did survive. By the early Christian period, the tower seems to have fallen out of use, but rather than being left to crumble into ruins like so many other buildings in the Roman *agora* (marketplace), it was saved from destruction through its conversion into the bell tower of a Byzantine church.

Following the capture of Athens by the Ottoman Turks in 1458 the tower had another lucky escape. No longer protected as a Christian site, the building was in danger of being demolished but the Turks, who treasured many of the surviving works of classical antiquity, wrongly thought they had stumbled upon the tomb of Plato and Socrates, whom they greatly admired.

So, while wars, earthquakes and the ravages of time took their toll on surrounding monuments, the Tower of the Winds survived, against all the odds and largely for the wrong reasons. Its remarkable state of preservation meant that by the 18th century, the tower found itself fêted by the architectural movement known as the Greek Revival, and its design inspired a number of copies from Oxford to Sevastopol – and even a tomb in a London cemetery.

With the birth of archaeology as an academic discipline in the 19th century, the tower was finally cleared of the centuries of earth and debris that had gradually built up around it and the Archaeological Society of Athens was called in to excavate. Today it stands much as it did in the first century BC, although now surrounded by ruins and shorn of its weather vane and water clock mechanism – a timepiece that has outlived its time.

The Antikythera mechanism, discovered in the sea off Crete in the early 20th century.

Plutarch both mentioned the 'celestial spheres', while the great Roman orator Cicero wrote that his friend and teacher Poseidonius '*recently made a globe which in its revolutions shows the movements of the sun and stars and planets, by day and night, just as they appear in the sky*'.

Now we know that such devices were a reality and not just theory in the Greek world, scholars have begun to rethink their ideas on what mechanism might have been housed in the Tower of the Winds. No crank handle was ever found with the Antikythera machine, and deSolla Price suggested it may even have been automatic, powered by one of Ctesibius's water clocks. As such, the Tower of the Winds may once have contained something far more impressive than a water clock and sundials – behind its Corinthian portico may have whirred the cogs and wheels of a complete mechanical calendar and model solar system.

The Rice Terraces of Banaue

An ancient wonder still in modern use

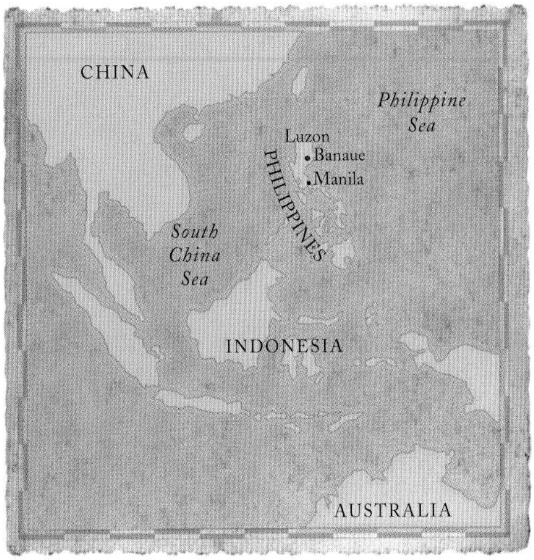

THERE IS ONE ANCIENT 'wonder' of the world that is unique, in so far as it has not only survived for at least two millennia but has remained continuously in use throughout that period, and still continues to fulfil its original purpose today. These are the rice terraces at Banaue on the Philippines.

The island of Luzon – which means 'big light' – is the largest landmass of the Philippines and home to the country's capital Manila, which lies in the south. North of this city stretches a 100-mile- (160-km-) long plain, the breadbasket of the island, before the land rises up into the northern mountain range of the Cordillera Central. Comprising precipitous slopes of up to 70 degrees and narrow valleys, the terrain here provides its inhabitants with a far harsher living, but it is the Cordillera Central that plays host to what Filipinos call the 'eighth wonder of the world' – the rice terraces of Banaue.

Rice is usually grown in paddyfields on flat floodplains, since it requires large quantities of water. However, the Ifugao people (whose name means 'people of the earth') have for millennia found a unique way of cultivating this crop in the most unlikely setting. Every mountainside where they live has been cut into a vast set of steps, catching the rainfall from the mountaintops and carefully channelling it down cascades of terraces in which small pockets of the local Tinawon rice are grown.

Exactly how this landscape was shaped in this extraordinary way can only be deduced from the limited amount of archaeology that has taken place in the area and from speaking to the farmers who maintain the tradition. Unlike so many ancient Mediterranean sites, we have no contemporary sources to tell us of their construction.

Reshaping the Landscape

The wholesale re-engineering of this landscape, which covers almost 4000 square miles (10,000 sq km), begins at the mountaintops, which are covered in thick rainforest. Heavy rain regularly falls here and filters through the forest and down the slopes in rivers and streams. To manage this plentiful

A section of the 2000-year old rice terrace system at Banaue on the Philippines. If placed end-to-end, the terraces would stretch for ten times the length of the Great Wall of China.

‘We cannot but do what our ancestors told us.’

Ifugao traditional saying

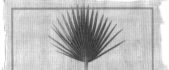

but irregular water supply, over the centuries the Ifugao have constructed an elaborate system of dams and sluices that collect the rainfall and then channel it through bamboo pipes to the highest level of terraces, some 1500 metres (4920 ft) above sea level.

The terraces themselves were made by locating any small hollow in the precipitous slopes and carving it out, filling in any cracks in the bedrock with gravel. To increase the area available dry stone walls up to 6 metres in height were then built up on the lower edge of each terrace turning what was a slope into a series of flat fields and near-vertical walls. Each terrace was then filled with layers of soil and finally connected to the irrigation system, with pipes coming into the field from the top and exiting through the retaining wall to the next level of terraces below. In this way the Ifugao and other terrace-building peoples of the island have slowly turned every available piece of land, no matter how steep, into a usable field and in the process have created enough retaining wall to reach half way around the world were the terraces to be placed end-on-end.

What is perhaps more extraordinary about this vast undertaking is that the Ifugao are not, and do not ever appear to have been, a highly centralized society with large quantities of available manpower, nor do they seem to have been influenced by outside cultures. Today they live as they probably have done for centuries, in small hamlets of five to ten dwellings, in among the terraces, in one-roomed houses on stilts, with steeply pitched pyramidal roofs.

While there is an aristocratic 'class' that retains its prestige through regular public feasts, Ifgao society is organized along kinship lines that can be traced as far as third cousins. There is no formal political organization in each hamlet and the various groups are bound together through marriage alliances and trading pacts. As such, the building of the rice terraces must have taken place piecemeal, with generations of each small hamlet slowly turning wild mountainside into workable fields. As Filipino architect Augusto Villalon has noted, this makes them unique, as '*the terraces are the only Philippine monument constructed without any foreign influence or intervention, and without enforced labour of any kind*'.

Harvest Festival

Having gone to such lengths to grow rice on mountainsides, it is perhaps not surprising that the main focus of the Ifugao year is the harvest. It is during this time that the *Hudhud* is chanted, an ancient epic poem recounting the battle between two invincible warriors. This oral tradition, which UNESCO calls a '*masterpiece of the oral and intangible heritage of humanity*' has certainly been practised since at least the 17th century and represents the method by which knowledge was passed down generations of terrace-builders before the adoption of writing.

The end of the harvest forms the most important feast of the year and is known as *tungul*, or 'day of rest' when no agricultural work can be done. This festival is celebrated with rice beer (*bayah*) and rice cakes and involves a complex ritual centred on a cosmology of over 1000 gods, of whom the most important is Bul-ol, the rice god. The blood of sacrificial chickens is poured over the image of this deity during the festival.

The end of the *tungul* festival also marks the beginning of the next yearly cycle, and the farmers must soon return to their precipitous fields to repair damaged walls and replace rotten bamboo pipes in preparation for planting their next crop of rice. Terraces that are left unmanaged quickly become overgrown and can collapse, endangering the whole fragile ecology of the slopes. In this way, little by little, the only surviving, still functioning wonder of the ancient world has been built and maintained.

TIMELINE

1st century AD Banaue terraces first created by indigenous farmers for the cultivation of rice

1973 The Philippines government pledges to preserve the unique ecosystem of the terraces

1995 The Rice Terraces of the Philippine Cordilleras are designated a World Heritage Site by UNESCO

2001 Philippines rice terraces listed as being an endangered World Heritage site

2007 UNESCO threatens to delist the terraces as a World Heritage Site unless the Philippines government undertakes urgent conservation work

A FRAGILE ECOLOGY

The rice terraces of Banaue form just one of the more spectacular parts of a much wider region known as the Rice Terraces of the Philippine Cordilleras, which consists of clusters of terraces separated by buffer zones of forest managed by tribal custom. They offer the chance to maintain an extraordinary system of agriculture that has operated successfully for over 2000 years. Yet they now find themselves at risk.

In the 20th century the delicate ecological balance of the rice terraces was disturbed by the arrival of new rice varieties that cropped twice a year. Although they were introduced for the best of reasons – to improve the farmers' often tenuous livelihood – they required the widespread use of pesticides, which built up in the highly efficient irrigation system. The new varieties also began to exhaust the fragile soils, leading to erosion. This degrading of the soil of the terraces means that they may now be unable to support Tinawon rice, which many of the Ifugao are keen to reinstate, and which was grown without pesticides.

Other problems lie beyond the immediate control of the Ifugao. The forests that cover the tops of their mountains and which collect and slowly release the water that feeds their crops are in increasing danger from logging and clearance for farming. Deforestation could change rainfall patterns and spark flash floods that might overwhelm the terracing system and wash it away.

Moreover, the intrusion of the outside world into the region has changed the Ifugao culture forever. New farming practices do not match the old ritual calendar and this, combined with increasing missionary activity in the area, has led in places to a falling away of old beliefs. In addition, the younger generation is increasingly being lured away from a lifetime of back-breaking subsistence farming on the mountainsides of Banaue by the obvious attractions of city life. To counteract this, since 1973, the Philippines government has been committed both to protecting the physical environment of the rice terraces and, latterly, to promoting the traditional Ifugao way of life.

In a culture where farming knowledge is passed down orally from generation to generation, it is essential that these preservation schemes succeed in the next 50 years if the rice terraces are to survive. Just a single generation's break in the transmission of wisdom might bring the whole system to an end. Without the regular day-to-day maintenance of the retaining walls the terraces would soon collapse and the last living wonder of the ancient world vanish forever.

The effects of deforestation and soil erosion on the Cordillera Central.

The Great Serpent Mound

Ritual site of an early American culture

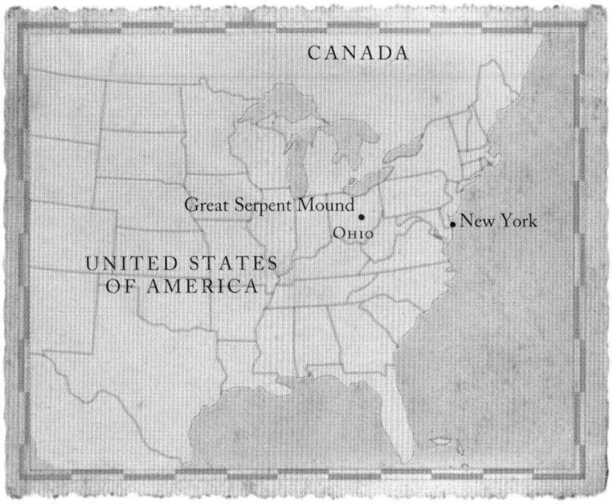

The Great Serpent Mound in Adams County, southern Ohio, is one of the most spectacular and least understood monuments in North America. Although this is the largest effigy mound in the world, its meaning, origins and even the identity of the people who created it are still matters of dispute.

The mound consists of a large earthwork in the shape of a snake with a tightly coiled tail at one end, leading through an undulating body to a head with an open mouth holding an unidentified object. This oval shape has variously been identified as an egg, a frog or even a star. The figure stretches some 382 metres (1253 ft) from the tip of its jaw to the end of its tail, and averages 6 metres (20 ft) in width and around a metre and a half (5 ft) high. It was constructed by heaping up clay and rock and then smoothing the surface using soil which is today under turf.

An Astronomical Site?

The siting of the serpent appears to be related to the local geology. The mound is built on an unusual promontory, which a recent geological study indicated may have been formed by a meteorite impact. Its peculiar contours may have suggested the shape of a snake and the effigy its makers created winds down the ridge to a cliff at the southwest end, where the head and 'ovoid structure' are located. Some sources claim there may once have been a platform here, although its purpose is unknown.

Indeed, the purpose of the entire monument is far from clear. To some of the early visitors to the preserved site, it clearly represented the snake from the Garden of Eden, as many early European settlers saw North America as a prelapsarian world. But more recent studies of Native American folklore from this part of the United States suggest that the Great Serpent was in fact a major cosmological figure whom people could call upon when they were ill or starving. This mythical creature was associated with the 'Beneath World' but could intercede, in various forms, in the human world and was often identified with the constellation we call Scorpio, especially the bright red star Antares, which was thought to be its eye. This is the star that some archaeologists suggest may be represented by the oval shape in the serpent's mouth.

The Great Serpent Mound is the largest of several such monuments built by early North American cultures. Found in Wisconsin, Minnesota, Illinois, Iowa and Ohio, they depict a range of animals, including bears, birds, turtles, deer and buffalo.

There also appear to be some astronomical alignments at the site, with the head of the serpent pointing towards sunset on the summer solstice. Likewise, it has been suggested that the tail and coils align with other astronomical calendar events, although the sinuous shape of the monument means a host of apparent alignments could be read into its position regardless of whether they were deliberate or not. What is certain is that this is not a burial mound; not a single artefact has ever been found in the structure nor is there any evidence of graves, so a ritual and astronomical use, which may be interlinked, seems more likely.

Difficulties of Dating

The lack of finds from the site does create another problem, however, since it has made it impossible to accurately date the figure. Traditionally the Great Serpent has been associated with the Adena culture (*c.*750 BC – AD 100) which gets its name from the home of an early governor of Ohio on whose lands their distinctive type of mound was first identified. The Adena were hunter-gatherers, rather than farmers, who lived in round houses with conical roofs made out of willow and bark, as well as making temporary camps in rock shelters. Typical Adena artefacts include stone hoes, axes and projectile points along with stone smoking pipes and simple pottery. They also traded with other cultures, importing copper, mica and seashells.

The Adena culture – along with the later Hopewell culture (200 BC – AD 500) – built numerous mounds in the Ohio River Valley which are famous for their complexity. In particular, the Adena buried their dead in conical mounds, which usually contain some artefacts. The presence of dozens of Adena burial mounds close to the Great Serpent is largely responsible for the traditional association between the two, despite the lack of finds from the serpent itself. Yet the discovery of three pieces of charcoal during recent archaeological work on the monument has cast doubt on this link. Carbon-14 analysis of two of these yields dates of *c.*AD 1070, suggesting that the Serpent was created by the much later Fort Ancient Culture (AD 100–1550). This culture takes its name from a series of earthworks in Warren County, Ohio, which somewhat confusingly was actually constructed by the Hopewell but later inhabited by the Fort Ancient people. This group, which was also based in the Ohio Valley, was known to construct mounds and there is a Fort Ancient village site and burial mound near the Serpent.

The third charcoal sample further confuses the matter by giving a date around the beginning of the first millennium BC, suggesting early Adena culture. However, this sample may have come from below the construction level of the mound. With no further evidence so far, most authorities remain non-committal, particularly as the site is home to burrowing animals such as groundhogs, which can transport material between archaeological layers in a process known as bioturbation. As many of these effigy mounds, which were once numerous in the region, have disappeared under the plough the mystery of who built the Great Serpent will remain unless a dateable object can be recovered from it.

'... a monument, which is to be forever protected where it was placed by its builders, an enigma for the present and a study for the future ...'

F.W. PUTNAM, LETTER TO THE *CINCINNATI POST* (4 JUNE, 1887)

TIMELINE

c.750 BC – AD 100 Adena hunter-gatherer culture is active in the Ohio Valley

200 BC – AD 500 Hopewell culture, which supersedes the Adena in the Ohio Valley, builds several mounds for ritual and burial rurposes

AD 1000–1650 Fort Ancient culture flourishes in southern Ohio

1846 Ephraim Squier and Edwin Davis are the first White Americans to find the site, during a land survey

1886–9 Frederic Putnam raises funds to purchase the Great Serpent Mound in order to preserve it as a historical monument; he then undertakes an extensive investigation of the site and two conical mounds nearby

1900 The mound becomes the first State Park in the United States

1967 Ohio Historical Society opens the Serpent Mound Museum

1993 Archaeologists Robert Fletcher and Terry Cameron map astronomical alignments which suggest that the moundbuilders may have used the Great Serpent as an astronomical calendar

2003 Geological survey suggests the outcrop on which the mound stands may be the result of a meteorite impact

PRESERVING AMERICA'S ANCIENT HERITAGE

The survival of the Great Serpent Mound into the modern world is largely thanks to the foresight of Frederic Ward Putnam (1839–1915), who is hailed today as the father of American archaeology.

The site had first been recorded by non-Native Americans in 1846, when Ephraim G. Squier and Edwin H. Davis stumbled upon it during a routine surveying mission. Fortunately these men recognized the value of what they had found and two years later brought it to world attention in their book *Ancient Monuments of the Mississippi Valley*, the first volume of the newly established Smithsonian Institution's 'Contributions to Knowledge' series.

Frederic Putnam was a tireless antiquarian, who directed digs in 37 US states.

It was 1885, however, before anyone noticed what a precarious situation the monument was in. In that year Frederic Putnam of the Peabody Museum of Archaeology and Ethnology at Harvard University was touring the Midwest, where he witnessed how the rapid development of the area, particularly the growth in farming, was destroying large parts of the region's archaeology. In particular the earth mounds of early Native American cultures were being ploughed out before they could even be recorded. On 4 June, 1887, after revisiting the Great Serpent, Putnam voiced his concerns in the *Cincinnati Post*:

> *'Last fall, in company with Mr. Kimball, I revisited the mound, and found that it had suffered much from wash-outs since my former visit. It was evident that if steps were not at once taken for its preservation it would soon be a thing of the past.'*

He added that he had circulated his letter to several newspapers to highlight the dire situation. In response, three Boston ladies agreed to start a fund to buy and preserve the site. The fund was a huge success and just a matter of months later Putnam was able to negotiate the purchase of 24 hectares (60 acres) of farmland surrounding the monument, including the Adena and Fort Ancient mounds and settlement.

With the site thus secure in the hands of the trustees of the Peabody Museum, Putnam set to work clearing the wheat that had overrun the Great Serpent, building up the mound where it had been damaged, and planting bluegrass lawns and an example of every tree native to Adams County. His intention was to turn the area into an idyllic place to visit to remind people of the history that was being lost all around them. In the park he built new paths around the monument, organized the construction of a road to improve access, and even designed a wooded glade, complete with a spring-fed fountain where picnickers might enjoy their lunch. His excavations of the mound itself failed to find anything that shed light on its makers, but his conservation of the mound from the plough and horse traffic at least ensured its survival.

In 1893 an exhibition of Putnam's work on the mound at the Chicago World's Fair brought the site to the attention of the wider world, which was then still largely unaware that North America even had an archaeological past. Since 1900, when it became the first State Park in the USA, the site has been under the protection of the Ohio Historical Society.

The Pont du Gard

Pinnacle of Roman hydraulic engineering

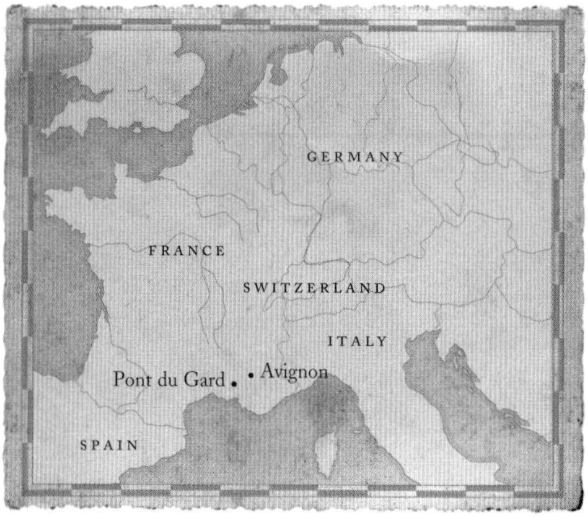

The Pont du Gard, near Remoulins in the south of France, is one of the most impressive feats of Roman engineering outside of the city of Rome itself: a huge aqueduct 275 metres (900 ft) long and as high as an 18-storey building. Yet astonishingly the name of the architect of this remarkable structure has not been preserved for posterity.

The only official inscription on the Pont reads MENS TOTVM CORIVM – 'the whole structure has been measured'. This bald statement is, however, the key to the Pont du Gard. The reason why there are no elaborate records praising the builders is that this is not a temple nor a decorative structure, but in the Roman mind simply a practical one.

Vital Water for Nemausus

The reason for the Pont du Gard's existence is the nearby town of Nîmes, which in the first century AD was known as Nemausus – one of the most important Roman cities in the province of Gallia Narbonensis. But Nemausus had a problem. The old Gaulish settlement, which became a Roman town in 45 BC, drew all its water from a local spring. As the city grew into a provincial centre and its population expanded (reaching around 20,000 in the first century AD), the spring could no longer cope with demand. Roman cities were water-hungry places, requiring not just drinking water and sanitation but a constant supply of water to the public buildings and facilities that were considered a key part of civilized 'Roman' life: there were public baths to fill, fountains to maintain and businesses to provide for. Nemausus was in danger of dying of thirst.

By the reign of the emperor Claudius (AD 41–54) the situation was critical and an engineered solution became imperative. This presented the Roman architects with a series of unusual and apparently insurmountable problems, however. Other than the town spring, there were no nearby water sources; indeed, the only other was the source of the Eure river 13 miles (20 km) to the north at Uzès. Yet even if it were possible to divert this spring, there was no clear route for it to flow down to Nemausus. In the first place, the spring was only 17 metres (56 ft) higher than the town, and a watercourse would have to run downhill all the way. But how could such a slight drop be engineered over a course of 13 miles? And even assuming this was achieved, the aqueduct would still have to cross the Garrigues de Nîmes mountains and the Gardon river.

The solution the architects found was typically Roman in its practicality. As the problems could not be circumvented, they would have to be surmounted. Roman surveyors, probably attached to the army, thus began marking out a route for the aqueduct that cut straight through the hills at so carefully constructed an angle that gravity alone would carry the water to the city.

Spanning the Gorge

At the Gardon river, however, they faced another problem. Here the Mediterranean landscape of olive groves, grape vines and evergreen oaks was cleft by a deep gorge that cut into the limestone bedrock. To cross this the watercourse would have to be suspended. But to do this at an angle that would still give enough of a drop on the other side to reach the city would entail a huge construction.

The imposing Pont du Gard took somewhere between three and five years to build, between around AD 40 and 60, and involved perhaps as many as 1000 workmen.

To create a bridge high enough to carry the aqueduct, the Romans settled on a three-tier design using decreasing arcades of immensely strong round arches. To begin with, the base of the gorge beneath the bridge was cleared down to the bedrock and stone foundations laid for six arches. The huge piers for these would have to support a further two arcades of arches above them, as well as cope with the fast-flowing river swirling around their base, so a source of limestone was found at the nearby Estel quarry

TIMELINE

c.AD 40–60 The Pont du Gard is built to carry the Roman aqueduct, running from the source of the Eure to the city of Nemausus, over the Gardon river

5th–7th centuries Local builders plunder the Pont for its masonry

1448 The Pont du Gard survives a major earthquake in southern France largely intact

1699–1704 The Languedoc State Council undertakes major restoration of the Pont, rebuilding the piers of the second tier to their original width to save the structure from collapse

1855–8 Extensive renovation works on the Pont ordered by Prosper Mérimée and carried out by engineer J.C. Laisné

1986 The Pont du Gard is declared a World Heritage Site by UNESCO

2000 Major redevelopment plan pedestrianizes the whole area around the Pont du Gard

that was easy to work but was also frost-resistant and would harden over time. For each level, the piers would be three blocks thick, requiring the lower courses to be cut into massive 6-ton blocks. These were carefully carved into the shape of the bow of a ship to allow the torrential winter floods to flow freely around them without eroding them.

Due to the immense weight of the blocks and the fact that, as the structure was built without mortar, each had to fit perfectly against its neighbour, the stones were cut to their exact shape at the quarry and marked with instructions to show where they should be placed, like a huge kit. On some of the less exposed stones on the bridge these scratched inscriptions can still be read, such as FRS II, denoting *frons sinistra II* ('front left 2').

The marked-up stones were then carried downstream to the building site, where wooden frames had been constructed to build the arches around. Cranes operated by men walking in treadmills attached to a series of blocks-and-tackle then hauled each stone to its predetermined position. The stones around it would then be doused in water, with the stone dust from the cutting forming a simple mortar when wet, thus helping bond the courses together before the new piece was lowered into place and bound in with iron clamps. As each course of masonry was laid, holes known as 'putlogs' were cut into their outer faces. Into these wooden scaffolding poles were inserted to allow the builders to work at each higher level. By the time the first bridge of six arches was completed, the structure was a massive 6 metres (20 ft) thick, but still some 29 metres (95 ft) below the required level of the aqueduct. So another bridge, this time of 11 arches and 20 metres (66 ft) high was built on top, followed by another of 35 arches, each 7 metres (22 ft) high, to give the familiar three-tier structure we see today.

Finally the bridge reached the requisite height to carry the watercourse across it, spanning a distance of 275 metres (900 ft) across the Gardon gorge. An enclosed channel could now be carefully built across the top using Roman cement (*puteolanum*), which is waterproof and so sets underwater. This channel had to be constructed with a gradient across the bridge of just 0.4 percent and linked with absolute precision to the channel on the far side. Once this had been achieved, the city of Nemausus had its lifeline.

Almost every statistic about the Pont du Gard is a record. Constructed of some 54,000 tons of limestone, it was the highest and widest aqueduct in the Roman world. The bridge itself formed just a small part of a watercourse that ran for a total of over 30 miles (50 km). Rather than being celebrated in inscriptions or recorded in histories, the lasting testament to this extraordinary engineering feat was the dramatic effect it had in revitalizing the city of Nemausus, whose water tower now received an additional 20,000 cubic metres (5 million gallons) of water a day. As for its architects and engineers, none has ever been identified, despite years of research. Today the aqueduct remains one of the greatest anonymous wonders of the world.

> *'I went over the three stories of this superb edifice with a sentiment of respect which made me almost fear to tread it; the echoes of my footsteps beneath its immense vaults seemed as if I heard the strong voice of those masters of the world who had built it.'*

JEAN-JACQUES ROUSSEAU – *THE CONFESSIONS* (1782–9)

A NATIONAL TREASURE

The Pont in around 1850. It had already become a major tourist attraction by the 18th century.

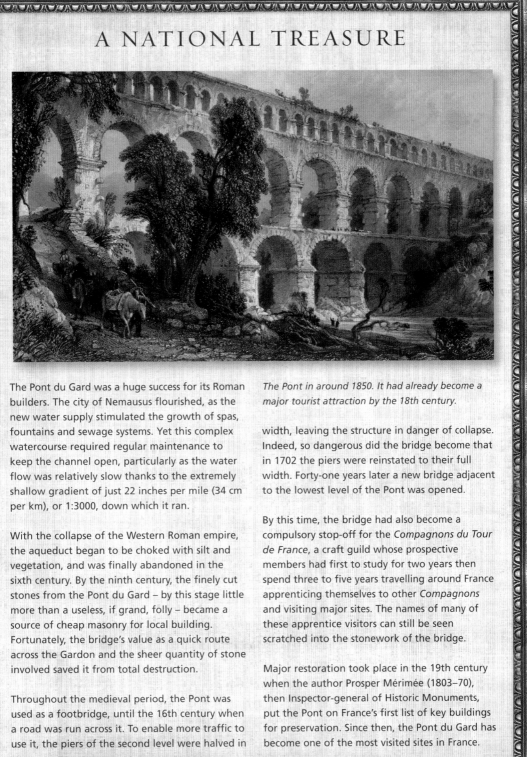

The Pont du Gard was a huge success for its Roman builders. The city of Nemausus flourished, as the new water supply stimulated the growth of spas, fountains and sewage systems. Yet this complex watercourse required regular maintenance to keep the channel open, particularly as the water flow was relatively slow thanks to the extremely shallow gradient of just 22 inches per mile (34 cm per km), or 1:3000, down which it ran.

With the collapse of the Western Roman empire, the aqueduct began to be choked with silt and vegetation, and was finally abandoned in the sixth century. By the ninth century, the finely cut stones from the Pont du Gard – by this stage little more than a useless, if grand, folly – became a source of cheap masonry for local building. Fortunately, the bridge's value as a quick route across the Gardon and the sheer quantity of stone involved saved it from total destruction.

Throughout the medieval period, the Pont was used as a footbridge, until the 16th century when a road was run across it. To enable more traffic to use it, the piers of the second level were halved in width, leaving the structure in danger of collapse. Indeed, so dangerous did the bridge become that in 1702 the piers were reinstated to their full width. Forty-one years later a new bridge adjacent to the lowest level of the Pont was opened.

By this time, the bridge had also become a compulsory stop-off for the *Compagnons du Tour de France*, a craft guild whose prospective members had first to study for two years then spend three to five years travelling around France apprenticing themselves to other *Compagnons* and visiting major sites. The names of many of these apprentice visitors can still be seen scratched into the stonework of the bridge.

Major restoration took place in the 19th century when the author Prosper Mérimée (1803–70), then Inspector-general of Historic Monuments, put the Pont on France's first list of key buildings for preservation. Since then, the Pont du Gard has become one of the most visited sites in France.

Nero's Golden House

An imperial palace on a grand scale

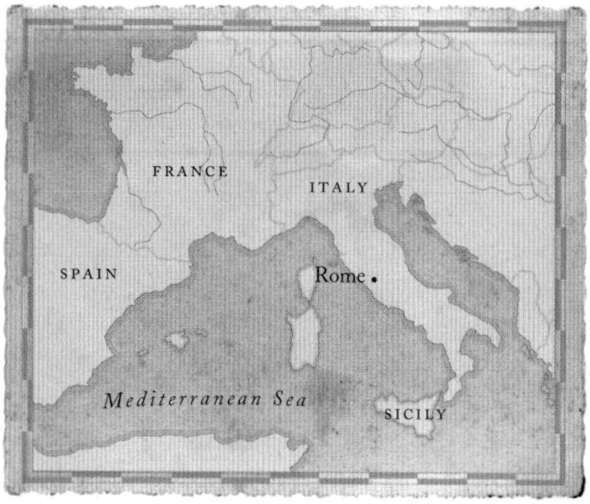

ALMOST TOTALLY FORGOTTEN and lost from view for many centuries, Nero's Golden House – known in Latin as the *Domus Aurea* – arose from one of the most infamous episodes in that emperor's terrible rule. Even in its incomplete state, this grand palace was for a time the most spectacular sight in the most powerful city on earth.

Nero is perhaps best known today for his role in the legend of the terrible fire that devastated Rome on 18 July, AD 64. The story goes that, as flames swept through the city, Nero played the fiddle (or lyre) and watched, refusing to offer help and instead dreaming of the wonderful new city he would build when the flames had done their work. The story is completely untrue – Nero wasn't even in Rome at the time of the disaster but at his villa in Antium – but it does preserve a folk memory of how the Romans felt about what happened next.

A Home Fit for a Megalomaniac

For Nero did indeed take the opportunity that the damage created by the fire presented to annex a huge swathe of the ruined city centre, where he set about building a palace fit for an emperor – the Golden House. The scale of the plan was vast. Because much of the site has still not been excavated to this day, we do not know exactly how large the house and grounds were, but it is estimated that they covered between 40 and 120 hectares (100 and 300 acres) between the Palatine and Esquiline Hills. Nero's plan was not simply to construct a palace but a whole private environment with lakes, woods and parks in the heart of the city. Once completed (which they never were), Nero's house and its grounds would account for no less than a third of the entire area of Rome.

The house was approached via a new colonnaded 'sacred way' leading from the Roman Forum to a vestibule containing a colossal bronze statue of the emperor himself. This Colossus of Nero, created by the Greek sculptor Zenodotus, stood over 30 metres (100 ft) high and gave its name to a building later constructed nearby – the Flavian Amphitheatre, which became known as the 'Colosseum' (see pages 132–137).

Around this lay the park, centred on a huge artificial lake and surrounded with porticoes, pavilions, baths and fountains, all set in an idealized landscape. Included in this parkland design was the unfinished temple to Nero's deified predecessor Claudius (r. 41–54), who was in all likelihood poisoned by Nero's mother Agrippina to ensure her son's succession. Nero ordered that the temple be demolished so he could use the platform on which it was built as a base for cascades and fountains for his garden. In his *Life of Nero*, the Roman historian and biographer Suetonius (*c.*75–130) describes the scene:

'There was a pond too, like a sea, surrounded with buildings to represent cities, besides tracts of land, varied by tilled fields, vineyards, pastures and woods, with great numbers of wild and domestic animals.'

An 18th-century copy of one of the fresco paintings found when the ruins of the Golden House were discovered during the Renaissance.

The main block of new buildings on the south slope of the Oppian Hill was built by the architects Severus and Celer. With unlimited funds at their disposal, their design diverged radically from traditional tastes. Built of concrete faced with brick, the 300 rooms of the main wing were designed around a complex geometry using arches, niches, domes and *exedrae* to create an interesting play of light on the interiors. In the centre, with the two main dining rooms to either side, stood an octagonal room, possibly the banqueting hall, with a giant concrete dome over it – the first time such a structure had been built for a non-religious building and including the first groined vault known in the Roman world. Exactly what all these rooms were used for is difficult to know, partly because the building is largely ruined but also as we have few records of what went on inside. As no latrines or kitchens have ever been found in the main wing, it may be that this was simply for entertaining and the other imperial palaces nearby, which were linked into Nero's grand scheme, provided the services for it.

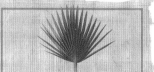

Sybaritic Opulence

The decoration of the rooms was also both lavish and revolutionary. The huge quantities of gold leaf used on the interiors gave the house its name but there were also large areas of fresco, created by the painter Famulus who, according to the writer Pliny the Elder (23–79), would only come to the palace to paint for a few hours each day when the light was perfect. Indeed, Nero commissioned so much of this painstaking work from Famulus that Pliny refers to the Golden House as the artist's 'prison'. For the first time, mosaics were also created on walls and ceilings, as opposed to just on the floors. This feature had never been seen before in the Roman world, but would later become a characteristic technique of Byzantine art.

Suetonius mentions strange mechanical devices in the building, designed to delight the emperor's guests: '*There were dining-rooms with fretted ceilings of ivory, whose panels could turn and shower down flowers and were fitted with pipes for sprinkling the guests with perfumes.*' Elsewhere, he describes the main banqueting halls as having a dome that '*constantly revolved day and night, like the heavens*'. This possibly refers to the octagonal concrete-domed room, whose remains now lie within the later Baths of Trajan. Here traces have been found of a water-powered device that may have turned this huge dome into a working planetarium, constantly revolving over the heads of Nero's dinner guests.

Suetonius further reports that, on entering one finished area of his palace, Nero apparently murmured that he could now at last begin to be housed like a human. Nero's megalomania and hugely sybaritic lifestyle did not endear him to the still-powerful ruling classes. The unpopular emperor was fated never to see his lavish plan come to fruition; in 68 the Roman senate, tired of his financial exactions and arbitrary executions, managed to have Nero declared a public enemy. His personal bodyguard, the Praetorian Guard, betrayed him and he was forced to flee to a suburb of Rome. Just before he was about to be captured he committed suicide by driving a dagger into his throat, aided by his secretary Epaphroditos. According to the second-century historian Cassius Dio, he then uttered the famous last words '*Jupiter, what an artist perishes in me!*'. And with the 'artist' died the Golden House.

TIMELINE

AD 64 The great fire of Rome destroys large parts of the city; Nero uses the Christians as scapegoats for the disaster and orders their persecution

65 Work starts on Nero's massive new palace, the Golden House (*Domus Aurea*) in the centre of Rome between the Palatine and Esquiline Hills

68 Nero is deposed by the senate and takes his own life

70 The emperor Vespasian begins construction of the Flavian Amphitheatre (Colosseum) on the former site of the huge artificial lake in the grounds of the Golden House

15th century Accidental rediscovery of the buried remains of the Golden House excites great interest from Renaissance artists

'Nero meanwhile availed himself of his country's desolation, and erected a mansion in which jewels and gold, long familiar objects ... were not so marvellous as the fields and lakes, with woods on one side to resemble a wilderness, and, on the other, open spaces and extensive views.'

TACITUS – *ANNALS* 15.42 (*c.* AD 117)

A SHORT-LIVED DREAM

After Nero's death, public opinion quickly turned against him. The ruling classes who had had their lands appropriated after the fire of AD 64 resented the presence of so lavish a construction, built, as they saw it, with their money on their land. The rumour was already current that Nero had started the fire deliberately; indeed, his attempts to deflect the blame witnessed the first major persecution of another group – the Christians - and earned their enmity. According to the historian Tacitus:

> *'Nero fastened the guilt and inflicted the most exquisite tortures on a class hated for their abominations, called Christians by the populace. Christus, from whom the name had its origin, suffered the extreme penalty during the reign of Tiberius at the hands of one of our procurators, Pontius Pilatus, and a most mischievous superstition, thus checked for the moment, again broke out not only in Judaea, the first source of the evil, but even in Rome, where all things hideous and shameful from every part of the world find their centre and become popular.'*

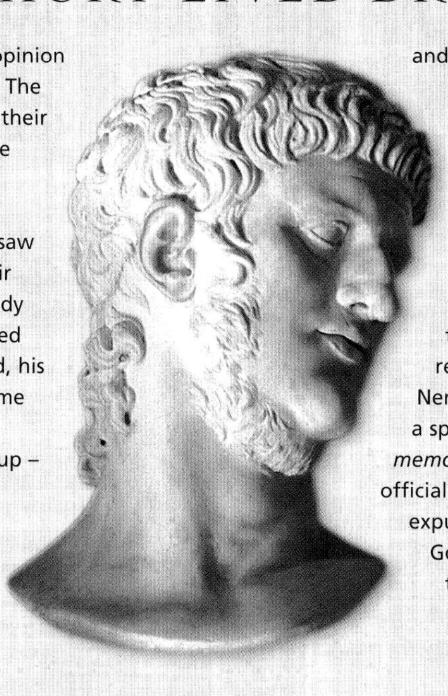

The extravagance and cruelty of the reign of Nero (seen here in a bust from the first century AD) made him deeply loathed.

Ultimately, however, responsibility for the excesses of Nero's reign was placed squarely at his own door. Within years of his death efforts were being made to eradicate all traces of the Golden House. The precious stones and ivory that decorated the interiors were stripped out and the landscaped parkland was levelled in preparation for building as this was prime and badly needed real estate. Beginning around AD 70, in the reign of the emperor Vespasian, Nero's great lake was drained and work began on constructing the Flavian Amphitheatre on the site. Vespasian also ordered that the head of the colossal statue of Nero, which stood nearby and which gave its name to the 'Colosseum', be remodelled to represent the sun god Sol, thus removing yet another reminder of the profligacy of Nero. (The Romans even had a special term – *damnatio memoriae* – to denote a person's official erasure from history.) The expunging from memory of the Golden House continued when the emperor Titus constructed a large public bath house on part of the site, while another, larger bath complex was built there by Trajan. Hadrian later added the temple of Venus and Rome, the largest temple in the ancient city, near the amphitheatre and in the process moved Nero's huge statue out of the way.

By 128 there was virtually no sign above ground that the Golden House, the largest complex ever built in the city, had ever existed. The ruins remained hidden until the 15th century when, legend has it, a local boy fell through a hole in the Avertine Hill and found himself in a painted grotto. Miraculously, in their haste to wipe out the Golden House, the Romans had simply built over it, so preserving many of the rooms and their paintings below ground. Their rediscovery at the beginning of the Renaissance was a revelation, and artists including Michelangelo and Raphael were lowered into the subterranean rooms to view the frescos. And so the emperor who saw himself as such a great artist posthumously provided some inspiration for the greatest artistic movement in history, and the Golden House once again evoked awe in those who visited it.

MASADA
Rugged symbol of Jewish survival

IN THE SOUTH OF MODERN-DAY Israel, on the eastern fringes of the Judean Desert where it overlooks the Dead Sea, stands Masada, a massive outcrop of dolerite rising some 400 metres (1300 ft) above the floor of the Jordan Valley and with a flat summit measuring over 7 hectares (17 acres). This wild, remote location was the scene of one of the most significant events in Jewish history, which still resonates today in this troubled region.

Baked by the desert sun, this exceptionally hostile environment, which has no natural water supply, led the Greek geographer Strabo, writing early in the first century AD, to claim that:

> '*... the country is fiery; for near Masada are to be seen rugged rocks that have been scorched, as also, in many places, fissures and ashy soil, and drops of pitch that emit foul odours to a great distance, and ruined settlements here and there.*'

Even so, despite its fearsome reputation for inhospitability, the hill – known as Masada, from the Hebrew *Metzada* ('fortress') – has a long history of occupation, for what it lacked in resources it made up for in strategic position and security. Its wilderness location has also meant that much of the evidence from one of the most tragic episodes in Jewish history remains visible on and around the rock. Yet while Masada will forever be associated with the siege that brought the First Jewish War (sometimes known as 'The Great Revolt') to an end and the extraordinary feats of engineering the Romans undertook to overwhelm its defenders, this event might never have taken place but for a remarkable building erected at the site over a century earlier.

Herod's Mountain Eyrie

In around 37 BC, at the start of his reign as Roman client king of Judaea, Herod the Great (r. 37–34 BC) chose Masada as the location for a palace. While Masada obviously had the benefit of being an easily defended site should his oppressed people stage a revolt, his clear intention in building here was also to impress, and the palace he constructed is one of the forgotten marvels of the age.

'There was a fortress of very great strength not far from Jerusalem, which had been built by our ancient kings, both as a repository for their effects in the hazards of war, and for the preservation of their bodies at the same time. It was called Masada.'

ROMAN-JEWISH HISTORIAN FLAVIUS JOSEPHUS – *THE JEWISH WARS* (*c.*AD 75)

The fortress of Masada. Excavations here in the 1960s uncovered the skeletons of 25 men, women and children, who were subsequently reburied at the site with full military honours.

TIMELINE

37–31 BC Rome's client king Herod the Great constructs a palace complex at Masada on the edge of the Judean desert

AD 66 Outbreak of the Great Jewish Revolt (First Jewish War) against Roman occupation

70 Jerusalem falls to the Roman commander (and future emperor) Titus; in reprisal for the revolt, Roman forces destroy the Second Temple (on Tisha b'Av, the same day in the Jewish calendar as the destruction of the first temple in the sixth century BC)

73 Siege of Masada comes to an end as Roman forces storm the summit; the Sicarii defending the site commit suicide

1842 Site of Masada was identified for the first time in the modern era by two American travellers

1958 Moshe Dayan, Chief of Staff of the Israel Defence Forces, inaugurates swearing-in ceremonies at Masada

1963–5 Masada is excavated by the Israeli archaeologist Yigael Yadin

2001 Masada is declared a World Heritage Site by UNESCO

Herod's 'Northern Palace' was built on three levels and appeared to hang over the precipitous cliff edge. On the top level were four bedrooms and a semicircular terrace that looked out over the Moab Mountains and the Dead Sea, which lay almost a quarter of a mile below. From this a hidden staircase cut into the rock led down to the next level with a large open room and a porch whose columns stood on the very edge of the cliff. From here more stairs descended to the bottom level with its large frescoed hall and colonnade.

Nearby another seven palace complexes are thought to have catered for Herod's family and guests who had the use of their own bath house, which incorporated the latest in Roman technology, including hypocausts (underfloor heating) and mosaic tiles. The whole top of the plateau was then surrounded by a massive wall, over 3.5 metres (10 ft) wide and 1300 metres (4265 ft) long, and studded with 38 defensive watchtowers.

Water in the Wilderness

Yet for all its panoramic views and impressive security, this site presented enormous logistical difficulties. There was no water supply on the plateau and no suitable land for growing food so supplies had to be transported there and carefully stored on site. To overcome the shortage of water Herod ordered that 12 large cisterns holding 40,000 cubic metres (8.8 million gallons) of water should be cut into the rock to catch any rain that might fall. If this proved inadequate – which, considering Masada's location and the huge quantities of water needed for the bath house, it probably did – then pack animals were used to haul water from the base. Food also had to be brought by pack animal to the site and 29 large store houses were built to hold this.

Fortunately for Herod, he never needed Masada as a last refuge and his palaces were only ever used for pleasure. The elaborate lengths he went to to provide for his guests, however, did make the site close to impregnable and this was his unknowing gift to the later Jewish defenders of the site – the last of his people to hold out against the Romans.

Masada and the Zealots

At the outbreak of the First Jewish War against Rome in AD 66, Masada was home to a Roman garrison, which used the outcrop as an observation post. Yet in the first year of fighting the site was wrested from Roman control by a Jewish group called the Sicarii (or Zealots), who established a fortified base there. Since history is famously written by the victors – in this case, the Romans – the exact nature of this religious group is uncertain. Romans portray the Sicarii as a fanatical splinter group who were fighting not only the Roman occupation but also other Jewish groups. Our principal source is the historian Flavius Josephus (37–100) who was descended from a family of Jewish priests and had himself taken up arms in the early days of the revolt. But when the rest of his garrison committed suicide (rather than be taken alive), he surrendered to the Romans and from then on provided them with intelligence, acting as an intermediary between the opposing forces during the siege and eventual capture of Jerusalem in 70.

This background gave Josephus a natural antipathy towards the more hardline Jewish groups such as the Sicarii. Significantly, during the period when Josephus was negotiating, the elders of Jerusalem expelled the remaining Sicarii from the city to try and ease tensions. These people soon found their way to Masada, which, after the fall of Jerusalem, was rapidly becoming the last major centre of resistance in Judaea. Herod's extensive works at this remote site , which the Roman garrison had later augmented, made it the ideal location for a dramatic last stand.

A TOUGH NUT TO CRACK

From the fall of Jerusalem in 70 to their final defeat three years later, the Sicarii remained a thorn in Rome's side, attacking both the Roman forces picketed around Masada and Jewish settlements that had come to terms with the Romans. Eventually, the Roman governor of Judaea, Lucius Flavius Silva, found himself forced to act. Marching the Tenth Legion ('Fretensis') to the base of the hill, he embarked on an engineering feat almost as impressive as that of Herod. Unable to breach the walls or scale the precipitous cliffs, the Roman engineers built a huge ramp, utilizing a rocky spur on the western side of the plateau, to create a walkable pathway from the desert floor to the plateau top. In the spring of 73 the legion marched up this incline, whose massive remains are still clearly visible today, and broke through the defensive wall with a battering ram.

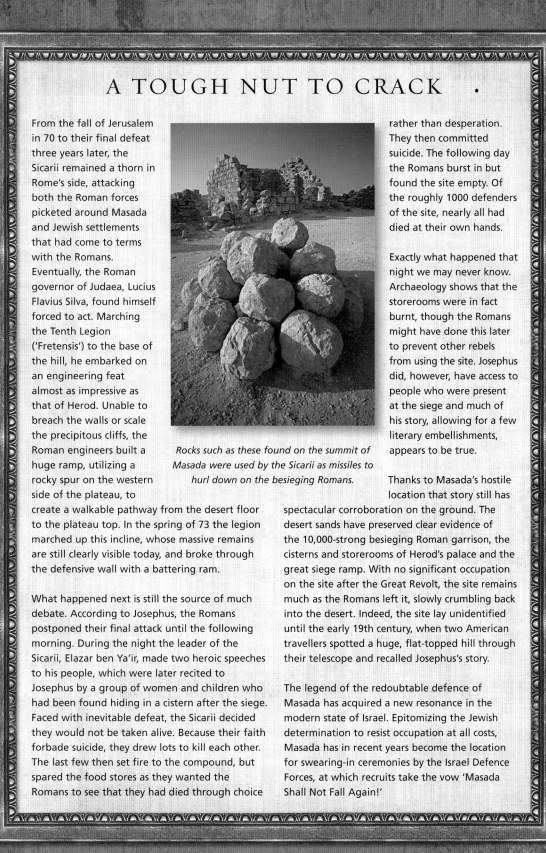

Rocks such as these found on the summit of Masada were used by the Sicarii as missiles to hurl down on the besieging Romans.

What happened next is still the source of much debate. According to Josephus, the Romans postponed their final attack until the following morning. During the night the leader of the Sicarii, Elazar ben Ya'ir, made two heroic speeches to his people, which were later recited to Josephus by a group of women and children who had been found hiding in a cistern after the siege. Faced with inevitable defeat, the Sicarii decided they would not be taken alive. Because their faith forbade suicide, they drew lots to kill each other. The last few then set fire to the compound, but spared the food stores as they wanted the Romans to see that they had died through choice rather than desperation. They then committed suicide. The following day the Romans burst in but found the site empty. Of the roughly 1000 defenders of the site, nearly all had died at their own hands.

Exactly what happened that night we may never know. Archaeology shows that the storerooms were in fact burnt, though the Romans might have done this later to prevent other rebels from using the site. Josephus did, however, have access to people who were present at the siege and much of his story, allowing for a few literary embellishments, appears to be true.

Thanks to Masada's hostile location that story still has spectacular corroboration on the ground. The desert sands have preserved clear evidence of the 10,000-strong besieging Roman garrison, the cisterns and storerooms of Herod's palace and the great siege ramp. With no significant occupation on the site after the Great Revolt, the site remains much as the Romans left it, slowly crumbling back into the desert. Indeed, the site lay unidentified until the early 19th century, when two American travellers spotted a huge, flat-topped hill through their telescope and recalled Josephus's story.

The legend of the redoubtable defence of Masada has acquired a new resonance in the modern state of Israel. Epitomizing the Jewish determination to resist occupation at all costs, Masada has in recent years become the location for swearing-in ceremonies by the Israel Defence Forces, at which recruits take the vow 'Masada Shall Not Fall Again!'

The Colosseum
Emblem of Rome's power and cruelty

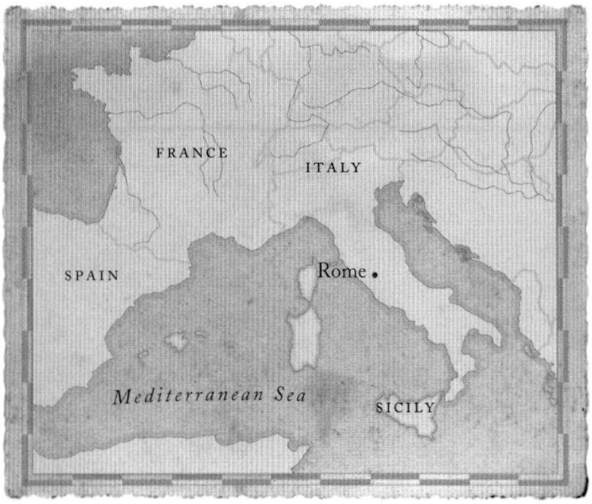

Together with the Great Pyramid, the Colosseum is perhaps the best-known monument to have survived from the ancient world. Its sheer scale, the high standard of its preservation and the terrible history of what once took place in its arena have all made it a source of fascination for some and a place of pilgrimage for others.

The Colosseum was not known by that name when it was first built, or for many years afterwards. Begun on the orders of the emperor Vespasian, (r. 69–79), the first ruler from the Flavian dynasty, and completed by his eldest son and successor Titus (r. 79–81) it was officially called the Flavian Amphitheatre (*Amphitheatrum Flavium*). The building was put up in celebration of the military successes of that family, notably the crushing of the Great Jewish Revolt of 66–73. It was only much later, during the reign of Hadrian (r. 117–38), after the colossal statue of the emperor Nero nearby was moved under the direction of the architect Decrianus and with the help of 24 elephants, that the building came to be known by asssociation as the Colosseum.

The Flavian Amphitheatre was the first such building not to be cut into a natural slope to provide support for the seating; instead, the new arena was to be a huge, freestanding structure, built over what was previously the ornamental lake in the gardens of Nero's Golden House (see pages 124–127). The location was significant, as it symbolized the Flavian emperors 'giving back' to the people of Rome the land that Nero had seized after the great fire of 64. It was also intended as the stage on which the might and generosity of the emperors could be daily demonstrated to their subjects.

Roman Society in Microcosm

Having first drained the lake, a series of doughnut-shaped foundations were laid in concrete under where the main walls and seating would be placed. On top of this were built a complex series of elliptical walls and terraces, connected by a labyrinth of passages and corridors beneath, all contained within a marble-clad retaining wall decorated with Doric, Ionic and Corinthian columns at each successive level. At the north end stood the imperial box, opposite the one reserved for the Vestal Virgins; each had its own private entrance. To either side of these, with the next best seats in

The Flavian Amphitheatre (Colosseum) was begun in around AD 70–72, with the aim of providing the Roman people with a major new venue where they might enjoy a variety of 'games'.

'Now all niceties were put aside, and it became butchery, pure and simple. The men had nothing with which to protect themselves, for their whole bodies were open to one another's blows, and thus each never fails to injure his opponent ... In the morning, men are thrown to the lions and bears, at noon they are thrown to the spectators.'

SENECA – *MORAL EPISTLES* VII, 4 (*c.* AD 60)

A TECHNICAL MARVEL

The Flavian Amphitheatre – the precursor of modern sports stadia and theatres – was a hi-tech building boasting many revolutionary features. The stage was wooden and covered in a deep layer of dry sand, sometimes dyed red, which was used to soak up the blood (hence the term 'arena', from the Latin word for sand, *harena*). Below this, Domitian built a complex series of tunnels (the *hypogeum*) holding cages as well as stage machinery that allowed exotic animals to be hoisted straight up into the arena and released through trap doors to 'surprise' the unfortunate performers. There was also equipment for raising scenery for the staged hunts, not unlike the modern scene-dock of a theatre. Some ancient sources mention that the arena could also be flooded for the staging of elaborate naval battles (*naumachiae*), though modern historians question whether this would have been feasible. On hot days an elaborate system of masts and pulleys on the top level of the walls was used to stretch a canopy, the *velarium*, over the amphitheatre to provide shade for the spectators. Emperors who did not receive the adulation they expected from their audience were also known to order the teams of sailors who operated the *velarium* to retract it, leaving the spectators to roast in the midday sun as a punishment for their lack of respect.

the house, was a podium on which senators (who were allowed to bring their own chairs) sat. On the raked level of seating immediately behind this sat those nobles who weren't senators, then behind them the ordinary citizens of Rome, with the richest at the front. Finally, in the top level, added by the emperor Domitian (r. 81–96) in 82, sat or stood the common poor, slaves and women. Within this highly stratified seating plan there were further divisions, with areas set aside for foreign embassies, scribes, heralds, priests, soldiers and tutors with their students, thus making the class divisions in Roman life visible to everyone. This does not mean, however, that 'everyone' went to the games; the audience mostly comprised those male inhabitants of the city who had the time and the inclination to attend. Moreover, certain groups beyond the pale in Rome's social hierarchy – grave-diggers, former gladiators and actors – were not allowed in the building at all.

The sheer size of the amphitheatre – 188 metres by 156 metres (617 x 512 ft) – which could easily accommodate 50,000 people and was as high as a modern 15-storey building, meant that special provision had to be made to get large audiences in and out without making them queue for hours or risking them getting lost in its cavernous interior. So, the Colosseum was provided with 80 entrances known as *vomitoria*. Four of these were reserved for dignitaries, while the rest were numbered; tickets for the games, in the form of broken pieces of pottery, had the entrance number marked on them to ensure people went to the right gate.

Theatre of Blood

The entertainments provided in the Colosseum are legendary; indeed, a good deal of pure legend has become mixed up with historical fact in certain accounts of them. When the amphitheatre opened in 80, the emperor Titus ordered 100 days of games, which were described by the poet Martial (40–103) in his book *De Spectaculi*. A typical day at the games

Beneath the arena, the layout of the underground hypogeum, *which formed the nerve-centre of the ancient amphitheatre, can be seen clearly in the preserved Colosseum.*

TIMELINE

AD 70 Emperor Vespasian's son and future emperor Titus follows in his father's footsteps as commander of Roman forces in Judaea, suppressing the Great Jewish Revolt

***c*.70–2** To celebrate Rome's military prowess, Vespasian orders construction of the Flavian Amphitheatre on the site of the former lake (now drained) of Nero's 'Golden House'

79 Death of Vespasian

80 Titus officially inaugurates the Flavian Amphitheatre with 100 days of games

82 Modifications made to the Colosseum during the reign of Domitian, including a top tier

217 Colosseum damaged in a major fire

1349 An earthquake causes severe structural damage to the Colosseum, which causes the outer wall on the south side of the building to collapse

1749 Pope Benedict XIV consecrates the Colosseum as a site of Christian martyrdom

1993–2000 Major restoration programme carried out at the Colosseum

began in the morning with the *venationes*, in which exotic animals such as rhinoceroses and lions were hunted. These hunts (or fights) might be conducted in elaborate reconstructed natural habitats known as *sylvae* ('woods'). At mid-day the executions would take place, if there were any condemned prisoners awaiting death. They might be dispatched in any number of horrific ways to entertain the crowd, including being burnt or crucified or set upon by animals (this latter punishment was called 'exposure to the beasts'). There is no conclusive evidence, however, that a single Christian was ever thrown to the lions in the Colosseum. In the afternoon the main event took place – the gladiatorial games – which could involve anything from a one-on-one combat to the spectacular re-enactment of entire battles or scenes from mythology. Contrary to popular belief, gladiatorial combats were not usually fought to the death. Games might last for several days or even weeks and involve thousands of gladiators and wild animals. According to the historian Cassius Dio (*c*.155–229), after the emperor Trajan's victory in Dacia (modern Romania), he ordered 123 consecutive days of games at the Colosseum during which 10,000 gladiators fought and 11,000 animals, both wild and tame, were slaughtered.

The Colosseum was undoubtedly the focal point for much of Roman life. Covering 2.5 hectares (6 acres) at the heart of the city, it provided a venue where Rome's citizens could be reminded of the might and reach of their empire and of the magnanimity of their rulers. For the eager audience, it was the epitome of what made Rome great, but in time it would come to stand for everything that was wrong with the empire.

A Symbol of Rome

The Colosseum was one of the most massive structures in Rome and its survival to this day largely intact is a testament to the skill of the architects who designed it. From its inauguration in AD 80 right up to the end of the Roman empire, it provided the main venue for public spectacle in the city. However, on a number of occasions, both its construction and the memory of what took place here have almost spelt its destruction.

Although the Colosseum was mainly constructed of stone and concrete, the seating, the arena and many of the internal structures were wooden, making them vulnerable to fire. In 217, the upper levels built by Domitian were destroyed following a lightning strike and were not repaired until 240. Further repairs are recorded throughout the Roman period up to the last known gladiatorial contest in the building, which took place in 404.

After this date the threat of invasion and the collapse of central Roman administration were not the only dangers facing the building. In 442 and again in 470 earthquakes hit the city, probably damaging the structure. Another such tremor is recorded in 523, which interestingly is also the last year that an animal hunt is known to have been held in the Colosseum; the interior wooden structures must therefore still have been in place at that date, although perhaps not for much longer.

By the tenth century the Colosseum was abandoned and the arena became a Christian cemetery, while the vaults and passages under the seating became shops and houses. After a brief period as the private fortress of the Frangipani family, who fortified the site, tragedy struck in 1349 when a major earthquake caused the collapse of the outer south side of the building, giving it the appearance it has today. As a ruin the Colosseum now became little more than a quarry, the tumbled-down rubble of the south side being taken away for new building, while the bronze clamps that held the mortarless stones together were melted down and its marble façades burnt to make quicklime.

By the 16th century the Colosseum had become an embarrassment to the papacy and the city – a huge, ruinous wreck taking up a valuable site in the middle of the town. Pope Sixtus V suggested turning it into a wool factory to employ reformed prostitutes and a century later bullfights were briefly authorized there. In 1749, however, Pope Benedict XIV announced that the Colosseum would henceforth be considered a sacred site in memory of those early Christians who had died in its arena. The removal of building material was stopped, the collapsing outer wall was shored up and the site became one of pilgrimage, marked inside with the 12 stations of the cross.

Since then the Colosseum has been fully excavated, consolidated and restored. Today, apart from hosting a few small events, it is one of Rome's main tourist attractions, but also serves as a reminder of the horrors that humans have in the past inflicted on each other. In particular it has become a symbol of the movement to abolish capital punishment – something it has witnessed so much of in its lifetime. Each time a death sentence is commuted anywhere on earth or a country abolishes capital punishment, the building is lit that night in golden instead of the usual white light. And so the Flavian Amphitheatre has gone from being a place of execution to a memorial to the executed.

By the 18th century, Rome had become one of the prime destinations on the 'Grand Tour' – a journey around the sites of classical antiquity by young European aristocrats seeking to further their education. This view of the picturesque ruins of the Colosseum by the Dutch artist Gaspar van Wittel (1653–1736) dates from this period.

The Pyramid of the Sun at Teotihuacán

Testament to a vanished culture

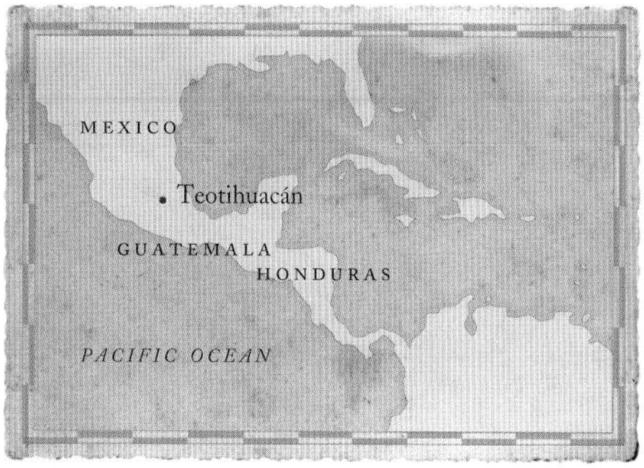

The city of Teotihuacán was the earliest city in the New World and the largest and most important in pre-Aztec central Mexico. At its heart lay the third largest pyramid on earth. Yet little is known either about the people who built this amazing structure or what became of them. Even the name of the city, meaning 'birthplace of the gods', is a later Nahuatl term invented by the Aztecs, as the language spoken by Teotihuacán's original inhabitants remains a mystery.

The area around Teotihuacán, which lies some 25 miles (40 km) northeast of Mexico City in the shadow of Mount Cerro Gordo, was first settled around 400 BC. The earliest signs of a permanent presence at the city itself comes from a century later but it was the first century BC before the city proper began to grow up. Exactly what inspired this building programme is uncertain, although an influx of refugees from the nearby settlement of Cuicuilco on the southern shore of Lake Texcoco, which was destroyed by a volcano at this time, may have provided the initial spur.

'Even though it was night/ even though it was not day,/ even though there was no light/ they gathered,/ the gods convened/ there in Teotihuacán.'

NAHUATL MYTH

An Early Metropolis

The city, like many in pre-Colombian Central America was highly planned, being laid out on a grid pattern with the most important religious and political structures aligned with a central processional avenue. This 'Street of the Dead' (a name given to it much later by the Spanish *conquistadores*) was 40 metres (130 ft) wide and ran for one and a half miles (2.4 km) directly towards Cerro Gordo. It was lined with stone platforms, which the Spanish believed were tombs but which are now thought to be temples and the residences of high-status inhabitants. Along the southeastern side of the street stands the 'citadel' – another Spanish name as it was believed to have been an ancient fort. In fact, this sunken plaza, standing at the crossroads of the two main streets in the city, was a ceremonial and political centre and home to the Temple of the Feathered Serpent, where archaeologists have discovered the remains of 18 men, possibly the victims of ritual sacrifice.

To the east of the street, and at the extreme north end stand the two largest structures on the site, and two of the most impressive buildings in the whole of the Americas – the Pyramid of the Sun and the Pyramid of the Moon. Exactly why these vast stepped structures were built remains uncertain and the attribution to the sun and moon are later inferences. Both

The mighty Pyramid of the Sun at Teotihuacán stands beside the Avenue of the Dead, so named by the Spanish in the mistaken belief that the buildings lining this route were tombs. Far from being a necropolis, in its heyday Teotihuacán was a thriving trading city.

pyramids were originally topped by altars or temples, but these have long since been destroyed and so it is now impossible to identify which deity was worshipped here. That they were sacred sites is clear, however, from the discovery of the sacrificed bodies of children, one under each corner of the Pyramid of the Sun. This pyramid is also built on an extant man-made cave and tunnel system, which runs under the pyramid and which some scholars believe to be a royal tomb. Others think it may be an older religious site over which the pyramid was deliberately built.

A Feat of Engineering

What is undeniable is that whatever its purpose, the Pyramid of the Sun was a monumental achievement requiring a huge investment in time and resources by the people of Teotihuacán. Begun around AD 100 and extended on several occasions, the pyramid in its final form rises in a series of four stepped platforms from a square base 225 metres (738 ft) long on each side to a height of 63 metres (207 ft), and is ascended by a staircase of 248 steps. Each level was constructed of layers of rammed earth and clay, clad in finely cut stonework, which was then plastered and painted. As none of the plaster or paint remain on the surface, we can only guess at the original appearance of the building but the nearby Temple of the Feathered Serpent is known to have been painted bright red, so the effect is likely to have been stunning.

In total, around 765,000 cubic metres (27 million cu ft) of building material are contained within the building. What makes this fact all the more astounding is that the pyramid, indeed the entire city, was built by what was effectively a Stone Age society, without the use of wheels, metal tools or beasts of burden.
Precisely who built the pyramid – slaves, conscripts or free citizens – again remains unclear. What we know of the people of Teotihuacán comes only from the finds that have been made in the city, the murals they painted on their walls and references to them in Mayan inscriptions. Archaeological work has shown that about two-thirds of the population, which reached between 100,000 and 250,000 at the city's peak between AD 150 and 450, were farmers and they must have provided much of the economic impetus of the city. The rest were craftspeople, manufacturing jewellery, obsidian (volcanic glass) tools and ornaments and pottery, which were traded by an large merchant class. While we have no texts from Teotihuacán to tell us of its links with the outside world, its cultural influence, in building styles and decoration, appears as far afield as Guatemala and Honduras.

Detail from a mural in the Palace of Tepantitla at Teotihuacán, showing a priest performing a rite. The shape emerging from the figure's mouth is believed to be a 'speech bubble' indicating that he is talking.

An Elusive Culture

The city's inhabitants lived in over 2000 single-storey apartment compounds around the central axis, each of which was home to between 60 and 100 people, giving an urban area of almost 8 square miles (20 sq km), rising to 32 square miles (83 sq km) if the outlying farming districts are included. This makes it possibly the largest city in the world at that time. Many apartments were decorated with vivid murals, which have been compared to Italian Renaissance frescoes in their quality. Some of the murals depict a 'Great Goddess', giving us a small insight into the religion of the people of Teotihuacán. Archaeological work

TIMELINE

c.400 BC Settled agriculturalists first begin to cultivate the region around Teotihuacán

200 BC The first buildings in Teotihuacán are constructed

AD 100 Probable date of completion of the Pyramid of the Sun

c.150–450 Teotihuacán at the height of its power

c.650–750 Decline of Teotihuacán, possibly as a result of growing social unrest

1320 The expanding Aztec empire takes over the abandoned city of Teotihuacán

1519 Spanish *conquistadores* under Hernán Cortés arrive in Central America in search of gold; military action and disease bring the downfall of the Aztec empire

1905–10 Mexican scholar Leopoldo Batres undertakes controversial restoration work at the site

1987 Teotihuacán named by UNESCO as a World Heritage Site

DESTROYED BY INSURRECTION?

The city of Teotihuacán flourished from the first century to the sixth century AD, becoming the largest city in the New World by 600. Yet by the time Europeans arrived in the Americas in the early 16th century the knowledge of who had built it and its former status had sunk into obscurity.

The decline and fall of Teotihuacán took around a century, beginning in 650 and culminating in a major fire in c.750. The cause of this fire was long thought to be an enemy attack, leading to the sacking of the city and its eclipse by neighbours, but recent research has shown that the blaze only destroyed the high-status buildings. This may indicate that the collapse of the city came from within, in the form of a revolt against the ruling classes. The discovery of malnourished skeletons from the sixth century points to severe droughts having brought famine to the region around this time. In such dire circumstances, dwindling resources in this massive urban complex may have led to political friction, which eventually brought the whole system tumbling down.

After 750 there is still some evidence of people dwelling in the city for another two centuries but the main public buildings are no longer in use and civic life seems to have ceased. Other nearby cities such as Xochicalco now filled the void and some of the former inhabitants may have moved to these newer centres. From 1000 to 1320 the site remained abandoned but then came to the attention of the expanding Aztec empire. The Aztecs gave the city its present name, Teotihuacán or 'the birthplace of the Gods', since their mythology claimed it to be the place where the current time-cycle began.

When Spanish *conquistadors* reached the city in 1519 only the myths remained to indicate what this place had been. But as a long-dead city with no economic significance, it remained little more than a curiosity until the first excavations began in 1884.

The Pyramid of the Sun, then largely overgrown, was first investigated between 1905 and 1910, when the architect Leopoldo Batres (1852–1926) was employed to restore it in time for the Mexican centennial celebrations of 1910. Batres's work – in particular his addition of a fifth terrace and his removal of large numbers of facing stones – has since attracted considerable criticism for having gone beyond restoration and into the realms of speculative reconstruction (like Arthur Evans's work at Knossos). Nevertheless, the restored pyramid certainly had the desired effect of bringing the city back to world attention. Excavations at the site continued throughout the 20th century, with the first accurate maps of the ancient city appearing in the 1970s. Since 1987 the city has been designated a World Heritage Site and archaeological teams have still only managed to probe a fraction of the total area.

has also identified human sacrifices – a common feature of pre-Colombian religions – as well as the live interment of wild animals including cougars, owls, eagles and snakes, which must have had some ritual significance to the population.

The rulers of this city who organized these massive construction projects are also an elusive group. Mayan texts talk about one leader known as 'spearthrower owl', who ruled the city for 60 years and in that time managed to install his family members in the ruling élites of several other large Meso-American cities. Whether this foreign influence was a product of diplomacy or outright warfare is not known. What does now seem to be the case is that this ruling class was eventually toppled. With their demise, the city of Teotihuacán collapsed and the Pyramid of the Sun was slowly reclaimed by the jungle.

The Forum of Trajan

Last and greatest of Rome's imperial fora

With its glittering imperial palaces, vast public baths and huge arenas, ancient Rome was full of remarkable sights. Yet there was another part of the city whose magnificence outshone even these. Today it is all but forgotten, but the Forum of Trajan, built in the early second century AD, was once regarded as a wonder of the age.

There had been fora in Rome since its earliest days. The central forum was the most ancient of these – a marketplace, shopping mall and the centre for politics, commerce and religion. From the late republic onwards, some of Rome's grandest families augmented these public spaces as the city grew. The Forum Julium was dedicated to Julius Caesar in 46 BC, while the first emperor, Augustus (r. 27 BC – AD 14), added his own forum to provide more room for law courts, plus a grand display area for bronze statues of those Roman generals who had helped shape the young empire. But by the late first century AD Rome was outgrowing even these spaces. The population of the ancient city was now at its height, perhaps close to one million people, and with the empire at its maximum extent, Rome needed – and believed it deserved – the sort of magnificent forum no city had seen before.

Spoils of War

Trajan's Forum was that emperor's gift to the city following the successful conclusion of his two wars of conquest in Dacia (modern Romania) in 101–2 and 105–6, conflicts that brought a massive amount of money flooding into the imperial coffers. The complex was designed by Apollodorus of Damascus, an architect and town-planner who had come to Trajan's notice as a result of his military engineering work during the Dacian campaign. He was responsible for building 'Trajan's Bridge' across the Lower Danube, which held the record as the longest arch bridge in the world for almost a millennium, despite being destroyed during the Roman withdrawal from Dacia in 275. Apollodorus soon become one of the emperor's closest advisors.

The site chosen, which lay between the Quirinal and Capitoline Hills, may already have been cleared by the emperor Domitian (r. 81–96) although his assassination cut short any building work planned there. Trajan's plan for the site followed the rules for such spaces laid down by the Roman architect Vitruvius in his famous 16-volume treatise *De Architectura* (*c.*15 BC):

> *'The size of the forum is to be proportioned to the population of the place, so that it be not too small to contain the numbers it should hold, nor have the appearance of being too large, from a want of numbers to occupy it. The width is obtained by assigning to it two-thirds of its length, which gives it an oblong form, and makes it convenient for the purpose of the shows.'*

'... a creation which in my view has no like under the cope of heaven and which even the gods themselves must agree to admire ... its grandeur defies description and can never again be approached by mortal men.'

AMMIANUS MARCELLINUS – *ROMAN HISTORY* (*c.*AD 375)

Trajan's Column – the emperor's magnificent monument to his victory in Dacia – seen from the colonnades that once surrounded the Basilica Ulpia (now demolished) to the south.

TIMELINE

AD 101 Trajan embarks on his conquest of the Dacians (completed 106)

104 Apollodorus of Damascus begins constructing Trajan's Forum

112 Trajan's Forum officially dedicated

113 Construction of Trajan's Column completed

117 Emperor Hadrian adds a triumphal gateway to the forum

357 Emperor Constantius II comes to marvel at the forum

663 Byzantine emperor Constans II plunders Trajan's Forum for remaining artefacts to take back to Constantinople

801 A massive earthquake destroys many of the buildings on the abandoned site of Trajan's Forum

1811 Archaeological work begins in Trajan's Forum, as French scholars working under Napoleon I excavate the site

1932 Italian dictator Benito Mussolini drives a major arterial road across half the site of Trajan's Forum

Within these broad parameters, however, Rome's position at that time as the largest and richest city in the world gave Apollodorus enormous scope. Given his previous experience, he is thought to have based his design on that of a military camp. The main forum covered an area of 185 metres (606 ft) by 310 metres (1017 ft) and was approached from the south through a triple gateway, added by Hadrian in 117. This gateway was surmounted by a statue of the triumphant Trajan in a six-horse chariot. Passing through the gateway, visitors found themselves in a wide plaza surrounded on all sides by colonnades, which housed the booths and stalls of merchants. This huge rectangular space was paved in white marble cobbles and centred on another statue of the emperor, this time on horseback. To the east and west lay two *exedrae* – semicircular six-storey buildings cut into the slopes of the Quirinal and Capitoline Hills. The *exedrae* contained large vaulted halls and 170 individual rooms, forming the Roman equivalent of a shopping mall, with offices on the higher levels and shops below selling olive oil, seafood, fruit, vegetables and wine. These buildings were separated from the forum itself by a high wall which acted as a fire break.

A Masterpiece of City Planning

To the north of the main plaza stood the Basilica Ulpia, a broad, double-aisled building with huge apsidal tribunals (semicircular platforms on which judges sat) at the east and west ends which served as law courts. The basilica also took its name from the emperor, whose family name was Ulpius. Behind it stood one of Rome's most famous monuments, Trajan's Column, a 30-metre- (100-ft-) tall pillar which depicted in a spiral relief the emperor's campaigns against, and final victory over, the Dacians. As well as providing a visual account of the wars that had funded the forum, the column also contained a stairwell leading up to a viewing platform at the top where the grateful inhabitants of the city could gaze out over Trajan's architectural achievements. This was the only place from which the whole forum could be seen, as Apollodorus had deliberately designed the complex in such a way that each part hid others from view. As visitors turned each corner and passed through each colonnade, they kept coming upon new vistas and new wonders in a seemingly endless procession.

On either side of the column stood another imperial gift to the city – two libraries, one for Greek works (to the west) and one for Latin works (to the east) whose windows also afforded a close-up view of the reliefs on the column. Finally, to the north of the column and libraries, lay the temple dedicated to the deified Trajan himself, although it is not clear if this was begun during the emperor's lifetime or commissioned by his successor and adopted son Hadrian (r. 117–38).

Trajan's Forum was dedicated in 112 and came to epitomize the grandeur and majesty of Rome, enhancing the reputation of an emperor who would go down in history as one of the very few unequivocally great Roman emperors. Apollodorus did not fare so well; though it was his masterpiece, Trajan's Forum would ultimately prove a millstone round the architect's neck. On Trajan's death, Apollodorus clashed with Hadrian, who found a pretext first to banish and then to execute him. But his forum survived, never surpassed, and continued to inspire admiration in Rome's rulers and people for centuries to come. The fourth-century historian Ammianus Marcellinus describes a visit to Rome by the Balkan-born emperor Constantius II (r. 337–61), during which he stood awestruck at the sight of Trajan's Forum, which by then was over 200 years old. Ammianus recounts Constantius's despair at ever being able to match Trajan's achievement:

> *'Therefore giving up all hopes of attempting anything of this kind, he contented himself with saying that he should wish to imitate, and could imitate the horse of Trajan, which stands by itself in the middle of the hall, bearing the emperor himself on his back.'*

FADED GLORIES

The history of Trajan's Forum is intimately bound up with that of Rome itself. The complex seems to have survived the classical period intact. So long as there was an empire to rule, with Rome as its hub, there remained a need for Trajan's Forum.

By the seventh century, however, the Roman empire that Trajan had known was but a distant memory and the infrastructure needed to support this huge complex no longer existed. By now only one of Rome's aqueducts was still working and the inhabited part of this frequently sacked city had shrunk to the banks of the Tiber. The great public baths built by Diocletian and Hadrian were defunct and served as burial grounds, while the population had shrunk to just 20,000–30,000. By the time the Byzantine emperor Constans II (r. 641–68) visited the site in 663 – the first 'Roman' emperor to set foot in Rome for two centuries – the city was little more than a papal enclave, and he spent his visit stripping the remaining ornaments and bronze from the derelict buildings, including Trajan's Forum, to take back to Constantinople.

Although the forum was now abandoned, it was still largely intact. This changed in 801 when a huge earthquake hit the city, toppling many of the surviving ancient buildings. After this the site became little more than a quarry, as its marble pavements were lifted and reused in other buildings. By the 11th century the site was home to a small chapel, built up against Trajan's Column and cutting into its side. However, in 1162 Pope Alexander III, realizing that Rome's architectural heritage was disappearing fast, issued a decree protecting the monument. Sadly, other parts of the derelict site were not protected and continued to be plundered, not least by the Church itself. Four of the columns from the portico of the Basilica Ulpia found their way into the transept of St Peter's, where they remain to this day.

Interest in Trajan's Forum was reignited when Napoleon invaded Italy. In 1811 the French emperor's academics, who at the time were also busy unearthing the wonders of ancient Egypt, began excavating at the site. Today Trajan's Column and the tumbled remains of his forum still occupy a central space in Rome, despite the fact that Mussolini drove his *Via Triumphale* across the site in 1932. One of Trajan's markets, Apollodorus's engineering masterpiece, cut into one of Rome's ancient hills, has fortunately fared better, and though reused and adapted over the centuries, still stands, hinting at the long-lost splendours of the entire complex.

East of the main plaza stands one of the exedrae *that once housed the markets flanking Trajan's Forum.*

The Pantheon

Uniquely intact reminder of ancient Rome

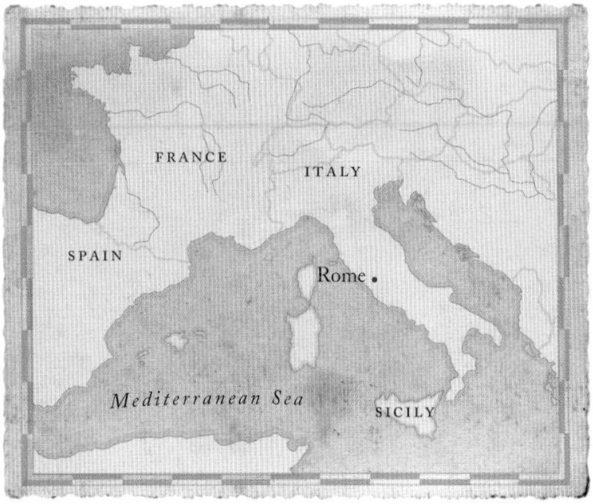

Rome's Pantheon – literally 'the temple of all the gods' – is without a doubt the world's best preserved Roman building, and probably the most intact structure from that period anywhere on earth. As the centuries have passed, so its renown has increased. Yet its modest exterior gives few clues to the astonishing feat of engineering that lies within.

Originally built by the first emperor Augustus's close ally Marcus Vipsanius Agrippa (*c.* 63–12 BC), the Pantheon was dedicated in particular to the seven deities representing the then-known planets – the Moon, Mercury, Venus, Sun, Mars, Jupiter and Saturn, all of which the Romans believed orbited the earth. Of this first building, only the inscription over the entrance still survives, which reads M·AGRIPPA·L·F·COS·TERTIVM·FECIT ('Marcus Agrippa, son of Lucius, consul for the third time, made this'), since the temple was largely destroyed in a huge fire that swept through Rome in 80, during the brief reign of Titus (r. 79–81). Titus's successor Domitian (r. 81–96) began rebuilding on the site but in the reign of Trajan (r. 98–117) it was struck by lightning and caught fire again. During the early second century AD, however, the emperor Hadrian (r. 117–38) decided to rebuild the temple, restoring the original inscription (as he frequently liked to do) but incorporating it within a wholly new building.

A Radical New Design

The Pantheon is entered through a large Corinthian portico or porch, supported on 16 11.8-metre (39-ft) high columns made of imported red and grey Egyptian granite. Above these, on the triangular pediment, there originally stood a huge bronze sculpture of the Battle of the Titans, long since looted, with only the fixing holes remaining to suggest what once stood there. Empty niches in the portico probably also held statues, perhaps of Agrippa, the emperor, or the gods, although again these have vanished, as has the original bronze ceiling – melted down in the 17th century on the orders of Pope Urban VIII (1568–1644) to cast cannons for the Castel Sant' Angelo. This act of vandalism inspired an anonymous contemporary wit to comment that '*what the Barbarians didn't do, the Barberinis did*' (Urban was a member of the Barberini family).

‘Shalt thou not last? – Time’s scythe and tyrants’ rods
Shiver upon thee – sanctuary and home
Of art and piety – Pantheon! – pride of Rome!’

LORD BYRON – *CHILDE HAROLD’S PILGRIMAGE*, CANTO THE FOURTH, VERSE CXLVI (1818)

This engraving (c.1815) by the English artist Matthew Dubourg shows the two bell towers added to the Pantheon in the 17th century by the baroque architect Giovanni Bernini. Dubbed the ‘ass’s ears’ by the people of Rome, they were removed in a major restoration in 1883.

TIMELINE

27 BC During his third consulship, Agrippa builds the first Pantheon in thanksgiving for Augustus's (Octavian's) victory over Mark Antony and Cleopatra at the Battle of Actium

AD 80 The first Pantheon is destroyed in a great fire

***c.*110** The reconstructed temple that Domitian orders built on the site is struck by lightning and burned

118–28 Emperor Hadrian constructs the Pantheon that still stands today

202 The Pantheon is repaired by the emperor Septimius Severus and his son Caracalla

609 Byzantine emperor Flavius Phocas Augustus donates the building to Pope Boniface IV, who consecrates it and dedicates it to the Virgin Mary

663 Byzantine emperor Constans II plunders many sites in Rome, including the Pantheon, for treasures to take back to Constantinople

***c.*1630s** Pope Urban VIII strips off the bronze ceiling of the Pantheon's portico to forge cannons and adorn the baldachin of St Peter's

The portico leads across the largest-known piece of Lucullan black and red marble to the 7-metre- (22-ft-) high bronze doors which, exceptionally, are original and the earliest of their type known anywhere in the world. When new they were covered in gold, the spoils from Trajan's wars in Dacia (Romania), although this has now gone. Yet it is only on passing through these doors that the true wonder of the Pantheon becomes clear. The sanctuary of the temple is covered by a dome so technically advanced that it still holds architectural records today. It rises 22 metres (72 ft) to an 8-metre (26-ft) opening at its apex known as the *oculus* (eye), which provides the only light to the interior. This bronze-lined hole obviously let the rain in, but a sophisticated drainage system below prevented the interior from flooding. As well as letting in light, the *oculus* also had the effect of air-conditioning the building, as the wind blowing across it created negative pressure within, drawing out the stale air and drawing in fresh air through the porch. But the dome itself is the true wonder of the Pantheon. With a span of 43.3 metres (142 ft), the dome was the largest in the world from its construction, in around 118–28, until the building of the Devonshire Royal Hospital in Buxton, Derbyshire, England in 1881, a record-breaking 1753 years.

The Pantheon as Microcosm

Originally the interior of the temple was decorated with coloured marble and the seven large apses probably held statues of each of the seven planetary gods. These, it has been suggested, would have been carefully arranged, with the Sun statue in the central apse, the male figures of Mars (the son), Jupiter (the Father) and Saturn (the grandfather) all to one side and on the other side the female (or androgynous) Venus, Mercury and the Moon. Two equilateral triangles were then formed by the good or favourable planets of the Moon, Jupiter and Venus and by the unfavourable ones of Saturn, Mercury and Mars. It could therefore be said that the whole building was a model of the Roman universe. Although we have no contemporary description of these statues, the Roman naturalist and historian Pliny the Elder, writing in around 77 (and hence about the original Pantheon before the fire) gives a hint as to how lavishly they were decorated. He tells us that the last queen of Egypt, Cleopatra VII (69–30 BC), owned a pair of earrings made from the two largest pearls ever known, which she had inherited from 'the kings of the East'. To show her lover Mark Antony how little such wealth meant to her, she removed one of these in his presence, dissolved it in vinegar and then drank it. Pliny then adds that after Cleopatra's death, the other pearl was taken to Rome, cut in half and placed on the ears of the statue of Venus in the Pantheon so that Venus should have at least 'half a portion'.

During the Roman period, probably around 202, the coffers in the dome were also cut, on the orders of the emperor Septimius Severus (r. 193–211). These five rows of 28 square sunken panels were not only decorative but also helped to reduce the weight of the dome. The whole temple had been built on the *Campus Martius* ('Field of Mars'), a marshy area on

the banks of the River Tiber. The instability of the ground here caused the foundations to crack and necessitated the construction of a second retaining wall around the dome. Despite these scares, however, the Pantheon did not collapse and today, save for some later internal decoration, this remarkable concrete structure remains exactly as it was when Hadrian commissioned it.

A Sturdy Structure

The fact that the Pantheon has survived for nearly two millennia is due to a variety of factors: the techniques used in its construction, the great admiration it engendered in later peoples and its rededication as a church.

Most important of all in the Pantheon's survival is simply how well the building was constructed. Hadrian intended to make a building to last and ordered the date – AD 123 – stamped on the bricks that make up the walls of the temple so that people far in the future might know when it was built. In spite of this, however, the building was never certain to survive. There is evidence of remedial repairs having been carried out on the structure even in

The high altar at the Pantheon, which was consecrated as a Christian church in 609. Writing in the early eighth century, the British ecclesiastical historian Bede commented: 'Once its horde of devils had been cast out, it became a memorial to the Company of Saints'.

MIRACLE MATERIAL

The dome of the Pantheon is a hemisphere, the height of the *oculus* above the floor being the same as the diameter of the dome. This means that if the dome were extended into a sphere it would sit perfectly on the floor of the building it stands within. Its construction technique is also unique. The dome is made not of brick or stone but Roman concrete, a combination of hydrate of lime, pumice from a local volcano and a sandy, volcanic ash called *pozzolana* (or *puteolanum*) from the village of Pozzuoli (Roman: Puteolanum) near Mount Vesuvius. This ash was one of the unlikely keys to Roman success, making a concrete of immense strength that would even set underwater. The renowned first-century BC architect Vitruvius gives a precise recipe for mixing concrete in his treatise *De Architectura*. The dome was slowly built up in rings of this concrete over a period of years, a slow process that allowed the concrete in each layer to fully 'cure' before the next was added. As the dome rose, the walls were thinned to reduce the weight and the stone aggregate in the concrete was also changed, using lighter and lighter pumices as the levels climbed. The end result was spectacular – a 5000-ton roof that is still the largest non-reinforced concrete dome ever made.

the Roman period, necessitated by the cracking of the foundations on their marshy base and the pressure of the lateral thrust exerted by the huge concrete dome. The repair work carried out in the early third century by the emperors Septimius Severus and Caracalla may have been as much to reduce the building's weight as to improve its appearance. This work is recorded in a contemporary inscription: '*With every refinement they restored the Pantheon worn by age.*'

At this point the temple was less than 75 years old, but their work seems to have prevented further deterioration and the building survived through the rest of the classical Roman period until it was handed over to the church by the Byzantine emperor Flavius Phocas Augustus (r. 602–10) in 609, a move that probably prevented it falling prey to the looting and quarrying away that was the fate of many of Rome's other great buildings. Phocas ordered that:

> '*...the Church of the Ever-blessed Virgin Mary and of all the Martyrs should be established in the old temple which was called the Pantheon, after all the uncleannesses of idolatry had been removed, so that where formerly the worship, not of all the gods, but of all the devils was performed, there at last there should be a memorial of all the saints.*'

Even as a church the Pantheon was not entirely exempt from despoliation, however, and in 663 the emperor Constans II (r. 641–68) sacked Rome and, according to Paul the Deacon (*c.*720–99):

> '*... pulled down everything that in ancient times had been made of metal for the ornament of the city, to such an extent that he even stripped off the roof of the church of the blessed Mary which at one time was called the Pantheon, and had been founded in honor of all the gods and was now by the consent of the former rulers the place of all the martyrs; and he took away from there the bronze tiles and sent them with all the other ornaments to Constantinople.*'

The Pantheon itself survived, however, and in the Renaissance gained new fame as artists and architects rediscovered Roman civilization. At this time a stucco frieze was added to the interior just underneath the dome to further enhance what Michelangelo claimed was a structure not of human design but built by angels. From this period onwards the Pantheon was also used as a tomb; various Italian kings as well as the Renaissance painter Raphael (1483–1520) and his fiancée are buried there. Even today the Pantheon is still a temple to a God – the Christian god – and masses, weddings and funerals are still regularly held in a building first dedicated almost 1900 years earlier.

The rings of lacunar coffering around the Pantheon's oculus were a later addition to lessen the weight of the dome. The thickness reduces from 6 metres (20 ft) at its base to 1.5 metres (5ft) at the top.

The Baths of Diocletian

The most luxurious spa ever built

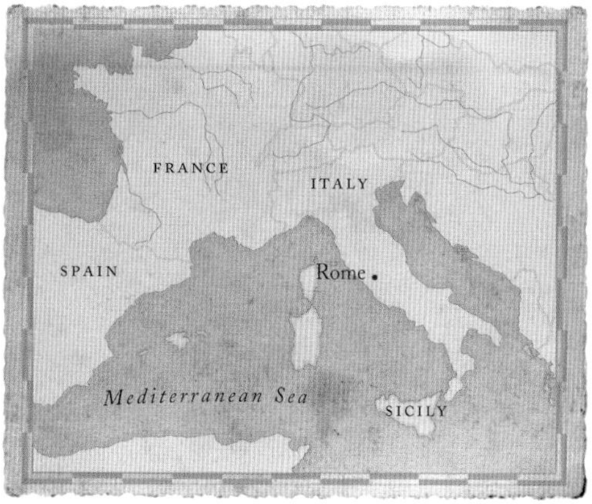

Roman emperors were renowned for their patronage of magnificent building projects, with the most lavish reserved for the capital Rome itself. Palaces, arenas and racetracks filled the city but nowhere was the largesse of the emperors more clearly seen than in the building of public baths (*thermae*). Of these, far and away the most magnificent were the monumental baths of Diocletian – the largest in the ancient world.

The first public baths in Rome, which set new standards for luxurious public architecture, were built by Agrippa (*c.*63–12 BC), son-in-law of the first emperor Augustus, around 20 BC on the *Campus Martius*. Not surprisingly many subsequent emperors followed suit, providing ever larger and more opulent facilities for the people, usually at some nominal charge. By the late empire there were nearly a thousand bath houses in the city, including imperial baths donated by Titus, Domitian, Trajan and Caracalla, but all of these were to be eclipsed by Diocletian's building.

By the time Diocletian (r. 284–305), who was of humble birth, took the imperial purple, the empire had been riven by political intrigues, social unrest and revolutions for 50 years. It is probably only thanks to the new emperor's decision to split control of the empire between four co-rulers and introduce a new administrative system of 'dioceses' that it survived at all. However, in this process of *de facto* devolution, the city of Rome lost influence. In fact, Diocletian never lived there, visiting the city only once, in the winter of 303, to celebrate his military victories and 20 years on the throne. Even so, Rome retained its status as an iconic city and the stage on which emperors demonstrated their power and wealth, so it was here, in 298, that work commenced on the greatest public baths ever built.

Last Word in Style

The Baths of Diocletian were not simply a series of pools for bathing, but an entire leisure complex, decorated in the finest style and offering the very latest in luxury. The site was enclosed behind a large wall marking off an area of 13 hectares (32 acres) in the centre of the city, near the Viminal Hill. Inside this colonnaded wall stood a pleasure garden, complete with fountains and sculptures and a running track in front of a huge semicircular recess known as an *exedra*. In the centre of these gardens stood the bath complex itself, arranged around a huge open-air pool – the *natatio* – which dwarfed even the largest of modern spas, being able easily to accommodate over 3000 guests at any one time. The baths were fed by the Aqua Marcia aqueduct, which brought water from a source 57 miles (91 km) away.

The main bathing facility comprised three vast rooms each kept at a different temperature – the cold *frigidarium* with its icy plunge bath, the warm *tepidarium* and the hot *caldarium*. The temperature was precisely controlled thanks to another Roman innovation, the hypocaust. This consisted of an enclosed fire, stoked by slaves, which produced hot air that was then ducted under mosaic floors supported on small pillars of tiles. Hollow tiles set into the walls channelled the hot air up and out though vents in the roof. By carefully controlling the flow of air through the rooms, each was kept at its correct temperature. In the case of the Baths of Diocletian, so huge were the rooms and so massive the walls that it took three days to get the building up to temperature.

Visitors to the baths would pass through an entrance in the stuccoed exterior walls, which were carved and polished to look like marble, and enter a vestibule area called the *apodyterium*, where they would undress completely save for a pair of sandals to protect their

This engraving (1721) by the 18th-century Austrian architect Fischer von Erlach indicates the enormous scale and elaborate design of the Baths of Diocletian.

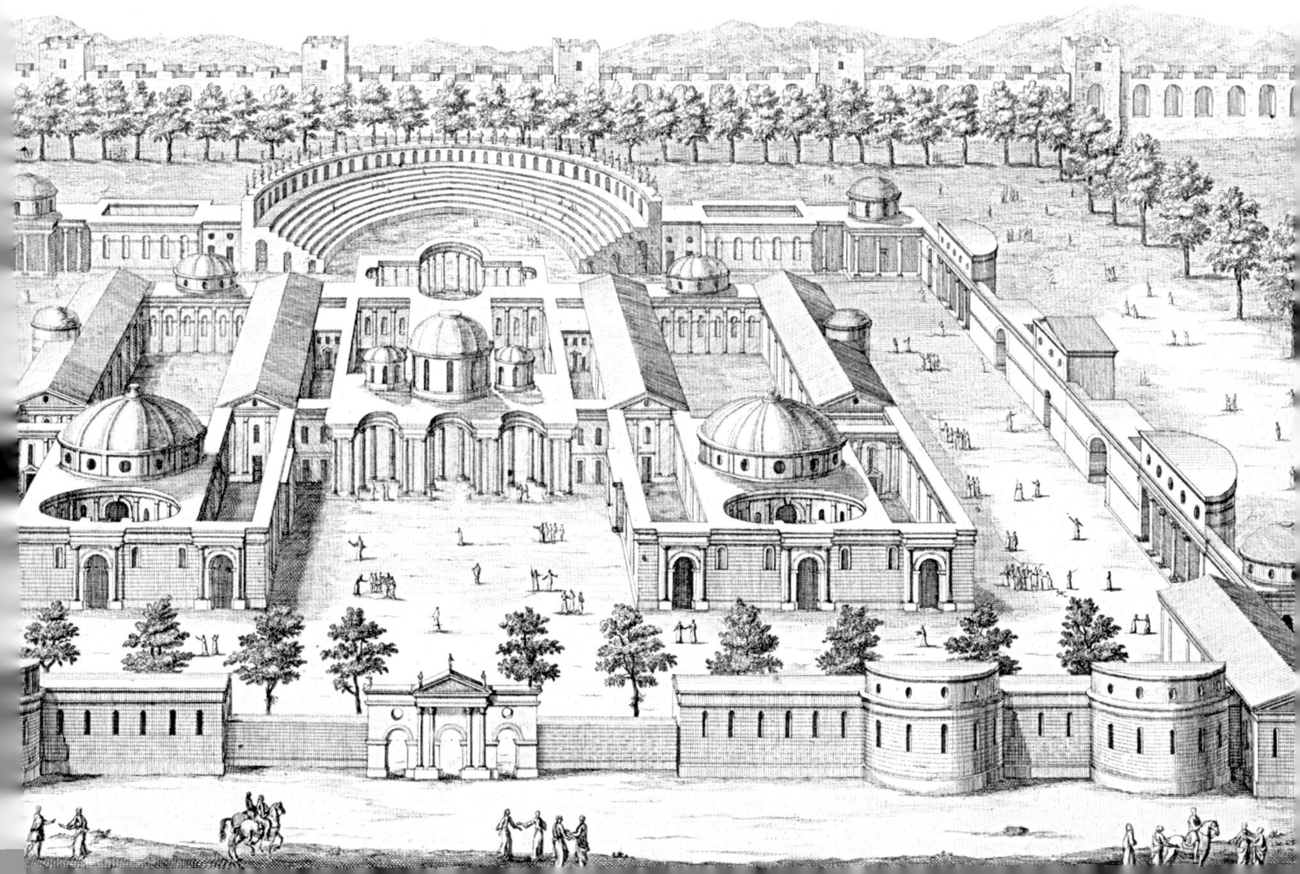

TIMELINE

c.20 BC Agrippa constructs the first public baths in Rome

AD 298 Work commences on the Baths of Diocletian, possibly involving the forced labour of 10,000 Christians

306 The Baths of Diocletian are dedicated and opened to the public

537 Baths cease to function in their original role, as invading Goths cut the aqueduct supplying them

1563–6 Michelangelo converts the *tepidarium* of Diocletian's baths into the church of Santa Maria degli Angeli e dei Martiri

1598 The church of San Bernardo alle Terme is built in one of the *spheristeria* (ball-game arenas) of the baths

1889 The National Roman Museum is housed in part of the former Baths of Diocletian

feet from the hot floors. Having stowed their clothes in a pigeonhole, or got their slave to do it for them, they were then ready to begin the bathing process. In exactly which order the various rooms were used is still a matter of dispute, and habits may have varied from country to country but probably the bathing began with some light exercise in the gymnasium to build up a sweat. The visitor would then pass into the *elaeothesium,* or anointing room, to be oiled with olive oil. Poorer visitors who could not afford oil might dust themselves with lentil flour instead. The visitor would then move into the most luxurious part of the building, the *tepidarium* where they might spend an hour or more talking to friends, and having a massage. From here they moved into the *caldarium* (from which we get the word 'cauldron'), the hottest room in the complex and closest to the furnaces, where there were baths for private bathing. Having sweated out the dust and impurities in their skin they then moved into the *laconium* where a slave – or a friend if you could not afford a slave – would scrape off the oil using a blunt, curved metal blade known as a strigil. Thus cleansed, the pores were closed with a dip in the icy cold pool in the *frigidarium.*

Ablutions formed only part of the experience of visiting Diocletian's baths, however. As well as bathing the guests could enjoy many other facilities, including private meeting rooms, theatres and concert halls as well as simply admiring the rare marbles that clad the walls, the finest mosaics on the floors or taking a walk among the classical sculptures of the gardens.

Social Nexus

Although Diocletian's baths were built as a gift to the city from the emperor, there was a charge to enter, but this was kept deliberately low to ensure that the facility was available to everyone. Those with money would come with their slaves, who moved around the complex through a series of underground passages, ensuring they were always discreetly available in whichever room their master or mistress required them. Less wealthy visitors would have to fetch and carry for themselves. For much of the history of the *thermae,* the sexes were separated – indeed, the emperors Hadrian and Marcus Aurelius banned mixed bathing altogether. Despite this, there are plenty of contemporary descriptions of men and women bathing together and in particular the presence of female courtesans in male baths. Attempts were also made to segregate the classes, with the baths being open at different times for slaves and freemen, rich and poor, the best time being considered the afternoon when the higher status members of society came.

Wealthy Romans would try to bathe every day if possible, not simply for reasons of cleanliness but because bathing was integral to Roman life and a major part of the social and political make-up of the empire. Diocletian's baths were a social nexus, a cultural centre and the informal meeting place where much of the business of the empire was actually done. They were also one of the last great statements of Roman imperial might, remaining in use for over 200 years and their demise would mark one of the final nails in the empire's coffin.

> *'Look at the cascades of water splashing noisily down from one level to the next. We have actually come to such a pitch of choosiness that we object to walking on anything other than precious stones.'*

SENECA – *MORAL EPISTLES*, 86 (*c.*AD 60)

FROM SECULAR TO SACRED USE

The Baths of Diocletian were built to last and some substantial parts of the complex survive to this day, although they are now given over to different uses.

The complex continued in use until 537, when the Goths severed the water supply to Rome by demolishing a part of the aqueduct supplying the vast quantities of water required by the baths. The enormous brick and stucco structure of the baths themselves, however, remained largely intact and was gradually reoccupied by tradesmen and families during the medieval period. But it was probably the papacy that ultimately saved and restored the progressively crumbling structure from demolition.

Diocletian notoriously presided over the last great persecution of Christians in the Roman empire, banning their religion and having their priests arrested and executed. It was rumoured that the vast baths in Rome had been built by thousands of Christian slave labourers, many of whom had died in the process. In memory of them, Pope Pius IV (1499–1565) commissioned the artist Michelangelo to convert the largest remaining part of the structure into a Christian church. Between 1563 and 1566 Michelangelo transformed the huge old *tepidarium* of the baths, with its 28-metre- (92-ft-) high vaulted Roman ceiling into the Basilica of Santa Maria degli Angeli e dei Martiri.

In doing so he preserved and restored the most luxurious part of the original complex. Its survival enables us to gain an insight today into just how spectacular the original baths must have been. In fact, when looking down the 90-metre- (295-ft-) long nave – once filled with the citizens of ancient Rome at their leisure – the only major difference other than the trappings of Christianity is that the pillars are now slightly shorter than their original height; Michelangelo had to build up the floor to the street level of his day, which was several feet higher than in the Roman period.

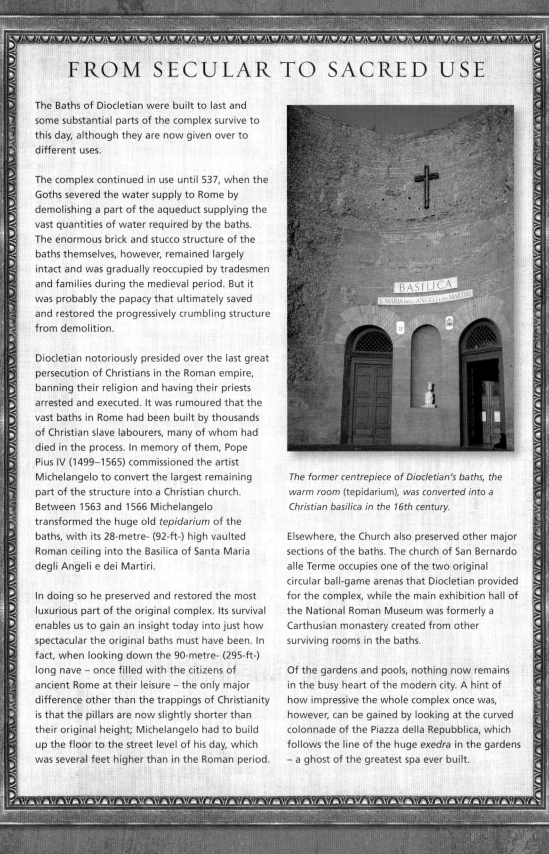

The former centrepiece of Diocletian's baths, the warm room (tepidarium)*, was converted into a Christian basilica in the 16th century.*

Elsewhere, the Church also preserved other major sections of the baths. The church of San Bernardo alle Terme occupies one of the two original circular ball-game arenas that Diocletian provided for the complex, while the main exhibition hall of the National Roman Museum was formerly a Carthusian monastery created from other surviving rooms in the baths.

Of the gardens and pools, nothing now remains in the busy heart of the modern city. A hint of how impressive the whole complex once was, however, can be gained by looking at the curved colonnade of the Piazza della Repubblica, which follows the line of the huge *exedra* in the gardens – a ghost of the greatest spa ever built.

The City of Tikal

Ancient metropolis in the rainforest

Tikal in the Guatemalan lowlands of Petén is located in one of the most densely wooded parts of Central America. Yet for over 1500 years this wilderness of giant kapok trees, spider monkeys, toucans and jaguars was home to one of the largest and most important cities in the Mayan world.

The oldest archaeological evidence for human occupation of Tikal comes from around 800 BC, when a small mound was built at the site. Over the following centuries, this was to expand into a huge complex of ceremonial and religious centres, royal palaces and ball-courts covering an area of over 0.7 square miles (2 sq km). These public buildings were surrounded by a residential area, which, although most of it remains to be excavated, probably covered 23 square miles (60 sq km), or 14 times the size of Vatican City, and was home to perhaps 60,000 people.

Royal and Ritual Centres

The earliest focal point for the city lay in what is now known as the 'Lost World' area of the site and centred on a 30-metre (100-ft) high pyramid structure, built from the local limestone. The present pyramid appears from archaeological investigations to be the fifth on the site, dating from between AD 200 and 400, the first having been built at least 800 years earlier. Just what this structure was for remains a mystery, although it stands in the 'Complex for Astronomical Commemoration', suggesting that it may have had something to do with the construction and maintenance of the highly accurate Mayan calendar. Whatever its original use, the Maya recognized this as an important place in the foundation of their city and continued to replaster, paint and maintain the structure for many centuries after it was built.

At around the same time, in what is known as the Early Classic Period, extensive developments were taking place elsewhere on the site. From AD 292 the city's rulers begin to have themselves represented in low relief on stone stelae, first in profile and then face-on. The Mayan hieroglyphics on these stelae provide us with the earliest first-hand account of the city. During this period, the rulers of Tikal were buried in the Northern Acropolis area and the site is full of stelae recounting their lives and events in Mayan history. Among them is one of the most famous Mayan monuments showing, on one side, the ruler Stormy Sky holding up a headdress to the people and a jaguar (representing the god who protected the city) on the other. The name Stormy Sky comes from the fact that we do not know the phonetic equivalents to many Mayan hieroglyphs, so instead have to use the words they portray. By contrast, scholars have determined the sounds that make up the name of Stormy Sky's grandfather, which can be rendered as Chak-To-Ich'ak.

Temple I, dedicated to the jaguar, at the Mayan city of Tikal.

'This is the first account, the first narrative. There was neither man, nor animal, birds, fishes, crabs, trees, stones, caves, ravines, grasses, nor forests; there was only the sky. The surface of the earth had not appeared. There was only the calm sea and the great expanse of the sky.'

MAYAN TEXT – THE *POPOL VUH* (*c.*1550)

TIMELINE

4th century BC Construction at Tikal of first ritual buildings by the Maya civilization

***c.*AD 200–400** Tikal grows in size and importance during the Mayan Classic period

562 Tikal conquered by the city of Caracol

seventh–eighth centuries Tikal reaches its zenith with the building of the Great Plaza; most pyramids at the site date from this period

tenth century Tikal largely abandoned by this time

1696 Andres Avendaño is thought to have sighted the abandoned city of Tikal while travelling through the Guatemalan rainforest

1848 Ambrosio Tut and Modesto Méndez visit Tikal and publish sketches of its buildings

1881–2 Alfred Maudslay conducts the first thorough archaeological survey of Tikal

1951 A new jungle airstrip facilitates investigation of the site

1956–70 Extensive archaeological work carried out at Tikal by the University of Pennsylvania

1979 Tikal is designated a World Heritage Site by UNESCO

The Northern Acropolis is only one of at least four in the city. The Central Acropolis contains the main palace buildings – a maze of 45 two- and three-storey buildings around six courtyards, which developed and was added to over a 200-year period. In this acropolis was also found a carving of a monkey mask. Monkeys appear frequently in Mayan mythology. For example, the *Popol Vuh* ('Council Book'), a narrative recounting the origins and history of the Quiché Maya people, tells how the twin brothers Hunahpu and Ixbalenque (known as the Hero Twins) were envied by their older twin half-brothers Hun Batz and Hun Chouen, who plotted to kill them. So, the Hero Twins tricked them into climbing a tree. As the tree grew taller and Hun Batz and Hun Chouen realized they couldn't get down, the Hero Twins turned them into monkeys, telling them to take off their loincloths, which became their tails.

The centre of the whole city, and the area which has been most extensively restored, is the Great Plaza with its famous opposing temples. These both consist of a pyramid approached by a staircase, as with the Lost World pyramid, but on the top of each of these is a temple. Temple I is 45 metres (148 ft) high and dedicated to the jaguar, as well as being the burial place of Ruler A, also known as Sawa Chaan K'awil. Excavations of his tomb revealed him to be almost 2 metres (6 ft) tall and buried with an impressive selection of grave goods, including 89 carved bones portraying the Mayan funeral mythology. They show the king being ferried to the underworld in a ritual canoe, paddled by twin gods and accompanied by an iguana, a parrot, a monkey and a dog. Opposite this structure is Temple II, which was built in 702 and is known today as the Temple of Masks. The wooden lintel of this temple shows a woman, leading archaeologists to speculate that this might be the last resting place of Sawa Chaan K'awil's wife, Queen Lady Twelve Macaw. The acoustics of the opposing temples are designed so that anyone speaking from the top of either pyramid can easily be heard in the plaza below. In addition, stelae at the site suggest that the steps of the temples provided platforms for musicians to play to the assembled crowd during ceremonies.

A Precarious Existence

The most extraordinary structure at Tikal, however, is not a temple or palace but the extensive system of cisterns (*chultuns*), storage pits and irrigation channels that kept this jungle city alive. Although Tikal was situated in a rainforest, there were no rivers, streams, springs or wells ensuring a constant source of water for the population. Instead, every drop of rainwater that fell had to be saved and carefully distributed via an elaborate system of canals to provide drinking water and irrigation for the vegetable gardens, fruit trees and breadnut crops.

This impressive engineering feat may also have been the cause of Tikal's downfall. Although the city was conquered by the city of Caracol (in modern-day Belize) in 562 it survived and indeed reached

Situated deep within the Maya Biosphere Reserve, the fourth largest continuous area of forest on the planet, Tikal long eluded the attention of archaeologists.

JEWEL IN THE JUNGLE

Buried in some of the world's densest rainforest, Tikal slipped out of view and memory very quickly after its abandonment. It does not appear again in western sources until 1696, when the Spanish friar Andres Avendaño, fleeing from the city of Tayasal to escape an attempt on his life, made an intriguing entry in his diary. He claims that while travelling through the forest to Mérida, he came upon an abandoned city full of temples and vaulted houses that still bore their whitewash.

While we cannot be sure that the site Avendaño stumbled upon was Tikal, the size and location strongly suggest that it was. This visit was not followed up, however, as the area was considered largely impenetrable. It would be nearly 150 years before the English architect Frederick Catherwood and the American diplomat John Lloyd Stephens heard rumours of the city while on an expedition in 1840 that eventually took them to the Mayan site of Palenque. Eight years later Ambrosio Tut, a gum collector, came close to the site and saw the tops of temples rising above the forest canopy, which he reported back to the governor of Petén province, Modesto Méndez. The two men went back to the site, taking with them an artist to sketch the ruins before publishing their discovery in the Guatemalan newspaper *La Garceta*.

In 1853 the Berlin Academy of Sciences published these findings and, in an era when the Western powers were competing to make spectacular archaeological discoveries, this soon came to the attention of British and American archaeologists. Sir Alfred Maudslay (1850–1931), who is considered the father of Mayan archaeology, made the first proper survey of the site in 1881–2 while camping in a palace in the Central Acropolis. His photographs, the first taken at the site, showed the world what would become the epitome of archaeological exploration – an entire city lost beneath a tangle of huge tree roots and holding secrets from a distant past.

Thereafter, American academics took a lead in studying the site; the Peabody Museum at Harvard University paid for a new map of the centre of the city, while the Carnegie Institution sent Sylvanus Morley (1883–1948) to make the first attempt at deciphering the hieroglyphics found in the ruins. However, it was only with the building of a small airstrip in 1951 that full-scale exploration of the site could begin. This facility meant that teams no longer had to make arduous treks through the tropical jungle, carrying all their supplies and tools. Between 1956 and 1969 a team from the University of Pennsylvania created a topographical map of 10 square miles (25 sq km) of the city, making it the largest excavated site in the Americas – an extraordinary feat in the dense undergrowth. Over a 13-year period, they plotted the location of over 4000 structures, although the vast majority of these could not be fully excavated. Even this huge effort probably represents under half the city's full extent, so the forests may hold on to many of Tikal's secrets for years to come.

its zenith with the building of the Great Plaza over a century later. But after 889 no further stelae were erected at the site and by the tenth century the area seems to have been abandoned. The reason for this may be a period of severe drought that began in the early ninth century, which left the city without sufficient rainfall. This chronic lack of water, combined with the overuse of fragile jungle soils by the agricultural demands of an ever-expanding population, seems to have precipitated an ecological crisis. In the years after the last stela was erected, the whole fabric of Mayan city society collapsed and the palaces were burnt down, perhaps by a population who no longer believed that their rulers had the physical ability or the spiritual authority to rule over them. Those people then moved away back to more sustainable modes of life and their huge city was slowly enveloped by the surrounding jungle.

The Buddhas of Bamyan

Devotional giants destroyed by zealots

The Bamyan Valley lies some 150 miles (240 km) northwest of the Afghan capital Kabul on a plateau rising over a mile (1.6 km) above sea level, hemmed in by the mountains of the Hindu Kush. Fifteen hundred years ago, however, this was no desolate outpost but rather a thriving staging post on the Silk Road at the heart of the Indian kingdom of Gandhara – and home to one of the great wonders of the age.

As a stopping-off point on the Silk Road, this area had been a cultural melting pot since before the days of Alexander the Great. The Silk Road provided the one vital link between the traders of the eastern (Chinese) world and the ancient and medieval West. Here you could meet envoys of the Roman empire, Chinese imperial officials, Persian merchants and traders from all over south and central Asia. Perhaps not surprisingly in this cosmopolitan environment, a unique style of classical art grew up here which fuses these eastern and western traditions. This style, sometimes known as Indo-Greek or Greco-Buddhist, found its most magnificent expression in the beliefs of the Buddhist monks who lived as hermits in the hundreds of caves – 720 at the most recent count – that line the south-facing cliffs for almost a mile (1.6 km) along the centre of the site. They gave their caves elaborate vaulted roofs and decorated the walls with vivid frescoes reflecting their adherence to the *Lokottara-vada* school of Buddhism. This taught that the Buddha was omniscient and eternal and that his presence on earth was merely an illusory projection designed to save other beings.

Labour of Devotion

The monks also created votive statues of the Buddha, two of which have made Bamyan famous. During the period of Kushan control of Gandhara, which began around AD 70, the region witnessed a golden age of Buddhist building, with the construction of large numbers of stupas and, in particular, the erection of several huge statues of Buddha himself, carved into the sandstone hillsides.

Of these, the two greatest were the Buddhas of Bamyan. Built after the shock of the invasions of the Huns, they were perhaps the swansong of the Kushite golden age, which was already fading

The smaller, and older, of the two Buddhas of Bamyan, pictured prior to their destruction by the fundamentalist Taliban regime in 2001.

fast. The smaller of the two statues is the oldest, having been recently dated using carbon-14 techniques to *c.*507. It was created by hollowing out a huge niche into the sheer rock face of the cliff and then carving within this a 37-metre (121-ft) tall image of a standing Buddha. Nearby, and just 47 years later, another similar image was carved but even larger, standing 53 metres (174 ft) tall, making it the largest standing stone Buddha ever created.

These huge figures must have stunned passing travellers, since they were not simply left as plain stone carvings. Although the bodies were hewn from the cliff face, the finer modelling, such as the lower parts of the arms and upper parts of the face, was done in wood, clay and straw, which was attached to the stone by pegs on massive frames. The whole finished statue was then covered in a layer of fine, smooth stucco before being vividly painted. The smaller of the two Buddhas appears to have been painted in various colours, while the larger was carmine red. This painted layer was then embellished with gold leaf and jewels.

Remarkably, we have a contemporary description of the Buddhas when they were at their best, by a Chinese Buddhist monk, Xuan Zang. Unhappy with the teaching of Buddhism he was receiving in China, he slipped out of the country, without permission, to undertake a pilgrimage to India, where he intended to visit all the sacred sites connected with the Buddha. Xuan Zang's journal of his travels has survived. En route to the Ganges, he travelled north past the desolate Takla Makan Desert, through Tashkent and Samarkand on the Silk Road, beyond the Iron Gates into Bactria and across the Hindu Kush into Gandhara. Around 630, this epic journey brought him to Bamyan, which he describes as being blessed with more than 1000 monks who had created huge statues of Buddha '*decorated with gold and fine jewels*'.

Intriguingly he also mentions a third statue, of a reclining Buddha, which he says was housed in a temple in the shadow of the other two and for which no archaeological evidence has ever been found. Xuan Zang claims this figure was nearly 305 metres (1000 ft) long. If true, this would make it easily the largest statue ever made, dwarfing the 46-metre (150-ft) high Statue of Liberty. Archaeologists have suggested that the original was made of clay and has either eroded away over the centuries or may have been hidden by the Bamyan monks to protect it from Islamic incursions. If this is the case, then a statue worthy of inclusion in the original list of Seven Wonders may still be lying buried in the foothills of the Hindu Kush.

The Resilient Buddhas

The Buddhas seen by Xuan Zang survived the period during which the area was under the nominal control of Huns, who oversaw a gradual move away from Buddhism towards Hinduism, before the region came under Muslim control in the eighth century AD.

The final destruction of Gandhara by the militant Muslim leader Mahmud of Ghazni (971–1030), who seized control of the region in the early 11th century, was accompanied by the systematic looting and desecration of Buddhist and Hindu monasteries throughout Afghanistan and northern India. However, the statues themselves remained untouched until the arrival of the Mongol ruler Genghis Khan (1162–1227) in 1222. As he swept through the region he destroyed the town of Bamyan and defaced the statues, probably removing some of the applied stucco and woodwork but, in the face of their sheer monumentality, could do little to the statues themselves.

Following in the footsteps of the holy warrior Mahmud of Ghazni, it was another group of latter-day *jihadists* who were to spell the final end of the Bamyan Buddhas in the first year of the 21st century.

TIMELINE

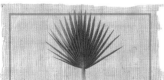

***c.*AD 507** Creation of the first and smallest Buddha of Bamyan by Buddhist monks

554 Second Buddha carved out of the rock face

630 Chinese Buddhist pilgrim Xuan Zang passes through Bamyan and describes the statues

***c.*1021** Turkish mercenary and Muslim leader Mahmud of Ghazni overruns the ancient kingdom of Gandhara

1222 Mongol ruler Genghis Khan sweeps through central Asia, destroying Bamyan and defacing the Buddhas

2001 The hardline Islamist Taliban regime of Afghanistan destroys the Buddhas with explosives

2003 The Buddhas of Bamyan are designated a World Heritage Site by UNESCO

WANTON DESTRUCTION

Despite attempts to desecrate them in the early Middle Ages, the Bamyan Buddhas survived and remained a tourist attraction into modern times, until the Soviet invasion of Afghanistan in 1979 effectively closed the country. In 2001, the Buddhas came to world attention once again, with news of their imminent destruction. The radical Islamist Taliban regime, which had seized control of Afghanistan in 1996, announced that it intended to dynamite the ancient statues.

The exact reasoning behind this decision remains somewhat unclear. Some sources claim that the threat to destroy the Buddhas was an attempt to extort money from the international community, while others believe it was part of a systematic programme of persecution of the local Hazara people, who claimed descent from the builders of Bamyan and who opposed Taliban rule. The official Taliban statement claimed that the destruction was simply a part of a general removal of what state clerics considered idolatrous images:

> *'Based on the verdict of the clerics and the decision of the Supreme Court of the Islamic Emirate (of Afghanistan) all the statues around Afghanistan must be destroyed. All the statues in the country should be destroyed because these statues have been used as idols and deities by the non-believers before. Only God, the Almighty, deserves to be worshipped, not anyone or anything else.'*

Despite a worldwide outcry the Taliban dynamited the Bamyan Buddhas in March 2001, filming the process so as to remove any doubt as to their fate. It took nearly a month of blasting to remove all trace of the two stone figures from the hillside niches where they had stood for nearly 1500 years.

Since the overthrow of the Taliban regime, there has been a concerted international effort to restore the site. This venture faces formidable problems: 40 percent of the statues are now entirely missing, having been blown to dust by the dynamite, while the remainder was left eroding, exposed to the elements, in the form of rubble ranging from fist-sized lumps to 90-ton boulders. Nearly 3000 fragments of surface plaster have also been recovered, along with the pegs and ropes that were used to hold it in place.

The destruction has at least allowed experts to understand how the Buddhas were constructed and has provided samples for carbon-14 dating, as well as uncovering a reliquary containing clay beads, a leaf, seals and parts of a Buddhist text written on bark, all of which are thought to have been sealed into a cavity in the chest of one of the Buddhas when it was built. The question now is, can all these pieces be reunited in restored figures?

Technically the project is feasible, though there is currently no crane in Afghanistan capable of lifting the largest fragments back into place. The cost, currently estimated at US$98 million, might also be hard to justify, especially in a war-ravaged country, many of whose populace live in poverty. Even then, there is the question of what a restoration would actually look like. If the site is to retain its UNESCO World Heritage Site status (ironically, only granted after the destruction of the Buddhas), only 'preservation' work, not new building, could be carried out. With 40 percent of the Buddhas missing, how this can be achieved remains uncertain. Currently plans are afoot to use anastylosis – a process approved by UNESCO and often employed with Greek and Roman temples – where small amounts of new building are allowed between original architectural elements provided the difference between new and original work is clear to see.

While the debate still rages over what to do with the Buddhas of Bamyan a temporary plan has been mooted to use lasers to project images of the statues onto the cliffs, but even this scheme is still awaiting approval. So for many years to come, all that visitors will find in the cavernous cliff niches of Bamyan is light.

The Hagia Sophia

Mother church of Eastern Orthodoxy

The Hagia Sophia (or 'Church of the Holy Wisdom') in Istanbul stands on the threshold between the ancient and medieval worlds and was considered by both to be one of their greatest achievements.

Despite its almost 1500-year history, the church we see today is not the earliest one to have been built on the site. The first, built by the man who converted the Roman empire to Christianity, the emperor Constantine (r. 306–37) was destroyed in a revolt in AD 404. (Some scholars believe that his son Constantius II [r. 337–61], who inaugurated this building in 360, was responsible for its construction.) A new church was soon built on the site but this too was burnt down during the Nika Revolt against the emperor Justinian I (r. 527–65) in 532. Once the uprising had been crushed, Justinian resolved to rebuild this central church at the heart of the Eastern Roman empire with such ambition and on such a scale that, despite the city's turbulent history, nobody would ever dare to destroy it again.

No Expense Spared

Justinian was adamant that no expense would be spared making this the largest and most lavishly decorated church in Christendom. He also intended it to be innovative, and so employed two of the greatest academic minds of the day to act as its architects. Isidore of Miletus (*fl.* 532–7) was a mathematician who is credited with the invention of the 'T' square and who could perform the complex mathematics necessary in building what was to be the largest church on earth. Anthemius of Tralles (*c.* 474–*c.*534) was a professor of geometry in the city whose book on conic sections made him the perfect choice as designer of the church's most spectacular feature – its huge dome.

Work on the church began in 532 and involved over 10,000 workmen, assisted by a legion of priests who prayed continuously during its construction. The plan of the church was 'basilican', that is having the same ground plan as the old public basilicas of the Roman empire. However, this oblong structure was to carry a round dome of the type previously used in Roman temples, such as the vast concrete dome on the Pantheon in Rome (see pages 146–151). It was a technology that had not been in widespread use for centuries; what is more, no one had ever attempted to place a circular roof on an oblong building before.

'Thus through the spaces of the great church come rays of light, expelling clouds of care, and filling the mind with joy.'

PAUL THE SILENTIARY – *DESCRIPTIO S. SOPHIAE* (*c*.550)

Without steel reinforcement, the weight and lateral thrust of the circular dome as it pressed down on the walls had to be supported by massive pillars; there are four such pillars in the Hagia Sophia, each of which has a floor area of nearly 100 square metres (1076 sq ft). These form the basis for four ribbed arches. Between each of them was placed what was at the time a completely revolutionary architectural feature: a 'pendentive', a concave triangular section of masonry transmitting the dome's thrust down onto the rectangular arrangement of pillars. This novel engineering solution was vital for the structural integrity of the building, since the planned dome was to be huge. When finished, it stood 55.6 metres (182 ft) high and over 30 metres (100 ft) across. Only the dome of the Pantheon (at 43.3 metres/142 ft in diameter) was larger. At the lower level, the dome was pierced by 40 single-arched windows, which allowed light to flood into the void within and made the whole roof appear to float.

Lavish Decoration

Finding suitable materials for such a massive project was not easy and the resources of the whole empire were quarried to build and decorate it. Ancient bronze doors, dating from the second century BC, were brought from Tarsus and the massive columns of the nave were clad in rare purple porphyry and green marble from Salonika, each topped with a white marble capital bearing the monogram of the emperor and his wife. Even some of the columns themselves were reused, as the building required no fewer than 107 of these on the ground and in the galleries. Eight ancient examples were even brought from the ruins of the city of

Rising resplendently on the First Hill, on the European shore of the Bosphorus, the Hagia Sophia is a masterpiece of Byzantine architecture and Istanbul's most characteristic landmark.

TIMELINE

AD 360 (15 February) First church on the site, begun by Constantine or Constantius II, is consecrated

532 Work begins on building the basilica of Hagia Sophia after the second church on the site is burned down in the Nika riots

537 (27 December) Inauguration of the Hagia Sophia

553, 557 Earthquakes damage the basilica, causing cracks to appear in the fabric

558 (7 May) Main dome collapses as a result of a major earth tremor

562 Hagia Sophia rededicated after reconstruction of the dome

994 (13 May) Basilica reopened after further earthquakes and a fire damage the building

1204 Priceless treasures stolen from the basilica during the sack of Constantinople by the Fourth Crusade

1261 Byzantines regain control of Constantinople from the Latin empire and rededicate the Hagia Sophia as an Orthodox church

1453 Ottoman Turks seize Constantinople and turn the basilica into a mosque

1847–9 Sultan Abdülmecid II orders a reconstruction of the mosque by the Italian architects Gasparo and Giuseppe Fossati

1935 Turkish president Kemal Atatürk turns the Hagia Sophia into a museum

The soaring interior of the Hagia Sophia is bathed in light from the many windows set in its walls and dome. Clearly visible are the leather medallions bearing the names of the prophet Muhammad and the first caliphs of Islam.

Baalbek in Lebanon. If the church of St Sophia was built too late to be considered one of the Seven Wonders of the Ancient World, it did at least contain a part of one of those wonders – one column also came from the Temple of Artemis at Ephesus (see pages 48–51), which the compiler of the original list, Antipater of Sidon, considered the greatest building of all. This survivor from a previous wonder lost none of its mystery in the new building, where it became known as the 'crying column', from the belief that miraculous tears were once seen seeping from a hole in it.

With the structure finished, no less time or money was spent on the decoration of the interior. The altar, pulpit and even some of the doors were plated in gold and silver and studded with jewels and ivory reliefs. The *iconostasis* – the screen between the nave and sanctuary in an Orthodox church, which is decorated with icon paintings – was 15 metres (49 ft) high and clad entirely in silver.

When Justinian walked through the bronze doors reserved solely for the emperor on 27 December, 537 to attend the patriarch's lavish consecration of the building, he was entering the largest church on earth – a title it would hold for almost another 1000 years, until the construction of the massive new cathedral in Seville, Spain in the early 16th century. It had taken just six years to build and only the intricate mosaics on the walls and dome remained unfinished. Henceforth, the Hagia Sophia would be the central church of the Byzantine empire and the place where her emperors were crowned. As such it was served by 80 priests, 150 deacons, 60 sub-deacons, 160 readers, 25 cantors and 75 doorkeepers. In his treatise on buildings, *De Aedificiis,* the scholar Procopius (*c.* 500–*c.*565), who witnessed its construction, wrote:

CHURCH, MOSQUE AND MUSEUM

The Hagia Sophia has survived a turbulent past, its preservation being partly due to the sheer awe it inspired in those who saw it and partly down to simple good fortune.

Fortune did not smile on the early history of the church, however. Within 20 years of its completion a series of earthquakes cracked the great dome and on 7 May, 558 another major tremor bought the whole roof crashing to the ground. Despite the vast cost of the original structure, Justinian was unperturbed and immediately ordered its rebuilding, this time under the control of Isidore the Younger, the former architect's nephew. Lessons had been learnt from the collapse and this time the dome was raised to ensure the weight was carried more vertically and lighter materials were used. The church was rededicated just four years later.

For the next 650 years the church continued to receive lavish spending, its walls and dome being gradually covered in the finest golden micro-mosaics that the Byzantine empire could produce. In 1204, however, the Eastern Orthodox city of Constantinople was sacked by the Catholic knights of the Fourth Crusade, who plundered much of its precious decoration.

The Hagia Sophia now became a Catholic church, remaining so until 1261, when the Byzantines retook Constantinople, returning it to the Orthodox faith until 1453. In that year the Ottoman conqueror Sultan Mehmed II (r. 1444–6; 1451–81) captured the city and turned the church into a mosque. Ironically, this sudden change of use may well have preserved much of the remaining interior decoration. The Christian figurative mosaics were carefully plastered over, so preserving some of the finest Byzantine artworks. The church was also renovated and enlarged to serve its new purpose, with the addition of an Ottoman library, schools, a clockhouse and the tombs of the sultans. During this period, four 7.5-metre- (25-ft-) wide leather medallions bearing the names of Allah, Muhammad and the Prophet's grandsons Hasan and Huseyn were also hung from the inside of the dome and four minarets were placed around the central building.

The Hagia Sophia continued to serve as one of the most important mosques in the Ottoman empire until, in the new secular Republic of Turkey, it was converted into a museum in 1935. With the carpets taken out of the nave and some of the plaster removed to reveal the golden mosaics beneath, the Hagia Sophia once again returned to something like its former Byzantine appearance. Today conservation at the site consists of a balancing act between revealing older elements of the structure and its decoration and preserving the evidence from all periods of this great building's long history.

'So the church has become a spectacle of marvellous beauty, overwhelming to those who see it, but to those who know it by hearsay altogether incredible. For it soars to a height to match the sky, and as if surging up from amongst the other buildings it stands on high and looks down upon the remainder of the city, adorning it, because it is a part of it, but glorying in its own beauty, because, though a part of the city and dominating it, it at the same time towers above it to such a height that the whole city is viewed from there as from a watch-tower. Both its breadth and its length have been so carefully proportioned, that it may not improperly be said to be exceedingly long and at the same time unusually broad. And it exults in an indescribable beauty.'

According to one source, Justinian put it more succinctly, simply whispering as he walked though his monumental creation, *'Solomon, I have surpassed thee'.*

The Basilica Cistern at Constantinople

Subterranean reservoir for a major city

ONE OF THE GREATEST architectural treasures in Istanbul was, for most of the city's long history, entirely hidden from sight and is only now beginning to be fully explored. Buried deep below the heart of the metropolis, its beguiling Turkish name is the Yerebatan Sarayı, or 'Sunken Palace'. In fact, its origins and use are far more prosaic, though no less impressive.

When the Roman emperor Constantine I (r. 306–37) founded his new capital at Constantinople (modern Istanbul) in 325, he was faced with a problem that previous Roman emperors had never had to deal with – water, or rather the lack of it. Rome was located in a temperate climate, surrounded by hills where plentiful rainfall was the norm, its aqueducts fed all year round by reliable and abundant rivers. The 'New Rome' of Constantinople, on the western fringe of Asia Minor, was an entirely different proposition. This city was prone to extended periods of intense drought, generally lasting from the summer to the early autumn, while in winter the rains could be dangerously torrential. As the first-century AD Greek historian Procopius put it:

> *'In the summer season the imperial city used to suffer from scarcity of water as a general thing, though at the other seasons it enjoyed a sufficiency. Because that period always brings droughts, the springs, running less freely than at the other seasons, used to deliver through the conduits a less abundant flow of water to the city.'*

If the new city was to be a success, this combination of feast and famine had to be turned into a regular, reliable water supply. In overcoming this natural impediment, the emperors of Constantinople commissioned a miracle of ancient hydrological engineering.

Constantinople's Lifeline

The immediate solution to Constantinople's water problem was to bring supplies to the city from the surrounding countryside via aqueducts, tunnels and conduits. The great 'Valens Aqueduct' – completed in 373 and named after the reigning emperor at the time, though probably begun under

The cavernous Yerebatan Sarayı lies 25 metres (82 ft) below street level, covers an area measuring 138 metres (452 ft) by 65 metres (213 ft) and can hold 80,000 cubic metres (21 million gallons) of water.

TIMELINE

AD 325 Emperor Constantine founds the *Nova Roma* of Constantinople

373 The Valens Aqueduct is built to bring water to the city

532 The Basilica Cistern is constructed by Justinian after the Nika Riots

1453 Constantinople falls to the Ottoman Turks; the Basilica Cistern is used to provide water for the nearby Topkapı Palace

1544–7 French traveller Pierre Gilles rediscovers the Basilica Cistern

1985 The Basilica Cistern is extensively renovated by the Istanbul Metropolitan Museum

Constantine or his son Constantius (r. 337–61) – still cuts across the suburbs of the city at the end of a water supply system that stretched for almost 100 miles (150 km) into Thrace, and which took 30 years to build. Other sections reached out to different water sources, so the city was never reliant on a single spring. The whole network covered some 250 miles (400 km) in total, including one stretch running 155 miles (250 km), via aqueduct and tunnel, to the plentiful springs of the Istranja Mountains.

The result was the longest water supply system anywhere in the ancient world. However, simply getting water to the city was not enough. In turbulent times, this precious resource also had to be stored in order to preserve supplies in time of drought and as a lifeline for the city if the aqueducts were to be damaged or cut by enemies. It was the solution to this problem that provided Constantinople with its hidden wonder – a system of vast and exquisite underground cisterns, as impressive as many cathedrals but never meant to be seen.

Various basins for retaining water were built in the city during the Roman period, including the above-ground suburban Aetios and Aspar Cisterns and the 'Elephant Stables' reservoir, which between them could hold over half a million cubic metres of water. But suburban cisterns were vulnerable, so from the earliest times the emperors also ordered the construction of huge subterranean water stores, of which around 80 survive to this day in the very heart of the city. According to tradition, the first of these was the Binbirdirek Cistern, built around 330 and known in Turkish as the '1001 columns', although the 5-metre (16-ft) high structure actually contains just 224 columns. But the greatest of all was the Basilica Cistern.

A Forest of Columns

Located just to the southwest of the Hagia Sophia (see pages 164–167), the Basilica Cistern is the largest of Istanbul's underground reservoirs. Indeed, it is one of the largest and most important buildings to have survived from the city's Byzantine period. It was constructed after the Nika Revolt of 532 – a week of rioting that left nearly half the city destroyed and tens of thousands of people dead, after a fight at a chariot race escalated into a serious attempt to overthrow the emperor Justinian (r. 527–65). After the riots, in which the Hagia Sophia was burnt down, Justinian set about rebuilding his city, beginning with the central market area. This took the form of an open-air forum or marketplace surrounded by a basilican hall. The eastern portico of this hall had collapsed as a result of a fire started during the revolt and so, according to the contemporary chronicler Malanas, Justinian's prefect Longinus took the opportunity to carve out a huge cistern beneath the basilica before it was rebuilt.

The cistern itself was excavated from the bedrock. Its walls were made of 4-metre- (13-ft-) thick layers of firebricks, pointed with a waterproof mortar, but the main problem facing the architects was how to support the enormous roof area. This was achieved by building one of the most sophisticated brick cross-vaults in antiquity, which in turn had to be supported on a forest of 336 marble columns, each 9 metres (30 ft) high, in

One of the two Medusa head sculptures in the cistern. They are thought to have been taken from the Temple of Apollo at Didyma on Turkey's Mediterranean coast.

A FORGOTTEN TREASURE

The Basilica Cistern provided water to Constantinople throughout the Byzantine period and has survived the city's many sieges, sackings and earthquakes for nearly 1500 years.

But while the cistern itself survived, the complex hydraulic system of which it formed a part began to deteriorate in the Middle Ages, probably due to earthquakes damaging the tunnels and aqueducts that brought water to the city. By the late 12th century the system was derelict and the Basilican Cistern, though still regularly filling with water from local rainfall, had fallen out of use.

In 1453 Constantinople fell to the Ottoman Turks. The city's new masters initially used the cistern as a well to provide water for the sultan's Topkapı Palace, but from the 16th century onwards the Ottomans built their own water supply system, which relied on sources in Halkalı and the Belgrade Forest to bring running water to the city. The Basilica Cistern became a reservoir to hold water for the gardens of the Topkapı Palace. Apart from the gardeners who worked there, common knowledge of it was lost.

The cistern was finally 'rediscovered' by the French traveller Pierre Gilles, who visited Istanbul between 1544 and 1547. While exploring the city he was told how people living on the First Hill drew their water from holes in their basements, through which they could even sometimes catch fish. Gilles managed to gain access to one of these 'wells' and descended into the cavernous interior with a small rowing boat and a torch, becoming possibly the first man to see the interior of the cistern since its construction.

Thanks to Gilles' publications, knowledge of the cistern grew and it soon became a necessary stopover for all visitors to the city. By the 20th century, however, the bustling modern city above the cistern had started to impinge on this subterranean world, with major cracks appearing in 1968. Urgent remedial work was carried out on the columns and roofs, and in 1985 a fuller restoration project was begun by the Istanbul Metropolitan Museum. During these renovations, the cistern was drained for the first time since Justinian's day, and in 1987 a metre- (3 ft-) thick layer of mud was removed, weighing 50,000 tons in total. Excavating this layer of silt brought to light the original brick pavement and the huge Medusa-head column bases. Today the cistern is one of the city's principal tourist attractions, with its forest of columns reflected in a mirror-like sheet of water providing the perfect backdrop for concerts and other public events.

12 rows of 28. As this was not a visible public building, there was no need to go to the expense of carving new columns and so ancient examples were scoured from around the region. As a result, the cistern today is a treasure-trove of architectural elements which might otherwise have been destroyed but which found a new life below the streets of Constantinople. Two of the columns are even supported on gigantic carved Medusa heads (a sea nymph from Greek mythology).

This vast columned hall was originally kept full of water, fed by pipes in the eastern wall, thus ensuring a constant supply of water to the public buildings in Constantinople's oldest quarter – the First Hill (the modern Istanbul district of Sultanahmet), which included the Hagia Sophia and the emperor's palace. With only the Corinthian, Doric and Ionic capitals of the pillars protruding above the 900,000 square metres (9.7 million sq ft) of water it contained, its sheer scale and architectural wonder lay hidden in subterranean gloom. Only nowadays, with the water depth kept at a constant 1 metre (3.3 ft), can the full magnificence of Justinian's 'Sunken Palace' again be seen.

Hôryû-Gakumonji

Early seat of Buddhist learning in Japan

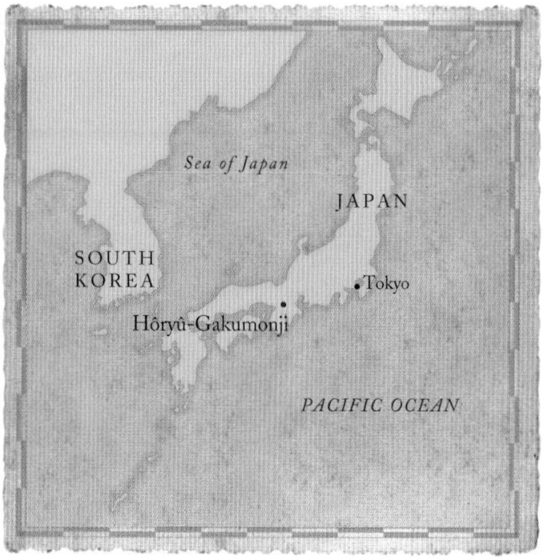

IN THE TOWN OF IKARUGA in Nara prefecture on the island of Honshu, Japan, stands a temple complex that has been in continuous use since at least AD 670. Built almost entirely of interlocking pieces of timber, held together without nails, its intricate halls and pagoda are thought to be the oldest wooden buildings anywhere in the world.

The Hôryû-Gakumonji complex was begun between 601 and 607, in the Asuka period, by Prince Shôtoku, (523–623; also known as Prince Umayado), son of the emperor Yomei (r. 585–7). In 593 he had become regent for his aunt (some sources say his mother) Suiko, the first woman ever to ascend to the Chrysanthemum throne of Japan. Working with her, Prince Shôtoku embarked upon a series of reforms in the country, instituting social welfare and building programmes and, most importantly of all, re-establishing trade and cultural links with China. By sending envoys to that country for the first time since the fifth century, he opened the way for Chinese craftsmen, artists and monks to come to his kingdom, where he eagerly adopted elements of their philosophy, religions and administration. Reforming the old hereditary legal system, he established 12 ranks of court official, each easily identified by their different coloured cap, and enacted the 'Seventeen Article Constitution' based on concepts of Confucian ethics.

But it was in religious matters that Shôtoku brought about the most profound change. Turning away from the native Japanese Shinto religion, he adopted Chinese Buddhism. According to the *Chronicles of Japan*, the emperor Yomei had originally vowed to erect the temple if he recovered from an illness. However, he had died and so it was left to his son and aunt to begin the work. The temple they built is a unique fusion of foreign and local influences, combining elements of Chinese Eastern Han and Northern Wei architecture, along with elements from the Three Kingdoms of Korea, all slightly subverted by a distinctly Japanese asymmetry.

The Pagoda and the Kondo

The temple consists of two main areas, the Sai-in to the west and the ancillary Tô-in to the east. In the cloistered courtyard of the Sai-in stands a five-storey pagoda, the oldest in Japan, which towers 32.5 metres (106 ft) over the site. The pagoda is built around a single huge timber, which dendrochronological dating has revealed was cut down in 594. As such, this may represent the sole surviving element from the first temple, which, according to the *Chronicles of Japan*, burned down in 670 and was replaced with the present structure.

'When the emperor who ruled the land from the Ikenobe palace fell ill, in the year hinoe-uma *[586?] he summoned the empress and Imperial prince, and made a vow that he would build a temple ...'*

INSCRIPTION ON THE YAKUSHI NYORAI IMAGE IN THE KONDO AT HÔRYÛ GAKUMONJI

This 30-metre (100-ft) cedar trunk is set on a central foundation stone, which is buried 3 metres (10 ft) below ground level and incorporates a small niche containing Buddhist relics. The rest of the building is then constructed around this central timber, rising in five roofed steps. There are no internal floors above ground level; the pagoda was never meant to be climbed, but instead represents a diagram of the Buddhist cosmos, the central pillar being the world axis that joins heaven and earth, the five storeys representing the terraces of the

The Hôryû-Gakumonji ('Learning Temple of the Flourishing Law') complex stands as a testament to Prince Shôtoku's adoption of the new creed of Buddhism, which was introduced into Japan from China. This building is the Yumedono, or 'Hall of Dreams'.

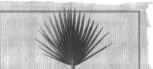

TIMELINE

AD 601–7 First temple of the Hôryû-Gakumonji complex is completed under the direction of Prince Shôtuku

623 Death of Prince Shôtuku

670 Fire razes the temple complex to the ground

714 Rebuilding of the temple complex is completed

739 The Yumedono (Hall of Dreams) is added to the complex

1374 The Hôryû-Gakumonji temple is extensively disassembled for repair

1943–54 Major period of reconstruction of the pagoda

1949 The Kondo is badly damaged in a fire

1993 Hôryû-Gakumonji is inscribed as a World Heritage Site by UNESCO

Buddhist universe and the nine rings – carved into the central post where it emerges from the top roof – signifying the nine heavens of the gods.

At ground level, in the centre of the pagoda, stands a plaster grotto representing Mount Sumeru, the mythical centre of the Buddhist terrestrial world, surrounded by four clay-figure scenes from the eighth century that draw on Buddhist legend, and which visitors to the temple can view from all sides.

Next to the pagoda is the two-storey Kondo, the main hall of the Sai-in. Originally this building contained seventh-century frescoes painted on 50 walls, but these were removed in 1949 after a fire. Also in this building, under a canopy representing heavenly paradise, is the Shaka Triad, created, according to the inscription on its base, in 623 to commemorate the death of Prince Shôtoku. The three (originally gilded) bronze statues show a lifesize image of the historical Buddha sitting between two enlightened beings (*boddhisattva*). Its exact meaning remains a mystery; the Buddha figure is making a hand gesture that is unique in Buddhist art, while the enlightened beings are shown holding some small nut-like objects that have never been identified. The symbolism may possibly relate to the deification of Shôtoku, who came to be regarded after his death as a Buddhist saint for his work in spreading the religion across Japan. The triad may therefore represent not just Buddha and his attendants, but also Shôtoku, his wife and his mother.

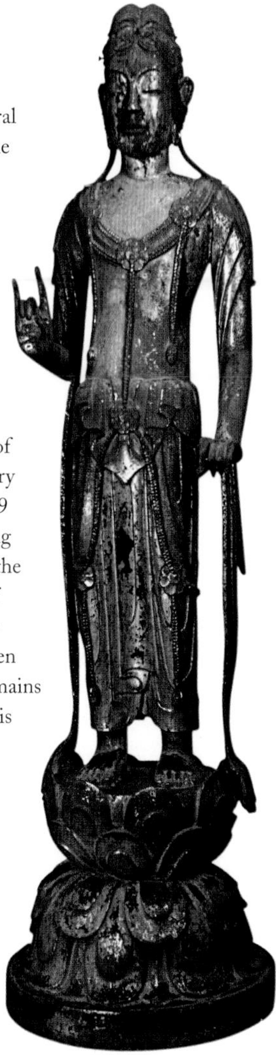

Alongside the statue of Kannon in the Yumedono, there are numerous other images of this boddhisattva *at Hôryû-ji. This carving dates from the seventh century.*

A Vengeful Spirit?

The main building of the Tô-in is the Yumedono or 'Hall of Dreams'. This octagonal structure was built on the site of Prince Shôtoku's palace in 739 as an addition to the main Hôryû-ji. Inside stands a unique statue of the enlightened being known in Japan as Kannon (and elsewhere as Avalokiteshvara or Guan-yin), who embodies compassion. What is unusual about this figure is that it was apparently never meant to be seen. For centuries it was covered in layers of silk until an American academic unwrapped it in 1884. While hidden statues are not uncommon in Buddhism, they are usually accessible to priests and honoured guests but this Kannon was apparently hidden from all eyes from the date of its dedication.

Why this should be is still a matter of much debate. The statue has several uncommon features, which have led some scholars to suggest that it may be another representation of Prince Shôtoku. As his family line ended in 643 with the forced suicide of his son, one school of thought suggests that his statue was wrapped up to cover the gaze of his vengeful spirit. It is also argued that this is why the figure's halo is not suspended on a post behind him, as is usual in such statues, but instead has been driven through the back of his head, voodoo style, on a metal spike. The proponents of this theory also point to the Chûmon or Middle Gateway at the Hôryû-ji, which, uniquely in Buddhist architecture, has a central pillar obstructing the main entrance. While some see this as just another example of the Japanese preference for a slight asymmetry in their architecture, others claim that the pillar deliberately blocks the doorway in order to keep in the angry spirit of Prince Shôtoku.

Nevertheless, the terrible consequences predicted by the Hôryû-ji priests when the statue was uncovered have not come to pass. Today, despite fires and 1300 turbulent years of history, the Hôryû Gakumonji remains Japan's oldest and most famous monastery and seminary.

DATING HÔRYÛ-GAKUMONJI

Hôryû Gakumonji (or Hôryû-ji for short) may well contain the oldest wooden buildings still in use today, but it has not survived the centuries entirely unscathed. One of the greatest controversies surrounding the site is the exact date at which the halls and pagoda were built.

Although a Japanese historical source maintains that the original Hôryû-ji was razed to the ground in 670, as there is no record of its reconstruction this claim was given little credence until the 20th century. In 1939, however, archaeological excavations located the site of the original Hôryû-ji, which lies 100 metres (330 ft) to the southeast of the present temple and which was laid out on a far more traditional Chinese plan.

Accordingly, it is now thought that the current site dates from the rebuilding of 670. Tree-ring dating of the temple's timbers has helped reveal the true age of each building. Apart from the huge cedar trunk at the centre of the pagoda, dated to 594, it appears that most of the pagoda wood was cut around 673, while the timber for the Kondo was felled slightly earlier, in 668–9, and the Chûmon gateway somewhat later, in 699.

Whether the cedar trunk in the pagoda survived the original fire or was simply another trunk kept in storage remains a mystery, but we do know that the rebuilt complex was finally completed by around 714, with the Yumedono and a lecture hall being added on the site of Shôtoku's palace in 739. From then on, the temple regularly appears in the records, with the addition of new buildings for the monks and the refurbishment of some old structures that may have either decayed or burnt down in the interim. These include the Yumedono, whose modern form dates from 1230.

However, the temple has remained in use throughout, and – possibly due to its relatively isolated position – has come through the worst upheavals in Japan's history unharmed. Its unique form of construction has contributed to its longevity; being built from wood without the use of nails, it has been a relatively straightforward task to disassemble, repair and rebuild it. For example, it is known to have been dismantled in 1374 and 1603, while the pagoda was taken down and repaired between 1943 and 1954. Almost miraculously this wooden wonder has not fallen prey to a major fire although the Kondo was badly damaged in a blaze in 1949, after which the delicate frescoes had to be removed from its interior. Today, however, the site remains in plan much as it looked in the seventh century, while the pagoda and Kondo are still functioning as their original imperial builders intended.

Borobudur

'Mountain of a thousand statues'

BOROBUDUR ON THE ISLAND of Java, which for much of its history was no more than a local myth about a 'mountain of a thousand statues', is now the most visited tourist attraction in Indonesia and one of the greatest Buddhist monuments on earth.

Lying in what was once deep jungle between four volcanoes in an ancient caldera in central Java, the Borobudur temple is shrouded in mystery. There are no inscriptions at the site to tell us who built it, no records of the architects, sculptors and stonemasons who designed it and no trace of the thousands of workmen who must have spent years working on it. All that remains is a local legend that the heavenly architect Gunadhama built Borobudur in a single day, laying a curse on anyone who might dare climb to the summit. From the similarities between some of the carvings at the site and drawings in royal charters, we may surmise that the temple was built at the height of the Shailendra dynasty sometime between 760 and 830. The Shailendra were a foreign ruling family, probably originating in southern India or Indochina, who came to power around 750 after the collapse of the mainland Southeast Asian Funan kingdom.

The Path to Enlightenment

During their rule, a particular form of Buddhism, known as Mahayana Buddhism, flourished on Java. One of the key tenets of this creed was that kings should do everything in their power to gain religious merit during their rule. Followers of Mahayana Buddhism, which developed around the same time as Christianity, did not aim to reach a personal Nirvana, as in other branches of the religion. Instead, they aspired to become *bodhisattvas*, or enlightened beings, who opted to remain in the cycle of birth, death and reincarnation so that they might help others to achieve Nirvana. These principles lay at the heart of the construction of Borobudur; the whole layout of the temple was a symbolic depiction of the path to Nirvana, which pilgrims to the site could follow, from the huge lower terraces of the temple to the silent stupas at the summit.

The temple takes the form of an artificial mountain, a representation of Mount Sumeru, the central world-mountain in Buddhist cosmology. Built of a local volcanic stone and probably once coated in vividly painted plaster, it rises like a stepped pyramid in three tiers. The square base measures 122 metres by 116 metres (400 x 380 ft) and is decorated with hundreds of reliefs

Stupas on the terraces of the Borobudur Temple on Java. The largest Buddhist monument in the world, Borobudur represents a map of the cosmos as conceived in Mahayana Buddhism.

'There was once a terrible drought, and a Brahman told the king he would have to sacrifice one hundred living beings to bring it to an end. Unable to do this the King proclaimed that he would select the necessary victims from amongst his worst subjects. At this news, his subjects all became virtuous, and the drought stopped.'

STORY TOLD ON A SECTION OF PANELS FROM BOROBUDUR

TIMELINE

c.AD 800 The Mahayana Buddhist temple of Borobudur is built on Java, during the heyday of the Shailendra dynasty

9th century Shailendra dynasty is expelled from Java; Borobudur goes into decline

1006 Eruption of Mt Merapi causes depopulation of the area around Borobudur

15th century Population of Java converts to Islam

1814 An expedition organized by Sir Stamford Raffles rediscovers Borobudur

1873 Publication of the first detailed study of the site at Borobudur

1975–82 Major project for the reconstruction of Borobudur undertaken by the Indonesian government and UNESCO

1991 Borobudur is designated a World Heritage Site by UNESCO

depicting earthly desires, in what is known as the 'realm of feeling'. This is the lowest realm of the Mahayana Buddhist universe and the reliefs show how good and bad deeds will affect the form of an individual's next reincarnation and demonstrate how foolish and wasteful it is to spend one's life in trivial entertainments.

Once pilgrims had walked around this level, a staircase (one runs up the middle of each face of the monument) then took them to the middle tier of five square terraces. Here the reliefs show the 'realm of form', portraying events from the life of the Gautama Buddha (the historical Buddha Siddhartha Gautama, *c.*563–483 BC) and stories from his previous lives. As pilgrims walked around each higher terrace, the scenes became more and more static, emphasizing the distance from the everyday corporeal world and the need for contemplation and meditation.

The final level, reached via another staircase, consists of circular terraces. The symbolic significance of this shape is that the temple, if viewed from above, is in the form of the mandala, a square (representing the earth) enclosing a circle (representing the heavens). On these higher levels there is very little decoration and the reliefs give way to 72 bell-shaped stupas – stone latticework enclosures containing statues of the Buddha. These denote levels of incomplete enlightenment, and lead up to the large central stupa at the very top, which is solid, meaning that the Buddha figure inside cannot be seen at all. This represents the realm of formlessness, a place free from the constraints of the material world.

For the Shailendra kings and all the people who assisted in the construction of Borobudur, building and visiting this site were acts of faith in themselves. The temple was the ultimate pilgrimage site where – in climbing to the summit and always keeping the reliefs to their right – the faithful were presented with a visual rendition of their beliefs and a roadmap of how to live their lives and reach a state of enlightenment, either in this life or future incarnations.

Reclaimed by the Jungle

The scale of the construction needed for such a project was vast. The whole monument is solid, with no internal structures, rising some 31 metres (102 ft) above its base and contains around 56,000 cubic metres (almost 2 million cubic feet) of stone held in place without the use of mortar. Adorning these terraces are 100 monster-headed waterspouts, which were designed to channel away the torrential tropical rain that falls on the site. There are 2670 reliefs, each panel a metre high, while originally, before looting, there were 504 statues of Buddha, 432 sitting in the lotus position and another 72 inside the smaller stupas. The proper pilgrimage route, taking in every relief, is a walk of 3 miles (5 km) and each level is carefully screened by retaining walls to ensure that until pilgrims reach the top tier they cannot see the other levels or the outside world. This helps them focus on the path to enlightenment.

One of the 2670 individual bas-relief panels at Borobudur. Many of these are arranged in narrative sequence, telling the stories of Buddhist seekers after enlightenment.

The sheer size of Borobudur created its own problems. The drainage system proved inadequate and the huge weight of the structure caused the temple to sink and the base to spread. To prevent a total collapse, early in its history the bottom level

RESCUED FROM NEGLECT

The fate of Borobudur during the Middle Ages is uncertain. The site is thought to have fallen out of use in the 11th century and was definitely abandoned by the time the people of Java converted to Islam in the 15th century.

The temple was not destroyed, however, probably due to the strong culture of religious tolerance on the island. When the British colonial administrator Sir Thomas Stamford Raffles (1781–1826) was appointed lieutenant governor-general of Java by the East India Company in 1811, he brought with him a fascination for local antiques and antiquities. Stories of the 'mountain of a thousand statues' spurred him on to arrange an expedition into the interior in search of this lost temple. He appointed a Dutch engineer, H.C. Cornelius, to lead the expedition, who, with a team of 200 men, set off into the dense jungle, guided by locals who knew of a site called Chandi ('temple') Borobudur near the village of Bumisegoro.

By the time Raffles was able to join it, the expedition had located what looked like a ruined pyramid with a bell-shaped structure on the top. Raffles immediately realized that this was a Buddhist temple and that the 'bell' was a stupa. He estimated, quite accurately, that it dated from between the eighth and tenth centuries.

Raffles wrote a brief description of his discovery in his *History of Java* (1830) but he was unable to describe the full extent of the site as it was largely covered in vegetation and layers of volcanic ash. Sadly, though, his publication did bring the site to world attention and soon antiquities dealers were looting Borobudur, smashing the stupas and decapitating the Buddhas to sell to Western museums to satisfy their craving for the exotic.

It was 1835 before the site was finally cleared of undergrowth and another 38 years before the first detailed study of Borobudur was published. By this stage the temple was becoming dangerously decayed. Looters were stripping the site of whatever decorations they could carry, while the incessant tropical rains had undermined the central core of the temple, causing its floors to sag inwards and its terrace walls to collapse. So parlous was its state of disrepair that in 1882 the chief inspector of cultural artefacts suggested dismantling the entire structure and placing the reliefs and sculptures in museums.

Thankfully this advice wasn't taken and small-scale restoration projects continued through the 20th century until Indonesian independence in 1945. The fate of this iconic structure temple now became a political issue, and in 1968 the 'Save Borobudur Campaign' was launched by the Indonesian government and UNESCO. In 1975 a full restoration programme began, involving the moving of over one million stones and the closure of the site for a decade. Despite a bomb outrage in 1985, the programme was a success and in 1991 Borobudur became a World Heritage Site.

was entirely encased in a new plinth, which acted as a retaining wall. This necessitated the covering up of the bottom level of reliefs; they remained forgotten until 1885, when their rediscovery allowed the accurate dating of the monument.

Of course, these repairs fundamentally compromised the whole purpose of the temple, and so Borobudur was in use for a relatively short period. In the mid-ninth century the Shailendra dynasty was driven from Java to Sumatra. At some point after this the site fell out of use, although there is no definitive evidence as to exactly when or why. Most scholars believe that the eruption of the nearby volcano of Merapi in around 1006 probably forced the local population to abandon the area, after which the temple was rapidly engulfed in jungle. Indonesia's greatest monument then remained hidden and neglected until the 19th century.

Ellora

Rock-cut shrines of three great religions

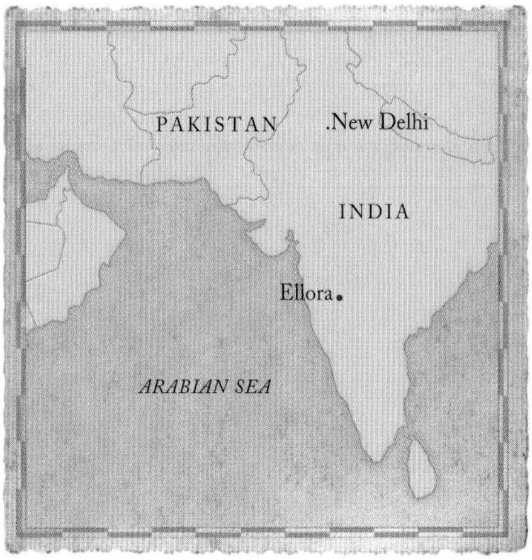

JUST UNDER 20 MILES (32 km) to the northwest of Aurangabad, in the Indian state of Maharashtra, runs a ridge of sheer basalt cliffs that are home to one of the most brilliant architectural feats of the ancient world. Here, cut into the living rock, stand the Ellora Caves, a series of 34 cave temples dating from the fifth to the tenth centuries AD, which mark the apogee of Indian rock art.

Nowhere on earth has more rock-cut temples than India. This tradition lasted for over a millennium, some of the earliest examples (dating from *c.*100 BC) being found at Ajanta near Ellora. The first Buddhist shrines in India were usually created from natural caves, extended and carved to mimic the architecture of earlier free-standing wooden shrines. But at Ellora this tradition was vastly expanded upon by three mutually tolerant religions – Buddhism, Hinduism and Jainism – all striving not simply to decorate caves but to mould the rock of the mountain into entire architectural schemes.

Grandiose and Intimate

The earliest temples in the south of the range are Buddhist *viharas* (monasteries) cut from the cliff face, in much the same way as the Nabataean monuments of Petra in Jordan (see pages 102–107). Beyond the façade of each lies a series of interconnecting rooms dug into the rock, including kitchens, dormitories and usually a shrine. These are not gloomy caves, however. Passing through the multi-tiered entrance to the Visvakarma Temple in cave 10 (known as the 'Carpenter's Cave') visitors suddenly find themselves in a cathedral-like void, a huge apsidal room, 26 metres (85 ft) long and nearly 11 metres (36 ft) high. At one end of this chamber is seated a 4.5-metre (15-ft) high statue of a Buddha at prayer. High above, the roof is carved into a series of ribs like the upturned hull of a ship, mimicking the roof beams of wooden temples.

To the north stand the Jain temples, the most recent structures at the site, which date from the eighth to 11th centuries. Their decoration is even more elaborate than in the Buddhist caves, although on a smaller scale, reflecting the more personal and ascetic devotion of the Jains. In marked contrast to the grandeur of some of the earlier caves, the lively carvings found here – which would originally have been painted in vivid colours – display a delicate eye for detail. This intricacy of execution chimes with the ancient beliefs of the Jains (the oldest surviving religion in India) in the sanctity of all life, human and non-human, and the immortality of the soul.

A Monolithic Masterpiece

But if the Buddhist and Jain monuments are impressive in their own right, they are truly modest compared to the mid-period (seventh and eighth century) Hindu monuments in the cliffs in the centre of the range. Begun under the auspices of the Rashtrakuta dynasty that ruled a substantial part of central and southern India from the sixth to the 13th centuries, they reached their pinnacle in the temple of Kailasanatha, commissioned by Krishna I (757–73). The scale and construction of this building has left many visitors speechless,

Vertically excavated from the mountainside, the Kailasanatha Temple at Ellora is a breathtaking example of rock-hewn architecture dating from the mid-eighth century.

TIMELINE

5th to 7th centuries AD Buddhist caves at Ellora (caves 1–12), including the 'Carpenter's Cave', are constructed

7th to 9th centuries Hindu caves at Ellora (caves 13–29) are created

8th century Krishna I of the Rashtrakuta dynasty orders construction of the Kailasanatha Temple

c.800–1000 Building of the Jain caves (caves 30–34) at Ellora

10th century Earliest traveller's account of a visit to the Ellora caves, by the Arab geographer Al-Masudi

12th century Tradition of rock-cutting edifices dies out in India

19th century The Ellora caves fall under the stewardship of the Hindu Holkar dynasty of Indore and thereafter the Muslim Nizams of Hyderabad

1895 James Fergusson and James Burgess of the Archaeological Survey of India publish a study of cave art at Ellora and other sites

1983 Cave complex at Ellora is designated a World Heritage Site by UNESCO

unable to comprehend how such a marvel could have been created. What is so spectacular about the Kailasanatha Temple is not simply its size or exquisite decoration but the fact that, rather than being built of cut stone or carved into the face of the cliff, the structure was cut out of the living rock from the top down, chiselling a whole mountain, by hand, into the shape of a temple. It is estimated that it would have taken 7000 labourers over 100 years to gradually carve away around 200,000 tons of hard basalt to leave the monument standing in its own 33-metre- (108-ft-) deep basin, which covers a total area five times that of the Parthenon in Athens.

The Kailasanatha Temple is in fact a whole religious complex dedicated to the god Shiva. After passing through an elaborately decorated two-tier gateway, the visitor crosses a stone bridge, also cut from the living rock, which leads to a galleried courtyard. This space is decorated with scenes from Hindu mythology and contains a huge image of Shiva's gatekeeper, the sacred bull Nandi, facing the temple. Beyond, across another stone bridge, lies the temple proper, whose plinth is carved to make it appear as though the building is resting on the backs of enormous elephants. This pyramidal structure is designed to represent Mount Kailash, a Himalayan peak in Tibet said to be the home of Lord Shiva (and which, in deference to that belief, has still never been climbed). The Kailasanatha Temple was originally covered in white stucco to mimic the snow-clad slopes of the mountain.

Inside, the assembly halls and temple rooms are decorated with images of the divine followers of Shiva and Vishnu along with scenes from the *Ramayana*, an ancient Sanskrit epic and an important part of the Hindu canon. Here we see Rama, an incarnation of the god Vishnu, battling with the demon Ravana, and Ravana uprooting and shaking Mount Kailash, disturbing Shiva and his wife Parvati. Central to the whole complex is the large carved *lingam*, a short cylindrical pillar, the traditional symbol of Shiva. Early Western visitors to the site wrongly took the *lingam* to be a crude phallic idol; writers such as John Seely in the 1820s euphemistically referred to it as an '*emblem of the generative power*' and drew a veil over the ceremonies performed around it, as they seemed to him to be of '*an impure kind*'.

If it had been carved from cut blocks of quarried stone, in terms of craftsmanship the Kailasanatha Temple complex would certainly be on a par with the finest medieval cathedrals of Europe, but given that its rooms, doors, piers pilasters, windows, relief and roofs are all cut from the very bedrock itself, it is unsurpassed in its sheer technical virtuosity. With nearly every face of every building, save for some plain galleried exteriors, covered with dynamic reliefs it is also a record in stone of the beliefs of the people of Maharashtra in the first millennium AD (and probably earlier). Its survival to this day in remarkable condition is also a testament to the religious tolerance of the era, which allowed Buddhist, Hindu and Jain monuments to stand alongside each other in peaceful coexistence.

> *'Each stroke of the chisel upon the surface of the interior was as delicate and exact as if a jewel instead of a granite mountain was being carved.'*
>
> William Eleroy Curtis – *Modern India* (1905)

A DYING ART

The temples of Ellora represent the high point of a long tradition in India of cutting buildings from the living rock. The practice probably dates back to early Buddhist missionaries, who began adapting caves as monasteries around the second century BC in the Western Ghats (a mountain range in northwestern India).

With trade came wealth, and soon these natural rock shelters were being enlarged and decorated, creating a unique style of architecture in which the natural walls and façades of caverns were chiselled into architectural forms that mimicked the wooden free-standing structures of the day. Indeed, so closely did these follow their wooden counterparts that some craftsmen went as far as carving the swirls of woodgrain into the walls and ceilings of their modified caves.

In the Palava kingdom of southern India (sixth to eighth centuries AD) architects took this idea a step further, and rather than simply expanding and adapting caves instituted the tradition of monolithic temple building. This involved carving lifesize copies of free-standing wooden temples not from caves but from single outcrops of rock. It was this technique and style that was employed at Ellora to create the most spectacular building there, the Kailasanatha Temple.

Eventually, the advent of a new technology – that of constructing free-standing buildings from quarried and cut blocks – brought an end to the tradition of rock-cut structures. The increase in speed, the reduction in cost and the flexibility of being able to build virtually anywhere proved irresistible. Some rock-cut work did continue, notably at Jain sites, where the sheer patience required to carve a building from bedrock was considered a form of devotion in itself, but temples on the scale of Kailasanatha would never be built again. Increasingly, the few remaining rock cutters turned their attention to purely civil engineering problems, such as building cisterns and cutting steps into cliff faces, and by the 12th century the tradition had died out.

Cave 10 (the 'Carpenter's Cave') in the Buddhist part of the Ellora cave complex is an exquisitely vaulted chamber containing a statue of the Buddha.

Ellora survived, however, thanks to its relatively isolated position and the sheer monumentality of its buildings. Beyond the decay of 1000 years of subsequent history, only the predations of the Mughal emperors and the occasional ignorant tourist have damaged the site, and then only to a minor degree, making Ellora one of the few ancient wonders to survive into the modern world virtually untouched.

Glossary

anastylosis An archaeological reconstruction technique, in which a ruined monument or object is restored after careful study and measurement, using original elements where possible.

aqueduct An artificial channel that conveys water from one location to another in particular any bridge that carries a watercourse rather than a railway or road.

Archimedean screw A machine consisting of a screw inside a hollow pipe possibly invented by Archimedes in around 250 BC and used to raise water from a lower to a higher level.

basalt A common volcanic rock rich in iron and magnesium. It is usually grey to black and fine-grained.

basilica A Roman public building usually located in the forum of a Roman town. In the early Christian period the term came by extension to refer to a large and important church with special papal privileges or conforming to the same architectural plan as a basilica.

bioturbation The mixing of layers of soil due to the action of animals and plants, in particular burrowing animals.

Bodhisattva In the Buddhist context literally 'enlightened existence'. In Mahayana Buddhism, it usually refers to a being that compassionately refrains from entering nirvana themselves in order to save others.

Bronze Age The period in the development of human civilization when the most advanced common metal technology was bronze. As a technological development it has no set dates, occurring in different parts of the world at different times where it has occurred at all. Where it is present, it occurs between the Stone Age and the Iron Age.

carbon-14 dating The scientific measurement of the amount of decay of the long-lived radioactive isotope Carbon 14, which is found in all organic materials and can be used to date the material.

cella The inner chamber of a classical temple.

chryselephantine Literally 'gold and ivory', a term for a type of classical statue built around a wooden frame with ivory plates used to represent skin and gold leaf or plate to represent clothing and hair.

cistern A receptacle for storing liquids, usually water. Large municipal cisterns are in effect covered reservoirs.

classical The art, language and culture of a civilization considered to be at its height. In archaeology the term is often used to refer to the ancient Greek and Roman worlds. In the New World it is applied to the height of Mayan civilization.

clepsydra An ancient Greek form of timer or water clock that operates by regulating the inflow and outflow of water from a vessel.

colonnade In classical architecture, a long sequence of columns joined by their entablature, either free-standing or around a building.

corbel In architecture, a piece of stone jutting out of a wall designed to carry any load above it.

cornice Generally any horizontal decorative moulding that crowns a building or furniture element. The cornice on a building is often designed to throw rainwater clear of the walls.

dendrochronological dating The counting of the annual growth rings in the trunk of a tree to calculate its age. As the width of each ring varies depending on the climate in a particular year in a particular region, a unique pattern forms and this can be matched to similar patterns in the remains of older trees found in the archaeological record and hence tree-ring lines can be extended back longer than any one tree has lived.

Doric/Ionic/Corinthian order The three orders or organizational systems of Ancient Greek or classical architecture. The Doric order is characterized by fluted columns with plain capitals, the Ionic order by scrolled capitals and the Corinthian order by acanthus leaf capitals.

entasis In classical architecture the gentle swelling or bulge in the centre of a column, which corrects the illusion of concavity produced by parallel straight lines.

exedra A semicircular recess, often crowned by a half-dome, which is usually set into a building's façade.

fresco A group of related painting types, in which paint is applied directly to plaster, usually whilst the plaster is still wet.

Hellenistic Relating to the influence of Greek culture and colonization over the non-Greek lands from the time of their conquest by Alexander the Great in the 4th century BC to the rise of Roman rule in the Mediterranean.

henge A prehistoric, usually circular, architectural structure enclosed by a boundary earthwork that usually comprises a ditch with an external bank. Internal components may include timber or stone circles, post rings, mounds and pits.

hypocaust An ancient Roman system of central heating by which air from a fire was conducted under floors and up through hollow tiles in the walls to heat a room.

hypogeum An underground, pre-Christian temple or a tomb often containing human remains.

(lacunar) coffering A panelled or coffered ceiling, decorated with a pattern of recessed panels.

lateral thrust The sideways force exerted on the walls of a building, often by the roof.

lingam A short cylindrical pillar, the traditional symbol of Shiva, which early western visitors to Indian archaeological sites often took wrongly to be a crude phallic idol.

low relief/bas-relief Carving in low relief in which objects project from the background less than half their true depth.

magnetometry The measurement and mapping of minute variations in the direction and strength of the Earth's magnetic field which can indicate the presence of buried structures and objects, notably magnetic metals such as iron.

megalith A large stone which has been used as an element in a structure or monument, either alone or together with other large stones.

Mesopotamia Literally 'the land between the rivers'. An ancient region between the Tigris and Euphrates rivers covering parts of present-day Iraq, Syria, Iran and Turkey.

metope In classical architecture, a rectangular architectural element that fills the space between two triglyphs in a Doric frieze.

mica One of a group of minerals that can form thin silicate sheets due to the hexagonal sheet-like arrangement of their atoms. The word is thought to be derived from the Latin word *micare*, to glitter.

Neoclassical A style of art, music and literature etc. based on classical models; used especially to refer to a style of 18th-century art and architecture influenced by the rediscovery of Roman sites such as Pompeii.

Neolithic The New Stone Age. The last of the three periods within the Stone Age. The period begins with the Palaeolithic (Old Stone Age), is followed by the Mesolithic (Middle Stone Age) and ends with the Neolithic (New Stone Age). The period is characterised by the advent of farming and ceramics and the development of finely flaked stone tools. It is followed in Europe by the development of metal technology leading into the Bronze Age.

obsidian A naturally occurring volcanic glass used in prehistory to form blades and projectile points as it can hold an extremely fine edge.

passage tomb A burial structure usually dating to the Neolithic and of megalithic form, where the burial chamber is reached along a distinct passage. The most simple form has one single chamber while other may have sub-chambers leading off from the main burial chamber. Externally the tombs are sometimes covered with a mound of earth or rocks.

pediment In classical architecture an element consisting of the triangular section found above the entablature, usually supported by columns. The triangular area within the pediment was often decorated with sculptures and reliefs depicting scenes of Greek and Roman mythology.

pendentive Triangular segments of a sphere that taper to points at the bottom and spread at the top to establish the continuous circular or elliptical base needed for the dome hence allowing the placing of a circular dome over a square room or an elliptical dome over a rectangular room.

porphyry A variety of igneous rock consisting of large-grained crystals, such as feldspar or quartz, dispersed in a fine-grained matrix. In the classical sense the purple-red form of this stone, prized in Egypt and later in Imperial Rome for its appearance.

portico The formal entrance to a building consisting of columns at regular intervals supporting a roof, either of or in the style of classical temples.

pozzolana (puteolanum) A fine, sandy volcanic ash, originally discovered in Italy near Vesuvius. When finely ground and mixed with lime it creates a hydraulic cement and can be used to make a strong mortar that will also set under water.

remote sensing In archaeology, a general term for a group of methods for locating buried features that are not readily visible on the surface. They include aerial photography, magnetometry, ground-penetrating radar and resistivity.

resistivity study A scientific technique in archaeology in which buried features are located by mapping the relative electrical resistance across a site, as this is affected by buried features such as ditches, banks and walls.

sarsen stone Blocks of sandstone found mainly on Salisbury Plain, the Marlborough Downs and in Kent. They are the remains of a now heavily eroded layer of sandstone that once covered much of southern England.

serpentine A group of common rock-forming hydrous magnesium iron phyllosilicate minerals, often with a mottled green appearance.

stele/stela A stone or wooden slab, generally taller than it is wide, erected for funerary or commemorative purposes, most usually decorated with the names and titles of the builder or person memorialized either painted onto the slab or carved into it.

stratigraphic excavation The excavation of an archaeological site, paying particular attention to the order and relative positions of layers (strata) of soils and sediments to deduce a sequence of events.

stupa A mound-like structure containing Buddhist relics.

stylobate In classical Greek architecture the top step of the stepped platform on which the colonnades of a temple were placed – in other words, the 'floor' of the temple.

triglyph An architectural term for the vertically channelled tablets of a Doric frieze, so called because the two vertical channels divide the tablet into three parts.

trilithon A structure consisting of two large vertical stones supporting a third stone set horizontally across the top, commonly used in megalithic monuments.

votive Something dedicated or given in consequence or fulfilment of a vow. Often applied in archaeology to objects deposited in a ritual context.

ziggurat A stepped tower or pyramid in which each successive stage is smaller than the one below. The term is most often applied to the distinctive stepped temple mounds found in Sumerian, Babylonian and Assyrian cities.

Index

Page numbers in **bold** type indicate main references to the various topics; those in *italic* refer to illustrations

S

T

U

V

W

X

Y

Z

Further Reading

Newgrange
O'Kelly, M.J., O'Kelly, C. *Newgrange: Archaeology, Art and Legend (New Aspects of Antiquity)* (Thames & Hudson,1988)

Stonehenge
Chippindale, C. *Stonehenge Complete* (Thames & Hudson, 1994)

Great Pyramid of Khufu and the Sphinx
Romer, J. *The Great Pyramid* (Cambridge University Press, 2007)

Mohenjo Daro
Kenoyer, J.M. *Indus Cities, Towns and Villages. Ancient Cities of the Indus Valley Civilization* (Islamabad: American Institute of Pakistan Studies, 1998)

The Great Ziggurat at Ur
Woolley, C.L. *The Ziggurat and Its Surroundings Ur Excavations, vol. 5* (London: Oxford University Press, 1939)

The Temple of Solomon
Hamblin, W., Seely, D. *Solomon's Temple: Myth and History* (Thames & Hudson, 2007)

The Palace of Ashurnasirpal II
Larsen, M.T. *The Conquest of Assyria: Excavations in an Antique Land, 1840–1860* (New York: Routledge, 1996.)

La Venta
Diehl, R.A. *The Olmecs: America's First Civilization*, (Thames & Hudson, 2004) .

The Hanging Gardens of Babylon
Roux, G. *Ancient Iraq (3rd ed.)* (London: Penguin Books, 1992)

The Temple of Artemis at Ephesus
Lethaby, W.R. *Diana's Temple at Ephesus* (London: B.T. Batsford, 1908)
LiDonnici, L.R. *The Images of Artemis Ephesia and Greco-Roman Worship: A Reconsideration* in *The Harvard Theological Review 85.4* (Harvard 1992)

Persepolis
Wilber, D.N. *Persepolis: The Archaeology of Parsa, Seat of the Persian Kings* (Darwin Press, 1989)

The Grand Canal
Needham, J. *Science and Civilization in China: Volume 4, Physics and Physical Technology, Part 3, Civil Engineering and Nautics* (Taipei: Caves Books, Ltd., 1986)

The Parthenon
Hurwit, J.M. *The Athenian Acropolis: History, Mythology, and Archeology from the Neolithic Era to the Present* (Cambridge University Press, 2000)

The Statue of Zeus at Olympia
Gialoures, N. *Olympia: Altis and Museum* (Schnell & Steiner, 1973)

The Mausoleum at Halicarnassus
Jeppesen, K., *et al. The Maussolleion at Halikarnassos, 6 vols.* (Denmark: Jysk Arkaeologisk Selskab, 1981 onwards)

Delphi
Burkert, W. *Greek Religion* (Harvard University Press, 1985)

The Colossus of Rhodes
Ashley, J.R. *Macedonian Empire* (McFarland & Company, 2004).

The Pharos of Alexandria
Pollard, J., Reid, H. *The Rise and Fall of Alexandria: Birthplace of the Modern World* (Penguin Books, 2007)

The Library at Alexandria
MacLeod, R. *The Library of Alexandria: Centre of Learning in the Ancient World* (B. Tauris & Co Ltd, 2002)
Pollard, J., Reid, H. *The Rise and Fall of Alexandria: Birthplace of the Modern World* (Penguin Books, 2007)

The First Great Wall of China
Waldron, A. *The Great Wall of China: From History to Myth* (Cambridge University Press, 1990)

The Tomb of the First Emperor
Wood, F. *The First Emperor of China* (Profile, 2007)

Petra
Taylor, J. *Petra and the Lost Kingdom of the Nabataeans* (Harvard University Press, 2008)

The Tower of the Winds
Noble, J.V., de Solla Price, D.J. *The Water Clock in the Tower of the Winds* (*American Journal of Archaeology* 72, 1968)

The Rice Terraces of Banaue
Wernstedt, F.L., Spencer, J.E. *The Philippine Island World.* (The University of California Press, 1967)

The Great Serpent Mound
Woodward, S.L., McDonald, J.N. *Indian Mounds of the Middle Ohio Valley* (McDonald & Woodward Publishing Company, 1986)

The Pont du Gard
Bossy, G., Fabre, G., Glard, Y., Joseph, C. *Sur le fonctionnement d'un ouvrage de grande hydraulique antique, l'aqueduc de Nîmes et le pont du Gard (Languedoc, France)* (Comptes Rendus de l'Académie des Sciences - Series IIA - Earth and Planetary Science, 2006)

Nero's Golden House
Ball, L.F. *The Domus Aurea and the Roman architectural revolution.* (Cambridge University Press, 2003)

Masada
Yadin, Y. *Masada: Herod's Fortress and the Zealots' Last Stand* (Phoenix, 1997)

The Colosseum
Hopkins, K., Beard, M. *The Colosseum* (Profile Books, 2006)

The Pyramid of the Sun at Teotihuacán
Coe, M.D., Koontz, R. *Mexico: From the Olmecs to the Aztecs* (New York: Thames & Hudson, 2002)

The Forum of Trajan
Packer, J. *Trajan's Forum: A Study of the Monuments.* (University of California Press, 1997)

The Pantheon
MacDonald, W.L. *The Pantheon: Design Meaning and Progency* (Harvard University Press, 1990)

The Baths of Diocletian
Aurigemma, S. *The Baths of Diocletian and the Museo Nazionale Romano* (Istituto Poligrafico Dello Stato, Libreria Dello Stato, 1974)

The City of Tikal
Harrison, P.D. *The Lords of Tikal: Rulers of an Ancient Maya City (New Aspects of Antiquity*) (Thames & Hudson, 1999)

The Buddhas of Bamyan
Sharma R.C., Ghosal, P. (eds) *Buddhism and Gandhara art* (Delhi: Aryan Books, 2004)

The Hagia Sophia
Mainstone, R.J. *Hagia Sophia: Architecture, Structure, and Liturgy of Justinian's Great Church* (W.W. Norton & Co Inc., 1997)

The Basilica Cistern at Constantinople
Tonguc, L. *The Basilica Cistern (Yerebatan Sarayi) and the other cisterns of Istanbul* (Key to Turkey Publications, 1988)

Hôryû-Gakumonji
Hall, J.W. *The Cambridge History of Japan "The Asuka Enlightment"* (Cambridge University Press, 1988)

Borobudur
Dumarçay, J., trans. and ed. by Smithies, M. *Borobudur*, (Singapore: Oxford University Press, 1991)

Ellora
Dehejia, V. *Early Buddhist Rock Temples* (Thames & Hudson, 1972)

Picture Acknowledgements

akg-images
64 © Hervé Champollion/akg-images; 69 © akg-images/John Hios; 89 © akg-images/Electa; 91 © akg-images; 172-173 © akg-images/ullstein bild

British Library
94 © 2008 The British Library

Corbis
11 © Gianni Dagli Orti/Corbis; 14 © Stapleton Collection/Corbis; 17 © Historical Picture Archive/Corbis; 21 © Historical Picture Archive/Corbis; 24-25 © Paul Almasy/Corbis; 26 © The Art Archive/Corbis; 28-29 © Dean Conger/Corbis; 31 © Bettmann/Corbis; 33 © Christie's Images/Corbis; 35 © Dave Bartruff/Corbis; 36-37 © Stapleton Collection/Corbis; 38 © Werner Forman/Corbis; 41 © Charles & Josette Lenars/Corbis; 44-45 © Bettmann/Corbis; 48-49 © The Art Archive/Corbis; 51 © Bettmann/Corbis; 55 © Bettmann/Corbis; 56-57 © Historical Picture Archive/Corbis; 59 © Corbis; 62 © Ted Spiegel/Corbis; 67 © Christel Gerstenberg/Corbis; 70-71 © Historical Picture Archive/Corbis; 73 © Werner Forman/Corbis; 76 © The Gallery Collection/Corbis; 79 © Araldo de Luca/Corbis; 81 © Bettmann/Corbis; 82 © Morton Beebe/Corbis; 84-85 © Historical Picture Archive; 87 © Robert Holmes/Corbis; 93 © Wolfgang Kaehler/Corbis; 101 © Charles & Josette Lenars/Corbis; 107 © Corbis; 109 © Michael Nicholson/Corbis; 117 © Richard A Cooke/Corbis; 123 © Gianni Dagli Orti/Corbis; 125 © Massimo Listri/Corbis; 128-129 © Nathan Benn/Corbis; 131 © Richard T Nowitz/Corbis; 137 © The Art Archive/Corbis; 140 © Robert Harding/Robert Harding World Imagery/Corbis; 146-147 © Historical Picture Archive/Corbis; 152-153 © Historical Picture Archive/Corbis; 155 © Lars Halbauer/dpa/Corbis; 161 © Charles & Josette Lenars/Corbis; 166 © Adam Woolfitt/Corbis; 174 © Burstein Collection/Corbis; 180-181 © Lindsay Hebberd/Corbis; 183 © Michael Freeman/Corbis

photos.com
43, 47, 127

Shutterstock
8-9 © Amra Pasic; 12-13 © Bryan Busovicki; 19 © Franck Camhi; 22 © Svetlana Privezentseva; 52-53 © Maza; 60-61 © Vangelis; 63 © Baloncici; 74-75 © Dr Le Thanh Hung; 96-97 © Goydenko Tatiana; 98-99 © Holger Mette; 103 © Clara Natoli; 104-105 Shutterstock Joseph Calev; 113 © Jonald Morales; 115 © Antonio V Oquias; 120-121 © Elena Elisseeva; 133 © Denis Babenko; 134-135 © mikari; 138-139 © Ian D Walker; 143 © faberfoto; 145 © David Davis; 148-149 © Motordigitaal; 151 © Roca; 157 © kschrei; 158 © Daniel Loncarevic; 164-165 © iNNOCENt; 169 © Daniel DeSlover; 170 © Daniel DeSlover; 177 © Morozova Tatyana; 178 © TAOLMOR

TopFoto.co.uk
111 © 2004 AAAC/TopFoto

Quercus Publishing has made every effort to trace copyright holders of the pictures used in this book. Anyone having claims to ownership not identified above is invited to contact Quercus Publishing.

Author's Acknowledgements

The acknowledgements for this book, were they to be written out in full, would form a book in themselves including, as they should, all the archaeologists and historians who have taught me and talked with me over many years.

But very special thanks must go to my wife, Stephanie, who did so much of the work in gathering together and sifting through the thousands of sources that are, by definition, the result of preparing a book that covers such a wide swathe of time and space. We have wandered through these lost worlds together.

For their support and help with this book I would also like to thank Richard Milbank, Richard Green and everyone at Quercus, Graham Bateman and the team at BCS, Julian Alexander at Lucas Alexander Whitley, Richard Foreman at Chalke and, as always, Connie for letting her dad write when she would rather he played.

For Helen, Barrie, Louis and Amber

non mihi, non tibi, sed nobis

Quercus Editions Ltd
55 Baker Street
7th Floor, South Block
London W1U 8EW

First published in 2008. This edition published in 2011.

A catalogue record of this book is available from the British Library

ISBN
UK and associated territories: 978 0 85738 663 2
Canada: 978 1 84866 144 8
Printed and bound in China

10 9 8 7 6 5 4 3 2